Part 3: Internal A[illegible] Knowledge Elem[illegible]

Book 2

Table of Contents

Section V: Management/Leadership Principles

This section is designed to help you:

- *Understand the importance of developing, implementing, and evaluating organizational strategy.*
- *Learn about global analytical techniques for market positioning, competitive analysis, and the formulation of competitive strategy.*
- *Become aware of the various types of industries and ways that competitive strategy can be adapted based on the industry environment.*
- *Become familiar with the strategic factors involved in business growth opportunities such as integration, entry, or expansion.*
- *Have a basic understanding of forecasting as a managerial planning tool and common forecasting methods.*
- *Have a basic understanding of total quality management (TQM) characteristics, measures, and tools and understand the costs associated with TQM.*
- *Describe methods and uses of decision analysis.*
- *Describe structures and configurations within organizational theory.*
- *Become aware of the organizational dynamics that influence organizational communication and behavior.*
- *Become familiar with motivational theories and their workplace relevance.*
- *Become aware of the characteristics of effective groups and the interpersonal and organizational dynamics involved.*
- *Apply the basic concepts, principles, and methods affecting human resources as they relate to individual performance issues in the workplace.*
- *Express the risk/control implications of different leadership styles.*
- *Measure organizational performance productivity and effectiveness.*
- *Lead, inspire, mentor, and guide people toward organizational commitment and an entrepreneurial orientation.*
- *Learn about leadership and management theories and their applications*
- *Recognize the importance of coaching and mentoring in the workplace.*
- *Create group synergy in pursuing collective goals.*
- *Gain an understanding of the methods used in building and assessing teams.*
- *Recognize triggers that cause conflict in the work environment.*
- *Become acquainted with conflict management and resolution strategies.*
- *Describe negotiation skills best practices.*
- *Learn about the added-value negotiation philosophy and its key steps.*
- *Describe the process of change management.*
- *Apply the basic concepts, principles, and methods underlying project management techniques.*

The Certified Internal Auditor (CIA) exam questions based on content from this section make up approximately 10% to 20% of the total number of questions for Part 3. All topics are covered at the "A—Awareness" level, meaning that you are responsible for comprehension and recall of information.

Section Introduction

Mastering management and leadership principles is another key aspect of being able to deliver value and insight to stakeholders. These principles apply to the leadership of the organization overall as well as to the leadership of the internal audit function. They are integral to being a good team leader so that the business function accomplishes the right tasks as efficiently and effectively as possible. When individual internal auditors also understand these principles, they can understand the organization's management and leadership actions better and also be better team players themselves.

Management and leadership has four key activities: planning, organizing, leading, and controlling. Exhibit V-1 shows how these activities form a cycle of continual improvement of the management process. It lists some activities that take place in each part of the cycle.

Exhibit V-1: Management and Leadership Cycle

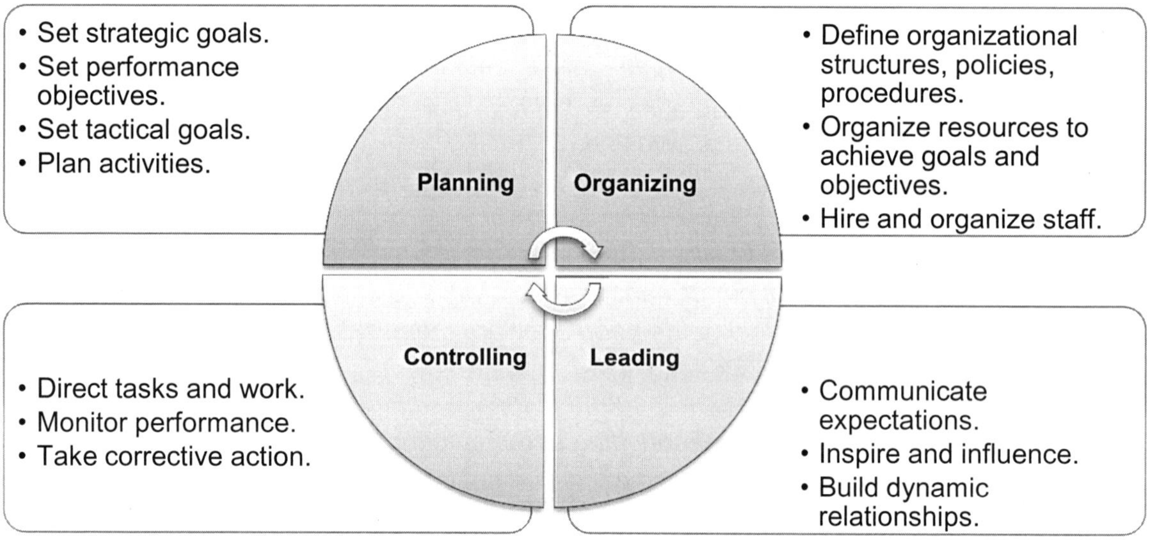

This section starts in the planning part of the cycle by discussing the importance of developing organizational strategy and managing the implementation of that strategy in Chapter A, "Strategic Management." The concepts of strategy formation vary in different parts of the world. This section starts with a focus on the management practices that relate to positioning and competitive strategy.

Chapter B, "Organizational Behavior," primarily addresses the organizing phase of the management and leadership cycle. This chapter addresses organizational theory, organizational behavior, group dynamics, and human resources to help CAEs understand how to best organize their teams. It also addresses leadership styles and performance measurement, which are part of the leading and controlling phases, respectively.

Chapter C, "Management Skills/Leadership Styles," addresses the overall concept of management but delves primarily into the leadership phase of the cycle. It addresses how to use leadership to develop organizational commitment and an entrepreneurial orientation, how to develop group synergy, and how to build effective teams.

Chapter D, "Conflict Management," is part of the controlling phase of the cycle. It involves developing an understanding of why conflicts occur so that they can be resolved. Negotiation skills are also addressed. Some leadership is also needed to build relationships that are amenable to conflict resolution.

Chapter E, "Project Management/Change Management," uses all phases of the cycle, since project management and change management involve planning, organizing, leading, and controlling for a specific project or change effort. Change management especially requires a healthy dose of leadership to ensure that people are ready for change.

Chapter A: Strategic Management

Chapter Introduction

Organizational strategy

In order for an organization to survive and thrive, it needs to answer some fundamental questions:

- What kind of business or businesses are we in?
- What industry or industries are we a part of?
- What are the future trends for our business and industry?
- With whom do we compete for customers and market share?
- How can we analyze the competition?
- What challenges or obstacles might we face?
- What competition and factors might we encounter in global industries?
- How do we make decisions about opportunities to expand or enter new markets?

The development and implementation of organizational strategy is of particular importance to the auditing role. Auditors must be aware of how an organization is managing risk and how current plans will affect business in the future.

Auditors can review strategic planning processes, structure audit plans to address business plan risks, and then help ensure that the organization is conducting activities to deal with emerging risks. Also, some of the best-practice audit groups are developing their own strategic plans in alignment with organizational goals.

It is helpful to understand the context of strategy development before focusing on the analytical techniques for strategic management. In general, strategy refers to the plans and means for developing advantageous positions and outcomes. Organizational strategy focuses on the entire organization and its plans for moving into the future and achieving its goals and objectives.

There are other types of strategy that align with and support an organization's overall strategy:

- Competitive strategy is the way an organization positions itself to compete in the marketplace.
- Strategic business unit (SBU) strategy is concerned with developing strategies for products and processes at the business unit level.
- Functional strategy is related to business functions such as marketing, research, financial, or operational areas.
- Comparative advantage strategy involves trading with other countries, regions, organizations, or individuals when a party has a comparative advantage. Comparative advantage refers to a party being relatively better at producing certain goods or services, and at a lower opportunity cost, in comparison to other goods and services it can apply its resources toward.

Strategic planning

Strategic planning is the process organizations use to determine where they want to be and how they will get there. There are numerous models and approaches for strategic planning. Depending on the organization, the planning may be done as often as twice a year, yearly, every three years, or some other time increment.

Strategic planning and implementation is a very involved process. For the purposes of this discussion, a simplified goals-based outline for formulating and implementing strategy is presented in Exhibit V-2. The main components are to:

- Establish organizational vision, mission, goals, and objectives.
- Develop strategic plans.
- Implement the strategy.
- Evaluate strategy implementation.

Exhibit V-2: Strategic Planning and Implementation

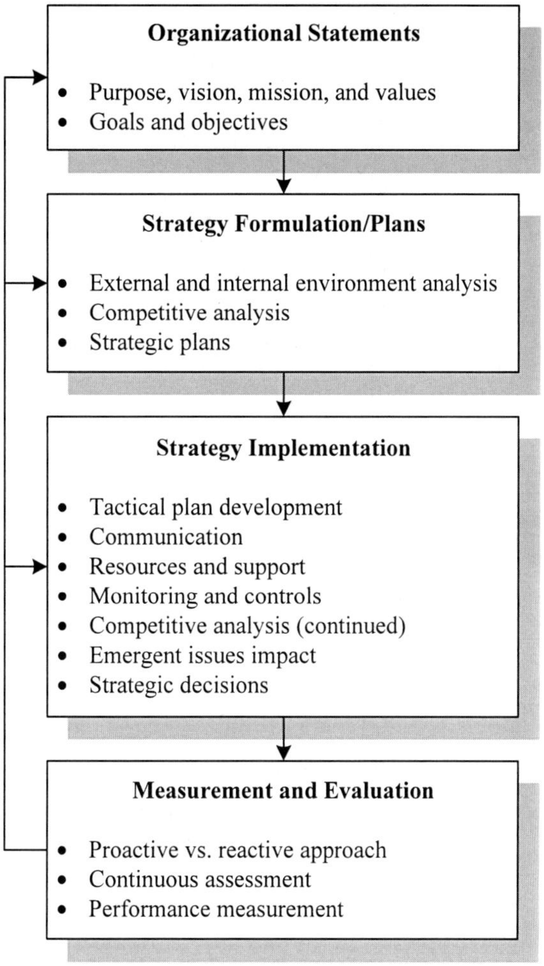

As shown in Exhibit V-2, each stage informs the other and should align with the overall organizational statements at the top. While this goals-based approach is usually seen as top-down, information is often fed back up through the process to impact the overall organizational strategy.

The evaluation component is particularly important because, while the process may look very rigid, it is actually dynamic. A number of factors can bring change, which then impacts the activities in one or more of the stages.

Organizational statements

An organization first needs to agree upon and document answers to questions such as:

- Who are we?
- What are our core values?

- What do we want to accomplish in the future?
- What does the ideal future look like?
- How will we go about reaching our goals?

An organization should work together to establish its:
- Vision for the future.
- Mission statement indicating purpose.
- Goals that support the mission and vision.
- Objectives that include measurable short-term results.

These statements then support the formation of organizational strategy.

Strategy formulation

Information gathering and analysis are the foundation for formulating strategy. Environmental analysis, or environmental scanning, is a process for analyzing external and internal factors that are important to setting and carrying out strategy. External analysis is a research process that gathers information on the external environment that might affect the industry and the organization, such as factors related to the economy, government, laws and regulations, societal and cultural concerns, and technology as well as specific industry or competitor trends. Internal analysis is a research process that collects information on the organization's resources, capabilities, structure, limitations, etc.

SWOT analysis

SWOT analysis is a common way to analyze internal and external information. SWOT stands for **S**trengths, **W**eaknesses, **O**pportunities, and **T**hreats.

In SWOT analysis, brainstorming is often used to generate lists of the organization's internal strengths and weaknesses and external opportunities and threats. The lists are placed in a SWOT matrix as shown in Exhibit V-3. Then new matches, or strategies, are made in the crossover shaded areas.
- SO strategies capitalize on internal strengths to maximize opportunities.
- WO strategies overcome internal weaknesses to maximize opportunities.
- ST strategies draw on internal strengths to reduce external threats.
- WT strategies reduce internal weaknesses to guard against external threats.

Exhibit V-3: SWOT Analysis

SWOT Matrix	**Opportunities** (external analysis)	**Threats** (external analysis)
Strengths (internal analysis)	***SO strategies*** Capitalize on internal strengths to maximize opportunities.	***ST strategies*** Draw on internal strengths to reduce external threats.
Weaknesses (internal analysis)	***WO strategies*** Overcome internal weaknesses to maximize opportunities.	***WT strategies*** Reduce internal weaknesses to guard against external threats.

Once generated, the new strategy lists need to be evaluated and prioritized for further action.

SWOT analysis action plans and the results of other competitive research can be used to develop strategic plans. A strategic plan is a document that indicates how an organization will carry out its mission, vision, goals, and objectives, given factors in the internal and external environments. The strategic plan spells out the direction for the organization—both for the short term and the foreseeable future.

Strategy implementation

A very important part of organizational success is the execution of the strategy and close management of the execution.

Implementation has commonly been conducted in a top-down approach, with the communication flow from top management throughout the levels of the organization. However, the approach will vary depending on how the organization is structured. For example, in an organization with a flatter hierarchy, both the development of strategy and its implementation may be done in a collaborative manner.

Implementation involves developing and communicating the operational or tactical plans. This often involves developing strategy on a business unit, functional, or departmental level as well.

Organizations do well to foster intra-organizational synergy, which involves sharing information and resources across the organization. Synergy is when informal or formal cooperative efforts bring about a result that is much stronger and advantageous than the sum of the individual parts alone. Synergy also applies in the case of mergers and acquisitions, global alliances, and other external partnership strategies.

These plans should align with the overall goals and objectives of the organization. Tactical plans are usually developed on an annual basis and include action plans, assignments, schedules, and budgets.

Part of the challenge with implementation is adhering to the plans set forth while at the same time remaining flexible to respond to changing circumstances. Getting an organization to move in a new direction is often met with a certain amount of resistance.

Evaluation and measurement

It is important to evaluate on an ongoing basis. Standards should be set, measurement approaches developed, and measurement results compared to the standards.

In our global economy, the pressures are keen. Organizations must constantly be on guard to keep their competitive advantage. It is much better to function in a proactive mode than a reactive, crisis mode.

Strategic management

Strategic management, which is the focus of this chapter, involves assisting with facets of strategy formulation, implementation, monitoring and controls, and evaluation.

Understanding the context for the business of the organization, continually evaluating and reevaluating, and acting in a proactive manner are important to ongoing success. In today's global business environment, strategic management also involves an understanding of global concerns that may impact industries and future direction. The following topics describe analytical techniques that can be used to assess industry environments, conduct competitive analysis, and make strategic decisions related to the organization's future. Effective strategic management is critical to optimizing the organization's future.

Throughout the chapter, the terms "product" and "service" are often used interchangeably. Also, while circumstances will vary, most principles apply to profit, not-for-profit, domestic, and international organizations.

Topic 1: Demonstrate an Understanding of Global Analytical Techniques (Level A)

This topic and the following focus on competitive strategy. The analytical techniques for strategic positioning can be applied generally and on the global front. Competitive analysis is part of the external environmental analysis discussed previously. The basic principles are to analyze the industry or industries that the organization is a part of, analyze the competition, and then use the information gathered to make strategic decisions about the organization's position.

A brief treatment of these principles is found here. For a more comprehensive study, refer to the landmark book *Competitive Strategy: Techniques for Analyzing Industries and Competitors* by Michael E. Porter and other sources on strategy analysis and development.

Structural analysis of industries

Industries vary in their levels of value creation and profitability. Industries have different structures, and the influences on those structures will affect profitability. For example, an industry that has a structure that provides niche products and services will likely have fewer competitors and higher profitability averages. Two types of industries may be very different, but if they have a similar industry structure that supports low profitability averages, their profitability may look similar.

Structural analysis is a method for analyzing the elements of industry structure and the factors that affect and drive industry competition. It is important because it gives an organization a framework to use in assessing its own strengths and weaknesses against the industry structure and the forces that affect the industry.

Porter developed a framework that is widely used for considering forces that impact competition in industries. Porter's five competitive forces are:

- The threat of new entrants.
- The threat of substitute products or services.
- The bargaining power of buyers.
- The bargaining power of suppliers.
- Rivalry among existing firms.

The first four forces listed ultimately impact the fifth—rivalry among existing firms. The combination of how all of these forces come together affects the competitiveness and profitability of an industry.

Structural analysis is a good way to forecast industry trends, and the research is critical to formulating an organization's competitive strategy. An organization will want to:

- Study its industry and the forces affecting competition.
- Identify organizational strengths and weaknesses based on the forces.
- Consider trends affecting competition and possible industry shifts.

- Determine a competitive position.
- Shape the overall competitive strategy.

Competitive strategies

Organizations determine competitive strategy to obtain a competitive advantage. A competitive advantage is the advantage that one organization has over competitors in realizing above-average financial performance. Sustained competitive advantage occurs when an organization carries its competitive advantage for a long period of time because other organizations are not able to duplicate its efforts.

Porter outlines three key generic strategies:

- **Cost leadership** is a low-cost-position competitive strategy. This means that an organization will minimize its development, advertising, and other costs in order to offer products and services at a lower cost than competitors.

- **Differentiation** is a competitive strategy to make an organization's products or services different and unique in the industry. A competitive advantage is seen when customers will buy based on that differentiation, even at costs above those of the low-cost competitors.

- **Focus** is a competitive strategy to appeal to a narrower segment of the industry. For example, the organization may try to move ahead by focusing on certain customers, geographic areas, or types of products. A focus strategy could result in either differentiation or cost leadership, or both, in those targeted areas.

There are other strategies and combinations of strategies that might be considered as well:

- **Pioneering** is an effort to be the first, or at least an early, entrant in a market and become the market leader. This can be a very effective and lasting strategy, and it relies on organizational creativity and innovation.

- **Synergy**, as defined earlier, is a strategy to draw upon internal resources, or internal and external resources, to create product and marketing advantages. It often involves collaborative internal partnerships between business units or special alliances with external parties. Synergy may also refer to the results of merging more than one competitive strategy for a stronger overall advantage.

These efforts may seem very straightforward. However, considering the advantages and disadvantages of various options, implementing the strategy and sustaining a competitive advantage in industries is quite complex.

Competitive analysis

Being successful in an industry has much to do with thoroughly understanding the nature of the competitors. One of the first steps is to identify who the current and potential competitors are. Then an organization needs to investigate each competitor, asking some of the questions that it used to develop its own strategies.

Questions such as the following need to be asked about secondary and emerging competitors:
- What type of organization is this?
- What are the current objectives?
- What are the future goals and objectives?
- What is the organizational structure?
- What are the internal strengths and weaknesses?
- Are assumptions made about the industry?
- Are assumptions made about the organization's place in the industry?
- What resources does the organization have?
- How profitable is the organization?
- Is the organization poised for growth?
- If the organization has multiple businesses, what is the performance of those businesses?
- Are mergers or acquisitions on the horizon?

Competitive intelligence is the data gathered about current and potential competitors. Data is available through public reports, presentations, trade shows, suppliers, customers, etc. Market research studies come at a cost but provide valuable comparative data.

Investigating the competition is extremely important and is done primarily to predict competitor direction, reactions to possible market moves, and adaptability and vulnerabilities. The intelligence should be analyzed and integrated into the strategy formulation process.

Market signals

Market signals are cues in the marketplace about an organization's actions or possible actions. They are yet another source of competitor information. Accurately reading the signals is as important as detecting them; some communication may be purposely misleading.

Porter outlines some examples of market signals:

- Announcements of moves, either before or after the fact
- Discussions of moves by competitors or others
- Information about tactical plans and implementation
- First moves for strategic changes, such as timing or prices
- Divergence from past goals or industry precedents
- Cross-parry situations (direct or indirect countermoves)
- Fighting brands (warnings or offensive brand campaigns)
- Private antitrust suits (to threaten, delay, or penalize)

The key to reading market signals is to understand the history of an organization with regard to past practices and past market signals.

Industry evolution

We've discussed the importance of industry structure in formulating competitive strategy. Another aspect of this is to recognize that industries evolve and change over time. Industries move through life cycles, not unlike the business development life cycle we learned about in Section III. Understanding where the industry is in the life cycle will aid in predicting industry changes and adapting competitive strategy.

Industry life cycles

A basic four-stage model for industry life cycles is shown in Exhibit V-4.

Exhibit V-4: Industry Life Cycle

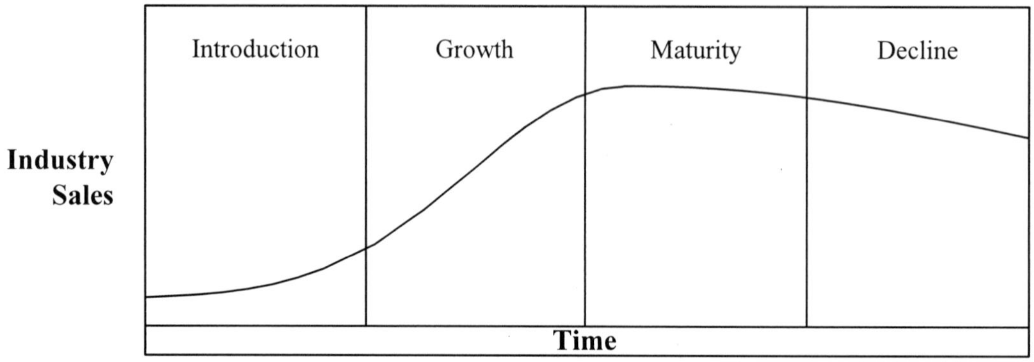

The exhibit shows the relationship of industry sales to time in the industry. How long the life cycle lasts, and the patterns of the cycle, can vary by industry. However, such a model is still useful for analyzing factors that can affect the structure of industries.

While many factors can be considered for the life cycle stages, a few parallel examples are noted here.

In the **introduction stage,** the industry is innovative and just being launched. Products and services are innovative and being tested. Buyers may be hesitant to buy at first. Profits are lower, given development and marketing costs. Competitors are few.

In the **growth stage,** interest builds and the industry expands. Products and services are in greater demand and are being refined. Buyers become educated, and interest builds. Profits are higher, with more and perhaps pent-up demand. Competitors come forth to be reckoned with, and alliances are formed.

In the **maturity stage,** the industry reaches maturity with experience and quality but starts to fall off in certain areas. Products and services are well developed. Buyers become more discriminating of quality and brands. Profits start to fall, with attention to cost control measures. Competitors start to exit.

In the **decline stage,** the industry trails off with less interest and perhaps overcapacity. Product and service quality declines. Buyer sales decline and overcapacity may result. Profits and prices are lower. Competitors exit the marketplace, and few competitors remain.

There are many influences that will change an industry structure, such as governmental policies and regulations, customer or supplier conditions, international alliances and trade considerations, innovation, and technology advances or changes.

To summarize, when developing a competitive strategy, an organization will want to study the structure of its industry or industries, the competitive forces affecting the structure, and the underlying causes of those forces. An organization will also want to pay close attention to the industry evolution and the life cycle stage of the industry. Doing so helps forecast the future of the industry. An organization should then assess its own organizational strategy in relation to predicted changes in the industry structure.

Topic 2: Describe Competitive Strategies and Global Competition in Various Industry Environments (Level A)

Industry types

As discussed, industries move through various stages of a life cycle. Industries are also described in terms of their focus. Industries might be classified as concentrated or fragmented. Geographically, industries might have a local, regional, country, or global focus.

This topic looks at industry characteristics and considerations for developing competitive business strategy for the following industry environments:

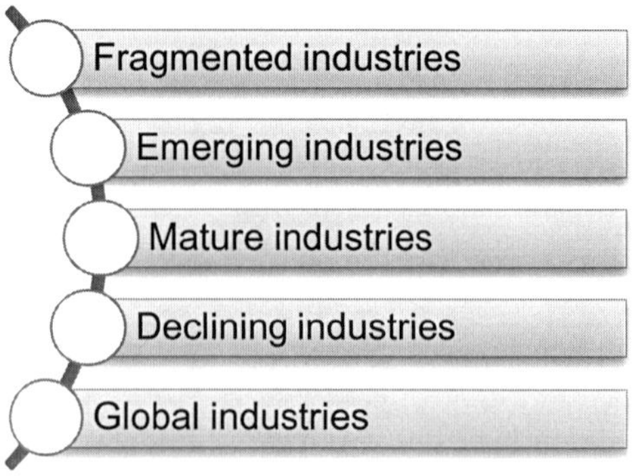

Fragmented industries

A fragmented industry is made up of a number of smaller competitors with no strong market leader. The structure of the industry prohibits it from becoming more concentrated. (A concentrated industry then is an industry with stronger and larger leaders that give it market focus.)

Agriculture, retail, service, and very innovative industries are examples of fragmented industries. These industries include many small and medium-sized organizations that are fragmented for several reasons:

- Barriers to entry are low, thereby encouraging smaller competitors.
- Products and services are delivered on a smaller scale.
- Competitor threats are relatively low.
- Operating costs are higher.
- Diverse or innovative products are developed more easily.
- Local or regional needs can be catered to.

Key competitive strategies suggested by Porter and others are to:

- Consolidate in the industry to gain a larger market share.
- Create economies of scale that increase output and decrease unit costs.
- Standardize a part of the industry.
- Specialize products and/or services for targeted customers.
- Create new ways to add value in the industry.

Before making such moves, however, an organization needs to carefully research the industry and determine whether new directions will be in their own best interest, with profitable projections.

Emerging industries

An emerging industry is in the early stages of development. Such industries are often inspired by technological innovation or new market needs. They might also be an outgrowth of an established industry. Computers and mobile devices are examples of industries that continue to emerge based on innovation in technology and new consumer demands.

Characteristics of emerging industries are:

- High creativity, innovation, and experimentation.
- Few competitors and competitor threats.
- Limited industry patterns, rules, and regulations.
- Much risk and speculation.
- Short window of opportunity.
- High initial costs.
- Steep learning curves.
- High marketing and advertising for visibility.

Strategies for competing in emerging industries suggested by Porter and others are to:

- Enter the market early to gain advantage.
- Enter the industry if initial and longer-term benefits are projected.
- Use forecasting methods, such as scenarios, to predict industry evolution.
- Research which buyers will be most receptive early on.
- Determine and make known the cost advantages of substitutions.
- Provide support services for new products and services.
- Promote the collective industry while keeping competitive advantage.
- Be on guard against new entrants and limit integration.

Emerging industries offer great prospects for an organization but often at a higher risk. There are numerous entry barriers to overcome, uncertainty on many fronts, and an industry structure that has yet to evolve. However, an organization that enters early and defends its place has the potential to ultimately become the market leader.

Mature industries

A mature industry is fairly well established. An example is the automobile manufacturing industry. There are strong leaders in quality, reliability, and safety. Makers need to continually keep up with competitors to stay ahead in the game.

A mature industry will reflect the following characteristics:

- Industry demand and growth slow.
- Innovation and new product or service development slow.

- Organizations must reduce or change output due to slower growth.
- Competition increases as a result of slower growth.
- Organizations become more customer-service-oriented.
- Organizations pay closer attention to cost control.
- Some organizations may consolidate.
- The industry faces greater international competition.

Strategies for managing mature industries suggested by Porter and others are to:

- Pay closer attention to product and service cost and pricing.
- Provide added value to current customers.
- Innovate without overshadowing current offerings.
- Consider whether products and services are competitive internationally.
- Reduce expectations and modify organizational plans accordingly.

It is important to note that mature organizations may have cycles of reinvention that extend their life in the industry. After time, however, environmental, technological, and other changes often push organizations toward a declining position.

Declining industries

As the title suggests, declining industries are those in which the demand for products or services is diminishing. Examples might be technology that is becoming obsolete or certain types of manufacturing.

The characteristics of declining industries are:

- Product and service demand continues to fall.
- Price competition is keen.
- Cash flow is maximized and investments are reduced.
- Output is decreased to avoid overcapacity.
- Organizations consolidate or form structured alliances.
- Larger or niche organizations increase market share.
- Organizations exit the industry.

Strategies for organizations in a declining industry suggested by Porter and others are to:

- Remain in the industry if financially advantageous over the exit barriers.
- Research competitors and find a niche to occupy.
- Take the lead in the market by forcing competitors out.
- Harvest (maximizing cash flow while minimizing or ceasing investments).
- Divest (selling off business units early in the decline stage by finding interested buyers).

In a declining industry, an organization first needs to recognize the signs of decline. Then it must carefully consider its own strengths against the strengths of competitors. If the organization has the ability to take a leadership position or focus on a niche segment, it may be beneficial to stay in the industry as long as possible. If the exit barriers, such as a low liquidation value, are prohibitive, this is another reason for remaining in the industry for a time. If the business unit in question is interrelated with other units, an organization will need to consider that impact as well.

The timing for an exit should be calculated carefully. For example, it may be more advantageous to divest early in the decline to find interested buyers than to wait until later in the decline.

Global industries

Interdependence of countries around the world and integration of economic, social, and other factors are increasing—thus our focus now on global competition. A global industry is one in which products or services are similarly created and distributed for markets in more than one country. This then fosters competition on a broad global basis.

A global industry is different than a multidomestic industry. A multidomestic industry is one in which the products and services are segmented by country and are not competitive from country to country. In other words, an organization may be considered multinational, which means it serves customers in various countries, but the competition may not be between those countries.

A global organization needs to focus on its competitive advantage, which often involves comparative advantage. As mentioned earlier, comparative strategy helps determine position in the global marketplace and involves product and service development comparisons to other nations.

Porter asserts that the five competitive forces mentioned earlier are applicable as well to global industries. However, an international competitive strategy needs to take into account certain differences:

- Foreign countries have different factor costs, such as labor.
- Foreign markets have differences to be aware of.
- Foreign governments have restrictions for business operations.
- Foreign competitors must be identified and monitored.

Competitive advantage sources

The following are some of the sources noted by Porter and others that support competitive advantage in a global industry:

- Comparative advantage, which occurs because one country has an advantage over another in resources, such as labor or technology
- Investment incentives, which may be offered by countries to enhance economic development
- Scale economies, which enable organizations to produce on a much wider basis for the global marketplace
- Global knowledge, which is increased by access to industry information in multiple locations and countries
- Cost savings, which results from shared production, services, marketing, purchasing, technology, and other proprietary developments
- Financial advantages, which result when profitable areas of the businesses can support less profitable or distressed areas

Competitive advantage impediments

Conversely, there are also impediments to competing globally. There are often, in reality, a number of differences between nations that make it difficult to standardize worldwide. A few of the impediments noted by Porter and others are:

- Differences in market needs by country locations.
- Strong leadership positions already established in a country.
- Existing distribution channels that vary by country.
- Lack of worldwide interest for products and services, creating short product life cycles.
- Marketing messages and brand received differently in cultures.
- Government laws and regulations for each country.

Evolution of global markets

It makes sense that in order for global industries to evolve at least some of the right conditions must be present to support competitive advantage. If innovation is encouraged, new market segments are identified, ample resources are available, and standardization is welcome, then industry development is supported.

A reduction in any of the impediments, such as relaxation of government regulations or changing of distribution channels, may also spur industry evolution.

Strategic alternatives

An organization needs to research whether becoming part of a global industry is in its best interest and, if so, how it will compete. It may be more prudent to compete in select national markets instead of broad global markets. An organization may decide to focus on a segment of a global industry, a specific national market, or a protected niche market (whereby the organization abides by government restrictions and receives certain protections).

Common ways to enter a foreign market include exporting, licensing and franchising, joint ventures, and foreign direct investment. Various types of global businesses are further discussed in Section VIII, "Global Business Environment."

Trends affecting competition

There are several trends affecting global competition today:

- Technology has leveled the playing field. Advances in technology and the World Wide Web have led to an explosion in communication, business, and e-commerce opportunities.
- Rapidly developing economies, such as in China and India, provide cost advantages with low-cost labor, raw materials, and other resources.
- Strategic alliances are increasingly important for minimizing risk and competing globally. A few of the advantages are access to markets and facilities, brand recognition, and avenues around trade barriers.
- Global harmonization is sought on many fronts to foster the free flow of goods, services, and capital around the world. One example is relaxation of some national trade barriers.
- Privatization, which is the sale of government operations to private investors, is a growing practice to increase investment and encourage competition.
- The risks and complexities of operating in foreign countries continue to grow, as further discussed in Section VIII, "Global Business Environment."

Topic 3: Analyze the Impact of Strategic Decisions to Integrate or Expand Capacity or the Business (Level A)

Making strategic decisions is a necessary part of strategic management. We have focused on competitive forces that affect the structure of industries, growth stages in industries, various types of industries, and competitive strategy options. Organizations routinely face decisions about growth strategies and whether to pursue integration strategies, expansion of operations, or entry into new markets.

Integration

Integration is a growth strategy used by many organizations to control aspects of product or service development or customer buying processes. The types of integration briefly discussed here are vertical integration, horizontal integration, and quasi-integration.

Vertical integration

Vertical integration is a circumstance where an organization owns and controls several different subsidiaries to promote cost and efficiency benefits. In order to help visualize vertical integration, it is useful to mention the value chain concept. The value chain, described by Michael Porter in the 1980s, is a model to analyze an organization's value creation activities. Another way to gain competitive advantage is to maximize value while minimizing costs.

The specific value chain activities vary by organization, but the primary categories are:

- Inbound logistics (receiving, inventory, etc.).
- Operations (assembly, maintenance, testing, etc.).
- Outbound logistics (warehousing, distribution methods, etc.).
- Marketing and sales (advertising, selling, pricing, etc.).
- Service and maintenance (customer service, repair, etc.).

Exhibit V-5 shows how these value chain activities relate to vertical integration.

Exhibit V-5: Vertical Integration

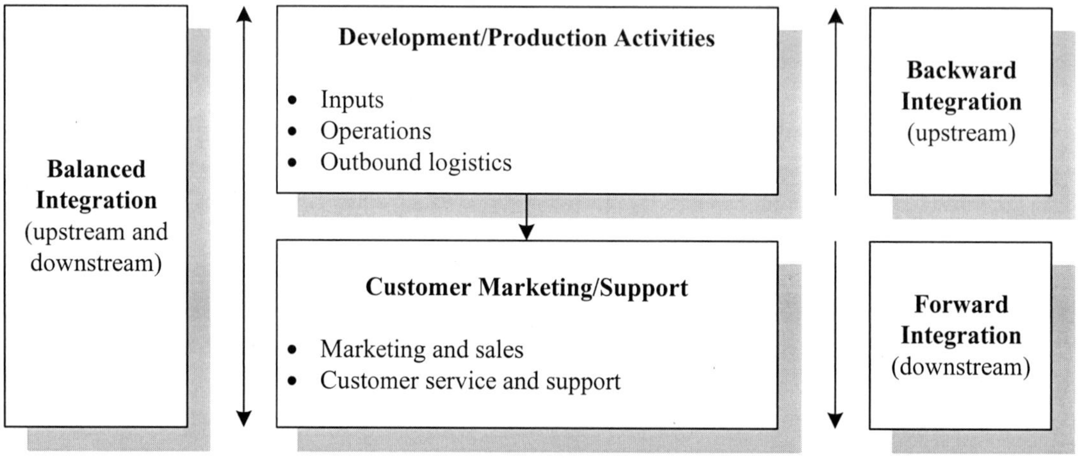

The basic principle is for the organization to maintain control of the activities in the value chain.

As indicated in the exhibit, an organization may choose to focus on one of three vertical integration strategies:

- **Backward vertical integration,** which is an upstream focus on the development and production activities
- **Forward vertical integration,** which is a downstream focus on customer buying activities, including marketing and support services
- **Balanced vertical integration,** which encompasses activities in both of the upstream and downstream areas

There are many benefits to vertical integration, which include:

- Less reliance on external suppliers and vendors (sometimes competitors).
- Flexibility in changing one aspect in the value chain and quickly adapting in other activities.
- Efficiencies in sharing information and merging certain operations and internal controls.

There are, however, implications for costs and flexibility to consider:

- Increased fixed costs with more activities conducted internally
- Change cost if activities are not being performed in a cost-effective or competitive manner and an external resource is engaged
- Increased capital needs due to more activities conducted internally
- Increased attention to the balance, effectiveness, quality, and future forecast for all of the activities under the organization's umbrella

Horizontal integration

Horizontal integration is a lateral approach to owning and gaining control of activities at the same level of the value chain. For example, an organization might decide to purchase products across the organization, acquire similar or substitute products, or even acquire competitors.

The benefits to horizontal integration include:

- Achievement of economies of scale.
- Improved business focus and expertise.
- Reduced competition and increased negotiating power.
- Increased synergy for production and/or marketing efforts.

Possible disadvantages of horizontal integration are:

- Monopolies and antitrust issues.
- Coordination complexities with multiple subsidiaries.
- Difficulty integrating substitute or similar products.

Quasi-integration

While vertical and horizontal integration are the most common integration methods, an organization may decide to operate in a quasi-integration mode. Quasi-integration refers to not having complete ownership and financial responsibility for the value chain areas. An organization may tailor the integration to suit their needs by creating alliances.

For example, a smaller firm may share trucking costs with another organization to allow them to take advantage of full truckload pricing. The less-than-truckload strategy makes it possible for each organization to benefit from economies of scale and density.

Strategic decisions related to integration are more complex than it might seem. Integration is a strategic choice to reduce the power of buyers or customers. An organization must thoroughly understand itself and its competitors and suppliers to make such decisions. Integration is not always cost-effective. Also, there are strategic management issues because there are many more facets that require special understanding to manage effectively.

Expansion

Another important strategic decision for an organization is whether to expand its capacity of products or services, i.e., increase market penetration. A delicate balance is required to prevent undercapacity or overcapacity. Future supply and customer demand is an issue as well as possible expansion moves by competitors.

For example, an organization may choose to follow a just-in-time strategy. (Recall the discussion of just-in-time manufacturing in Section III.)

When making strategic decisions about expansion, an organization should research several factors:

- The industry structure and competitive forces affecting the structure
- Global concerns that may affect the industry and the organization
- Trends or innovation, such as technology innovation
- Government incentives or pressures
- Predictions about industry supply and demand
- Possible expansion moves by competitors
- The organization's ability to preempt competitors
- The organization's overall strategic plans
- The organization's competitive strategies
- The organization's current capacity and resources
- The financial impact of expansion options
- The level of risk the organization is willing to take (risk appetite)

As identified by the list of research considerations, decisions about expansion require financial forecasting. Forecasting should take into account a number of other factors that will influence the bottom line.

New entry

Entry into a new business is yet another strategic decision because there is so much at stake. There are a number of ways to enter a new business in the same industry or in a different industry, including internal development in the same industry, acquisitions, joint ventures, strategic alliances, and gradual entry over time.

In foreign markets, an organization will enter through strategies such as exporting, licensing and franchising, joint ventures, direct investment, strategic alliances, and gradual entry over time. An organization entering a foreign market that is new to them will need to be assured that they are entering a high growth market and that they have both the finances and time window necessary to withstand the cost and potential setbacks of entering a new, unknown market.

While there are always financial, legal, administrative, and barrier concerns, studies indicate that it is most beneficial to enter an industry with some structural imbalances. If an organization enters an industry that is in balance, it will encounter costs in the barriers to entry, which already put it at a disadvantage with others in the industry.

Porter suggests looking for advantages when making strategic decisions about new business entry, including:

- Imbalances in the industry.
- Low or slow retaliation expectations.
- Low entry costs for the organization.
- Positive effects on the organization's businesses.

Risk response

Each of the strategic decisions discussed in this topic have positive impacts (opportunities) as well as inherent negative impacts (risks). It is up to management to channel the opportunities into their objective/strategy-setting processes—and to identify the risks, develop appropriate risk responses, and balance the rewards and risks. Risk responses could include 1) reducing the likelihood/impact of both via business decisions (e.g., invest in the technology needed to support the strategic decision), 2) sharing or transferring the risk (e.g., hedging or strategic alliances), 3) accepting the risk likelihood/impact, and 4) avoiding the risk (e.g., deciding not to carry out the original strategic decision or selling a product line).

Topic 4: Demonstrate an Understanding of Forecasting (Level A)

Description and purpose

An essential aspect of managing an organization, department, or project is planning for the future. The success of most ventures depends on how well planners and decision makers can anticipate the future and develop appropriate strategies. Analyzing past and present data in order to project the future is called forecasting. Forecasting is used in many different scenarios, including:

- Sales projections.
- Inventory demand.
- Cash flow.
- Capital needs.
- Cost estimation.

Forecasting methods can be classified as qualitative or quantitative. The type of forecasting method to use in a given situation depends on the objectives of the specific forecast and the existing conditions (such as the type of data available). There are many special-purpose forecasting software programs available that managers and others use to help them make business decisions.

Qualitative forecasting

Qualitative forecasting methods generally involve the use of expert judgment. For example, a panel of economists might develop a consensus forecast for the likelihood of higher fuel oil prices a year from now. The advantage of qualitative forecasts is that they can be used when:

- Information on the variable being forecast cannot be quantified.
- Historical data is either not available or not applicable.

Qualitative forecasting is useful in instances when a significant change in environmental conditions makes the use of past data questionable in predicting the future. For example, in the wake of a hurricane that destroys off-shore oil-drilling facilities, qualitative forecasting can be used to predict home heating costs for US consumers the following year, when the cost and availability of fuel oil raises questions about the validity of forecasting future fuel costs based on historical data.

The major disadvantage of using qualitative forecasting methods is the high cost due to the time commitment required from the people involved. Research has also shown that qualitative forecasting may be less accurate than more formal methods due to subjective biases such as optimism and overconfidence.

The four most common qualitative forecasting methods are:

- The Delphi method.
- Expert judgment.
- Scenario writing.
- The intuitive approach.

Delphi method

The Delphi method attempts to develop forecasts through group consensus. Typically, members of an unbiased, independent expert group are asked to respond to a series of questionnaires without knowledge of the identities or responses of any other members of the group. The responses from the first questionnaire are used to develop the second questionnaire, which contains information and opinions from the entire group. Each expert is asked to reconsider and revise his or her response in light of the group information provided. This process continues until the facilitator determines that a consensus has been reached. The goal of the Delphi method is to produce a narrow spread of opinions with which the majority of the experts involved agree.

Expert judgment

Expert judgment is a forecasting method used when conditions in the past are not likely to hold in the future. This method can provide valid forecasts in many situations, particularly when the forecasts are based on the judgment of at least five and ideally up to 20 experts. Essentially, expert judgment involves a group of experts each considering information and then weighing in with an opinion or conclusion regarding a specific forecast. This is the method used by financial experts at major US stock brokerages to forecast stock market averages and the prime rate each year.

Scenario writing

Scenario writing consists of developing a conceptual scenario of the future based on a well-defined set of assumptions. Different assumptions are used to formulate different scenarios, and the decision maker must decide how likely each scenario is and make decisions accordingly.

Intuitive approach

The intuitive approach is a subjective technique based on the ability of the human mind to process information that may be difficult to quantify. It includes things like brainstorming sessions or "charrettes" where individuals come together to share information and strategize the future without fear of criticism, peer pressure, or restrictions.

Quantitative forecasting

Quantitative forecasting often makes use of statistical or mathematical models designed to simulate reality and help in decision making.

Quantitative models depict interrelationships among factors or variables and are classified in three different ways:

- Descriptive—showing relationships among variables
- Predictive—predicting how variables will behave when one or more of them is changed
- Planning—determining the best way of combining or changing relationships to achieve a desired result

Quantitative methods can be used when:

- Past information about the variable being forecast is available.
- The information can be quantified.
- A reasonable assumption is that the pattern of the past will continue into the future.

This section will discuss the following quantitative forecasting methods:

- Time series analysis
- Smoothing methods
- Causal methods
- Learning curve analysis
- Sensitivity analysis
- Simulation

Time series analysis

Time series analysis involves a series of measurements taken at successive points in time or over successive periods of time (hours, days, months, etc.). It is used if the data is restricted to past values of the variable that is being forecast. The objective of a time series analysis is to discover patterns in the historical data and then extrapolate these patterns into the future. For example, a store manager may track sales to determine whether they increase or decrease during certain seasons in order to forecast inventory needs. A university may track annual freshman enrollment in order to forecast staffing needs, and a city may track daily flows in a river in order to provide its citizens with flood warnings should the need arise.

The benefits of time series analysis include:

- Showing patterns that are clearly upward or downward.
- Helping decision makers project future developments.
- Allowing organizations to plan production and expenditures to match the market by tracking cyclical or seasonal trends.

The limitations of time series analysis include:

- Assuming that past patterns will continue into the future, which is not always the case.
- Allowing missing variables to impact results without measuring them.
- Realizing that analysts cannot predict irregular events such as natural disasters or wars.

In time series analysis, four components combine to provide the overall pattern or behavior of the data: trend, cycles, seasonality, and irregular variations.

Trend

Time series data may be taken at any regular interval. Although the data typically shows random fluctuations, it may also show gradual shifts or movements to relatively higher or lower values over time. This is called a trend. A long-term trend is usually the result of changes in the population, technology, or consumer preferences.

Cycles

Time series often show alternating sequences of points below and above the trend line. Any recurring sequence of such points lasting more than a year can be attributed to the cyclical component of the time series. This includes overall cycles of the economy, which may include a variable in the form of an economic indicator or index.

Companies that do better in a poor economy (such as those that sell inexpensive and necessary goods) are known as countercyclical businesses or industries because they go against the normal economic cycle. Industries that do better in a good economy, such as producers of luxury items, are known as cyclical businesses. Noncyclical organizations, like those in the food industry, are more constant.

Seasonality

Variability in the time series data due to seasonal influences is called the seasonal component. This component may be used to represent any regularly repeating pattern that is one year or less in duration. This includes the predictable sales peak each winter for the ski industry and each summer for swimming pool manufacturers. It can also reflect fluctuations in daily traffic volume.

Identifying seasonal variations is necessary to predict volume over a period of time more accurately. Planning must be synchronized with accurate forecasting. Failure to account for seasonal increases in business could result in understaffing or out-of-stock situations due to insufficient production. Basing annual sales and production estimates on data from a seasonal peak period will probably result in missed quotas, overstaffing, overpurchasing, excess inventory, and cash flow problems.

To remove the effect of seasonality from a time series, the original series value is divided by the seasonal factor (the typical change one might expect, based on previous data). For example, a restaurant knows it spends an average of $1,000/month on produce, but the seasonal factor for the month of January is 0.8. Since $1,000/0.8 = $1,250, any increase above $1,250 for the month of January must be due to factors other than normal seasonal increases in produce prices—perhaps a spike in transportation costs.

Irregular variations

Random variability in a time series is any irregular deviation of data from trend, cyclical, and seasonal components. Irregular variations are caused by short-term, unanticipated, and nonrecurring factors such as the weather, natural disasters, or terrorist attacks. For example, after a hurricane there may be a spike in sales of generators and bottled water. Analysts cannot predict the impact of irregular factors on time series analysis.

Smoothing methods

Smoothing is an analytical method in which random fluctuations from the irregular component of the time series are averaged out. Smoothing methods are helpful for stable time series that do not exhibit significant patterns due to trend, cyclical, or seasonal effects. They generally provide a high level of accuracy for short-range forecasts such as a forecast for the next time period. They are generally easy to use and require few data points, so they are well suited to manufacturing environments that require forecasts for thousands of items weekly and monthly.

There are three smoothing methods:

- Moving averages
- Weighted moving averages
- Exponential smoothing

Moving averages

The moving averages method uses the average of the most recent data value set for a given time period. The term "moving" indicates that as a new observation becomes available for the time series, it replaces the oldest observation and a new average is computed; the average will change as new observations become available.

Weighted moving averages

In the moving averages method, each observation is given equal weighting in the calculation. In the variation known as weighted moving averages, the assumption is that the most recent data has more power of prediction than data that came before, so more weight is given to the most recent data.

Exponential smoothing

Exponential smoothing uses a weighted average of past time series as the forecast. It selects only one weight, that of the most recent observation. The weights for the other data values are automatically computed and get smaller and smaller as the observations move farther into the past.

Exponential smoothing has minimal data requirements and is used when forecasts are required for a large number of dependent variables. Not all past data needs to be saved in order to compute the forecast for the next period. Once the smoothing constant has been selected, the exponential smoothing method requires only two pieces of information to compute the forecast: the forecast and actual values for the last (current) period.

Causal forecasting methods—regression analysis

Causal forecasting methods are based on the assumption that the variable being forecast exhibits a cause-and-effect relationship with one or more other variables. For instance, sales volume for many products is influenced by advertising expenditures.

Regression analysis is a causal forecasting method used to develop forecasts when time series data is not available. It is used to examine relationships among two or more variables in order to make a prediction. It is a statistical method used for obtaining an equation that best fits a set of data. Regression analysis is often used by management accountants to analyze cost behavior (for example, to determine the fixed and variable portions of a total cost) or to forecast future events such as sales levels. It is often used to disclose business trends and identify aberrations. Internal auditors can use it to help managers make predictions or to test management's predictions.

Regression analysis creates a linear equation based on the relationship between a dependent or response variable and one or more independent or predictor variables. The dependent variable is the value being forecast, such as sales or total costs. The independent variables are the factors that are assumed to influence or drive the variations seen in the dependent variable.

There are two basic types of regression analysis:

- Simple linear regression involves one independent variable and one dependent variable; the relationship between the variables sometimes can be approximated by a straight line.
- Multiple regression analysis involves two or more independent variables.

In simple linear regression, the relationship between two variables can be plotted on a graph called a scatter diagram. The items plotted show the trend or historical information. The independent variable is normally plotted on the horizontal axis, and the dependent variable is plotted on the vertical axis. The line fitted to the scattered dots represents the relationship between the variables. Exhibit V-6 shows an example of a scatter diagram.

Exhibit V-6: Scatter Diagram

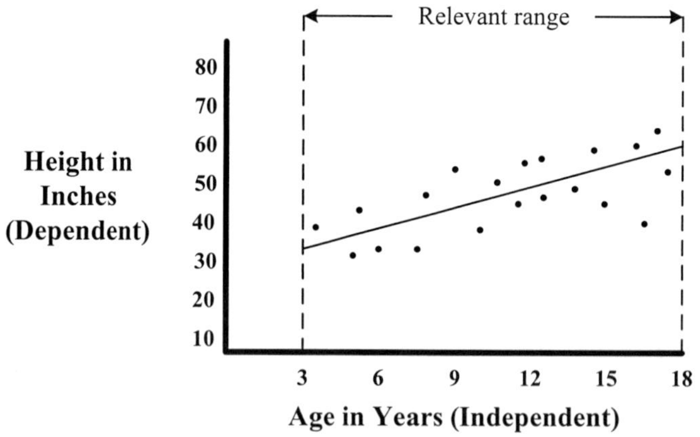

Source: *Sawyer's Internal Auditing,* fifth edition, by Lawrence B. Sawyer, et al. Used with permission.

Least squares regression analysis is based on the idea that the value that best represents (or fits) a given set of quantities is one that minimizes the sum of the squared differences between itself and these quantities. Least squares regression analysis equations systematically reduce estimation errors by fitting a line (the regression line) though data points. This line minimizes the difference between the line (prediction) and the data point (actual), making it a fairly reliable forecasting tool. The statistical formula that the regression is based on produces the least amount of error between the two items.

Regression analysis makes the following assumptions:

- There is a linear relationship between one dependent variable and one or more independent variables. (This can be problematic in the case of learning curves, which are discussed below, or different relevant ranges of activities that cause variables to shift.)
- There is only one independent variable that causes changes to the dependent variable. (There is a chance another variable might be missing from the equation.)
- Past relationships between dependent and independent variables will hold in the future. (It is important to evaluate and adjust the forecast for changes in the relationship between variables over time.)

The benefits and limitations of regression analysis include:

- It is useful as an objective measure in evaluating the precision and reliability of estimations.
- It is useful with a collection of data points, preferably 15 or more, to ensure accuracy. Data can be skewed by unusual data points (outliers), so it is important to graph data before using the regression analysis method.
- It is not useful to answer why something occurs because it does not prove cause and effect.
- It is useful if the reasonableness of the relationship between the dependent and independent variables is evaluated to determine if the equation makes sense.

Learning curve analysis

Learning curve analysis (also called the experience curve) is a systematic method for estimating costs based on increased learning by an organization, group, or individual. As a group or individuals gain experience, they learn and become more efficient at completing tasks. As a result, costs will decrease as learning increases. However, this happens only up to a point before costs level off. Learning curve analysis is commonly used by industries where learning is likely to occur during repetitive operations, such as manufacturers of semiconductors, aircraft, and automobiles. It can also be used to improve cost estimates of project managers when the projects involve repetitive operations.

Calculation of the learning curve is based on the learning rate, which is the percentage by which average time (or total time) falls from previous levels as output doubles.

The learning curve can be measured in two ways: the incremental unit-time learning model and the cumulative average-time learning model.

- **Incremental unit-time learning model.** The incremental unit-time learning model measures increased efficiency by adding the incremental time for each unit to the previous total time. Average time per unit is then calculated by dividing total time by the number of units.

  For example, if a new worker can assemble a widget in ten hours, it would take two new workers a total of 20 production hours (ten hours each) to assemble two widgets. However, if the same worker assembles both widgets, the first will take the ten hours, but due to the worker's learning curve, the second widget may take only eight hours, or 80% of the time it took to build the first one. The total time to build two widgets is 18 hours (10 + 8), so the average time per widget is nine hours. The learning curve and the learning rate do not stay constant. Learning increases efficiency to a point at which productivity reaches equilibrium and then levels off.

- **Cumulative average-time learning model.** The cumulative average-time learning model also measures increased efficiency due to learning. It calculates cumulative total time by multiplying the incremental unit by the cumulative average time per unit. So in our widget example, the cumulative total time for assembling two widgets would be 16 hours (eight hours times two units). The individual unit time for the last unit then is six hours (16 hours total cumulative time minus the previous total of 10 hours).

Exhibit V-7 shows an example of learning curve analysis.

Exhibit V-7: Learning Curve Analysis

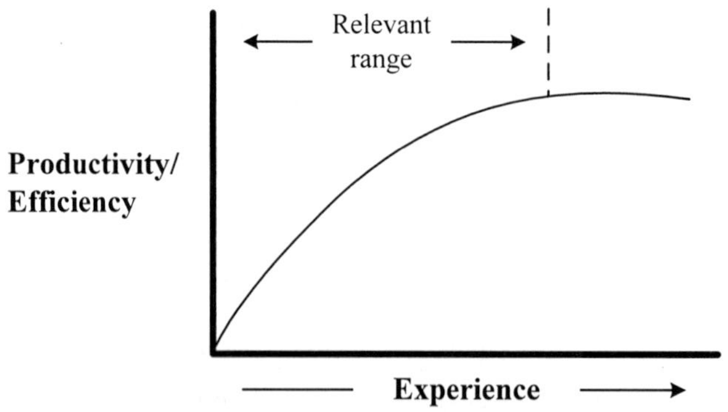

Source: *Sawyer's Internal Auditing,* fifth edition, by Lawrence B. Sawyer, et al. Used with permission.

The following are benefits and limitations of learning curve analysis:

- It can enhance the ability to predict costs when learning occurs.
- It is appropriate for labor-intensive operations that involve repetitive tasks for long production runs.
- It is not appropriate for operations involving robotics or computer controls designed for maximum flexibility and fast set-up times. These require relatively little repetitive labor or opportunity for learning.
- It assumes that the learning rate is constant, which may not be true in actual applications. It is important to update projections based on the observed progression of learning.
- It may cause unreliable conclusions because observed changes in productivity might actually be a result of factors other than learning, such as a change in the labor or product mix.

Sensitivity analysis

Sensitivity analysis describes how changes in probabilities and/or payoffs affect a recommended decision alternative. It is a form of what-if analysis because it is conducted by plugging in different variables and building what-if scenarios with the various possibilities. It is popular in financial applications, risk analysis, and other areas where models are developed. It can help identify which points of input are critical (sensitive) to the choice of the best decision alternative.

The solution to a particular problem is sensitive to a particular input if a small change in input results in a change in the recommended decision alternative. If this is the case, this input must be as accurate as possible to help make decisions. The solution to a particular problem is not sensitive to a particular input if a small, or even large, change in the input does not result in a change in the recommended decision alternative.

Sensitivity analysis can be used in many applications. It can be used to:

- Identify critical assumptions.
- Compare alternative model structures.
- Guide future data collections.
- Detect important criteria.
- Optimize the tolerance of manufactured parts in terms of the uncertainty in the parameters.
- Optimize resource allocation.

The following example illustrates the use of sensitivity analysis in demonstrating the possible effects of variations in the certainty of results.

A company manufactures machinery used in recycling paper products. For each possible level of sales, it assigns a level of probability. It then multiples the expected profit level at various levels of production by the probability factor and totals these sums to identify the level with the most profit potential. The process is shown in Exhibit V-8. As the analysis shows, the most profitable level of production would be 50 units:

$$(.1 \times -10 = -1) + (.2 \times 10 = 2) + (.5 \times 30 = 15) + (.2 \times 30 = 6) = 22$$

Exhibit V-8: Sensitivity Analysis and Forecasting

Demand	10 units	25 units	50 units	100 units	
Probability	0.1	0.2	0.5	0.2	

Units built	**Expected Profit (in thousands)**				**Profit**
10	10	10	10	10	10
25	0	20	20	20	18
50	<10>	10	30	30	22
100	<30>	<10>	10	50	10

The following are benefits and limitations of sensitivity analysis:

- It illustrates how susceptible the outcomes of decisions are to changes in any parameter or estimate.
- It allows for making a "best guess" estimate of how an unexpected occurrence might impact decision outcomes. For example, if airline workers strike, what will be the impact on an airline's bottom line.
- It allows for unreliable results as a change in one estimate or parameter could have an impact on another. It is important to account for this mutual relationship or the results of the sensitivity analysis will not be reliable.

Simulation

Simulation is one of the most widely used quantitative analysis techniques. Various software tools have been developed to model the operation of a system and perform various computations. Simulations are another form of what-if analysis. Once the simulation model is developed, different what-if values are plugged into the program to simulate the effects of changed assumptions.

Most computer simulation programs share the following characteristics:

- They model development.
- They generate values from probability distributions.
- They maintain a record of what happens during the simulation.
- They record and summarize the simulation output.

There are also a variety of special purpose simulation packages available that have simplified methods for generating probabilistic inputs and procedures for collecting and summarizing the simulation output.

Simulation models have two inputs: controllable inputs (decisions) and probabilistic inputs (states of nature), which are randomly generated. In a simulation model exploring whether an organization should introduce a new product line, the controllable inputs might include information based on market research such as the selling price and administrative and advertising costs. The probabilistic inputs might include the cost of labor per unit, parts cost per unit, and demand. Assigning each input a value and running simulations that generate random numbers within an expected range for the probabilistic inputs will illustrate how the outcome changes based on changing variable inputs.

Exhibit V-9 shows an example of a computer simulation model.

Exhibit V-9: Computer Simulation Model

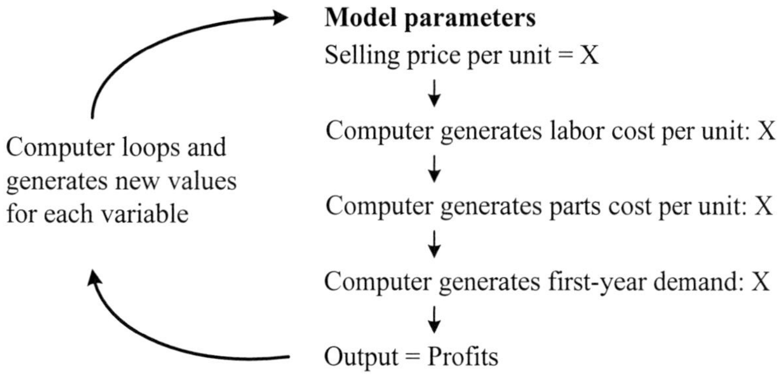

A simulation that involves randomly generating values for the probabilistic inputs is often referred to as a Monte Carlo simulation because of similarities between that type of model and gambling games played in casinos.

Simulations can be applied in numerous ways, including:

- Analyzing where a new product will be profitable.
- Determining the number of reservations an airline should accept for a flight (determining probability of overbooking).
- Creating a policy for ordering inventory (when and how much).
- Analyzing traffic flow.

The following are benefits and limitations of simulation models:

- They are easy to understand, and they can be used to model and learn about the behavior of complex systems that would otherwise be difficult to analyze.
- They are flexible and can be used to model systems without the assumptions often required for mathematical models.
- They enable testing of how changes in assumptions will change a system and its final outcomes.
- They are most appropriate for testing systems with many probabilistic inputs.
- Modeling a complex system might be time-consuming and expensive.
- Simulation data provides estimates of how a real system will operate. It does not guarantee an optimal solution.

Exhibit V-10 on the next page summarizes the different qualitative and quantitative forecasting tools explained in this section and describes their uses.

Topic 5: Demonstrate an Understanding of Quality Management (Level A)

Definition and characteristics of quality

Given the rigors of the global marketplace, continuous improvement in quality is a way of life for many organizations. Global competition gives consumers abundant choices, and they demand high-quality products and services at a reasonable price. Customer expectations are the key to understanding the concept of quality, defined as "fitness for use" by quality guru Joseph Juran. Quality is products or services that match or exceed customer expectations at an anticipated price.

To survive and be successful in today's marketplace, organizations must manufacture quality products and offer quality services. The marketplace has shown that product quality and profitability are closely related. Businesses that offer high-quality products and services are more likely to have larger market shares and a higher return on investment.

Exhibit V-10: Qualitative and Quantitative Forecasting Tools

	Definition	Uses
Qualitative Tools		
Delphi method	Forecasts developed through group consensus using a series of questionnaires	Produces a narrow spread of opinions with which the majority of the experts involved agree
Expert judgment	Experts weigh in with an opinion or conclusion regarding a specific forecast	Used when conditions in the past are not likely to hold in the future
Scenario writing	Conceptual scenarios of future based on defined set of assumptions	Decision maker decides likelihood of scenarios
Intuitive approach	Subjective method based on ability of human mind to process hard-to-quantify information	Examples are brainstorming sessions and "charettes"
Quantitative Tools		
Time series analysis (trend, cycles, seasonality, irregular variations)	Series of measurements taken at successive points or over successive periods	Uncovers patterns in historical data, which are then extrapolated into the future
Smoothing methods (moving averages, weighted moving averages, exponential smoothing)	Average out random fluctuations from irregular components of time series	Accurate for short-range forecasts and well suited to manufacturing
Causal forecasting (regression analysis)	Statistical method used for obtaining equation that best fits a set of data	Used when time series data is not available; examines relationships among two or more variables in order to predict the expected
Learning curve analysis (incremental unit-time learning model, cumulative average-time learning model)	Estimates costs based on increased learning by organization, group, or individual	Used by industries where learning is likely to occur through repetitive operations
Sensitivity analysis	A form of what-if analysis that describes the effects of changes in probabilities and payoffs when different variables are plugged into different scenarios	Used in financial applications and risk analysis to identify which input points are sensitive to different choices
Simulation	Computer software that models system operations and performs computations using different values	Most widely used what-if analysis that simulates the effects of changed assumptions

Advantages of quality

Cost, quality, and time are key factors in determining an organization's success. An organization with low production costs and high-quality products and services will typically enjoy the following benefits:

- Decreasing product returns and customer complaints
- Decreasing warranty costs, service calls, and repair expenses
- Decreasing inventory levels for raw materials, components, and finished products
- Increasing reliability in manufacturing schedules and processes
- Decreasing manufacturing costs by reducing or eliminating rework and increasing productivity
- Increasing number of customers perceiving higher value in products and services, which allows the organization to increase the price of products or services and increase market share and ultimately revenues and profits

Conformance

As mentioned earlier, Juran's "fitness for use" emphasizes quality as the reliability of a product or service for its users. To ensure a reliable level of quality throughout an organization, every individual, department, and subdivision must conform to specifications set by customer expectations. Conformance means reducing and eliminating variations (defects) from the desired outcome (the target value).

There are two primary types of conformance:

- Goalpost or zero defects conformance means achieving a quality specification expressed as a specified range around a target.
- Absolute or robust quality conformance requires all products or services to meet the target value exactly, with no variation.

However, achieving quality is not simply a matter of reducing or eliminating variations in order to produce quality products or services efficiently. A quality product or service must conform to a design that meets or exceeds customer expectations at a competitive price that customers are willing to pay. For example, a customer who requests a deluxe car wash and who is willing to pay the added cost for a wax and polish will not be satisfied with a basic car wash that includes nothing beyond a wash and dry.

Total quality management

Total quality management (TQM) is an integrated quality management system that involves managers and employees and uses quantitative methods to continually improve an organization's processes. Because quality costs are often a substantial share of sales revenues, many firms integrate TQM efforts with their strategic planning efforts.

Implementing TQM takes a significant long-term commitment on the part of everyone at an organization. It is an ongoing, time-consuming task, and it can take several years before the benefits of TQM become tangible. Individual organizations develop TQM strategies suited to their individual goals and culture; the characteristics common to most TQM programs are shown in Exhibit V-11.

Exhibit V-11: Critical Success Factors for TQM

Critical Success Factor	Description
Focus on the customer	• Identify internal and external customers. • Determine their needs, requirements, and expectations. • Solicit customer feedback to measure satisfaction.
Continuous improvement	• TQM as way of life, not finite goal. • Continuous improvement is company-wide philosophy. • Encourage ongoing processes that find and eliminate problems and eliminate waste.
Involvement of the entire workforce	• Systematic problem solving. • Empowerment at every employee level. • Teamwork such as quality circles to identify problems and implement solutions.
Active support and involvement by top management	• Involvement at every level of organization. • Top leaders must demonstrate commitment to TQM at every opportunity. • TQM is present in every decision.
Clear and objective measures	• Quality requires institutional changes. • Analyze both good and bad processes. • Conformity (design quality into products and services to minimize variations). • Embrace measurable objectives such as key performance indicators with related targets or goals.
Quality achievements recognized in a timely manner	• Incentives are important to success of TQM. • Encourage pride and teamwork. • Tie compensation to TQM objectives. • Use both financial and nonfinancial rewards. • Reward quality through publications, awards, and seeing suggestions implemented.
Continuous TQM training	• TQM is cultural change that requires continuous reinforcement. • Ongoing training and education at every level demonstrate management commitment. • Employees need specific skills to succeed at TQM.

The role of teamwork in TQM

Teamwork is one of the key elements of TQM initiatives. Teams provide a vehicle for identifying common problems that are holding the organization back, drawing on shared knowledge and experience to solve those problems and providing group support through the implementation process. Teams may be temporary (to address specific problems) or ongoing.

Effective teams will benefit from:

- A clear charter, a work process, and deadlines, if appropriate.
- Support from senior management.
- Sufficient resources (both materials and time) to accomplish the charter.
- Vehicles for communication that ensure ease and openness of exchanges between team members.
- A leader or rotating leaders who can engage and coach team members and create a constructive, supportive atmosphere.
- Recognition and accountability for team members.

Exhibit V-12 summarizes some of the benefits and challenges of teams.

Exhibit V-12: Benefits and Challenges of Teams

Benefits	Challenges
• Applies a diversity of perspectives, skills, and experience • Generates more practical solutions with greater chance for success • Often results in greater ease in implementing team-developed solutions and workplace acceptance	• Requires time and resources to train team members in process • Requires strong facilitation/leadership skills to focus efforts and manage disagreements • May take more time to reach consensus on actions to be taken

TQM quality measures

To achieve its goal of meeting or exceeding customer expectations, an organization must have quality measures in place to determine whether quality efforts and actions are helping the organization achieve its goal.

Typical TQM quality measures include:

- **Product design,** assessed through the number of new parts and the number of total parts in an organization's products. This can also be applied to procedures and operations in a service-oriented organization.
- **Vendor rating systems,** analyzed through the number of defects and on-time delivery.

- **Customer satisfaction,** evaluated through surveys and warranty expenses.
- **Manufacturing,** analyzed through defect rates, scrap, rework, and on-time delivery.

Statistical process control measures tend to look at two dimensions of quality:

- Whether the process is in control, thus stable and predictable
- Whether the process is in compliance, or within the specifications required for the product or by the customer

Costs of quality

Along with having quality measures in place, organizations must understand the costs associated with quality processes in order to make tradeoffs among quality decisions. The costs of implementing quality initiatives can be a substantial part of revenue. Yet part of the TQM philosophy is that gains in efficiency and effectiveness can also be realized with no net increase in costs and can ultimately create significant cost reductions.

Costs of quality are the activities associated with the prevention, identification, repair, and rectification of poor quality. They also include the opportunity costs from lost production time and sales as a result of poor quality. Exhibit V-13 lists some of the most common costs of quality.

Exhibit V-13: Costs of Quality

Quality Cost Type	Quality Cost Components
Prevention costs (incurred to eliminate defective products before they are produced)	• Reengineering and design • Use of high-quality parts • Improved processes • Employee training
Appraisal costs (incurred to identify defective products before they are shipped)	• Inspecting and testing raw materials and work in progress
Internal failure costs (incurred when defects are discovered before sending products to customers)	• Handling and fixing products or disposing of them • Opportunity cost of not being able to sell disposed-of products
External failure costs (incurred when customer receives defective products)	• Cost of returns • Warranty work • Product liability claims • Opportunity cost of lost sales from damaged reputation

Quality tools and techniques

A variety of tools and techniques are available to help organizations, managers, quality circles, and work teams analyze quality problems in specific processes and operations.

Benchmarking

Benchmarking is a methodology in which an organization compares its practices with internal best practices/goals or historical data or the best practices of other organizations and adapts these best practices for its own use. Measurements that are used are referred to as benchmark metrics because of their quantifiable nature.

Broadly speaking, benchmarking can be understood as a continuous process, as depicted by the plan-do-check-act cycle (also known as the Deming Wheel) in Exhibit V-14.

Exhibit V-14: Plan-Do-Check-Act Cycle Applied to Benchmarking

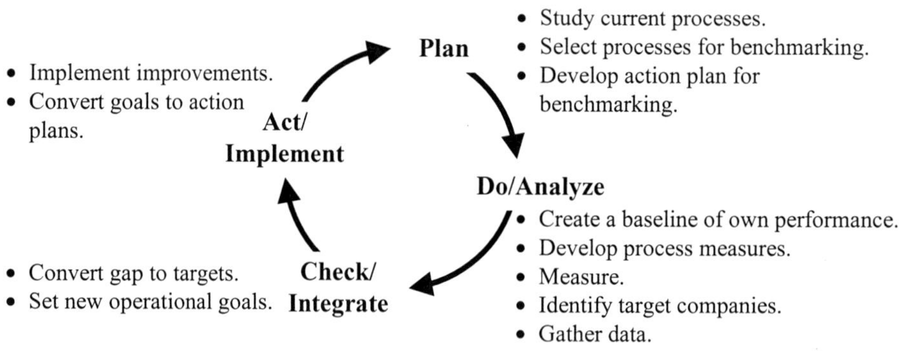

Note that many of the cycles discussed elsewhere, for example, the cycles presented in Section III, Chapter B, "Typical Activities in Various Business Cycles," are also variations on the plan-do-check-act cycle.

Innovations in benchmarking, such as comprehensive benchmarking tools like the Global Auditing Information Network (GAIN), make it much easier to access benchmarking information.

Quality audits

A quality audit is an in-depth review of a company's processes and strategy from a quality standpoint, including analysis of best and worst practices. Quality audits include systems or process audits and product audits.

The results of the audit are compared with analyses of other companies with similar processes as part of a benchmarking study. The result is a long-term plan for strategic quality improvement.

Gap analysis

Gap analysis frequently follows a quality audit in order to identify specific problems and set distinct targets for improvement. It looks at the gap between the organization and the benchmark competitor that has the best quality in the industry.

Process flow analysis

Process flow analysis (also known as a flowchart) is a two-dimensional graphic representation of an operation in terms of the flow of activity through the process. This is a method of analyzing operations for efficiency and control.

Flowcharts are discussed in more detail in Part 1, Section III.

Control charts

A control chart is a statistical process that illustrates variations from normal in a situation over time. It has upper and lower control limits drawn on either side of a process range, which allows users to see if the process is out of range.

Exhibit V-15 shows an example of a control chart.

Exhibit V-15: Control Chart

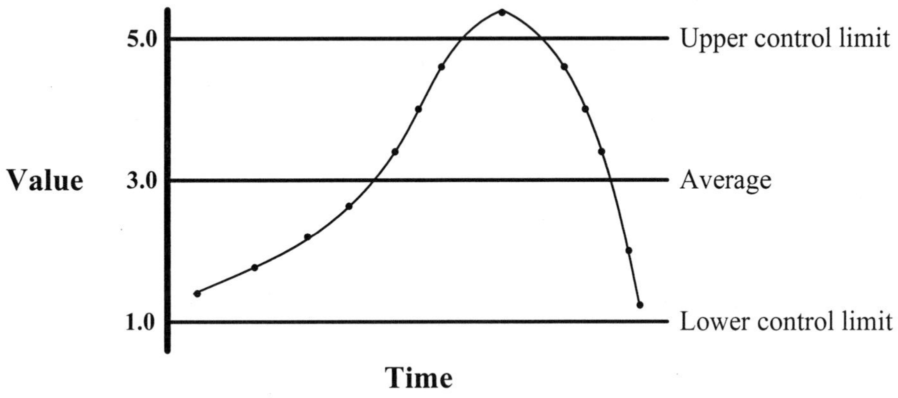

Control charts are also discussed in more detail in Part 1, Section III.

Cause-and-effect diagrams

A cause-and-effect diagram (also called a fishbone or Ishikawa diagram) uses a visual to map out a list of factors that are thought to affect a problem or a desired outcome. An audit team might use such a diagram to determine the root cause of a process with many problem elements.

An example of a cause-and-effect diagram is shown in Exhibit V-16.

Exhibit V-16: Cause-and-Effect Diagram

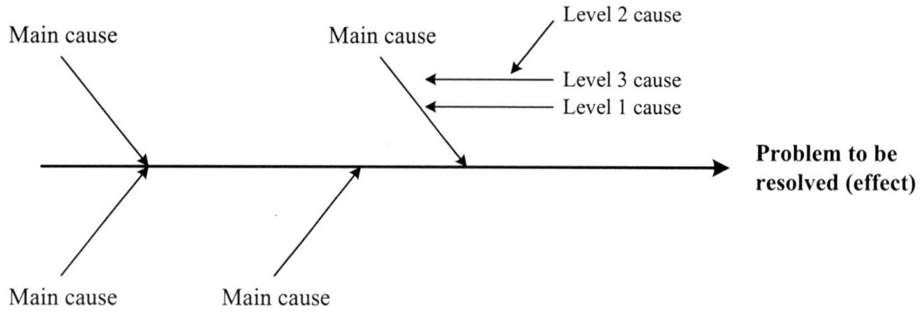

Histograms

A histogram is a measurement of the frequency of particular elements contributing to an overall set of data. A Pareto diagram is a quality histogram that breaks down quality problems into their various causes and lists them from most to least prevalent. Pareto diagrams can be useful in making management decisions that provide the greatest results. In auditing, a Pareto diagram might be used to determine the areas with the greatest number of defects in a process to assist with scoping decisions.

Check sheets

Check sheets are simple visual tools used to collect and analyze data. A check sheet could be used by an audit team to manage the engagement plan.

Run charts

Run charts illustrate trends and results over a period of time. For example, the run chart in Exhibit V-17 graphically portrays the number of opinions and deficiency audit findings over a period of five years and differentiates between control and performance opinions and between major and minor deficiencies.

Exhibit V-17: Example of a Run Chart: Summary of Deficiency Findings, Year 5

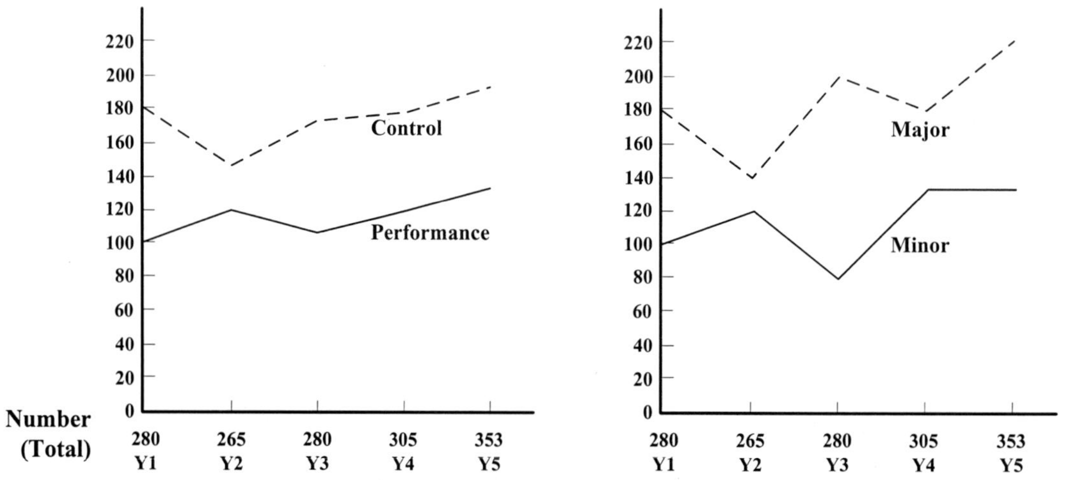

Source: *Sawyer's Internal Auditing,* fifth edition, by Lawrence B. Sawyer, et al. Used with permission.

Six Sigma

Another quality tool is Six Sigma, a disciplined, data-driven approach and methodology for eliminating defects. To achieve Six Sigma, a process must not produce more than 3.4 defects per million opportunities. A Six Sigma defect is defined as anything outside of customer specifications. A Six Sigma opportunity is the total number of chances for a defect. Six Sigma processes are explained further in Section III, Chapter C.

Topic 6: Describe Methods and Uses of Decision Analysis (Level A)

Decision making is the process of identifying feasible options and selecting the optimum option for a given situation. Decision analysis is a method of quantifying the optimal option for a given situation using statistical tools and mathematical models of actual business problems.

Methods

The methods chosen for decision analysis will be selected based on the type of decision being made. Some examples include a SWOT analysis (described in the introduction to this chapter) for strategic decision analysis, linear programming (described in Section III, Chapter C) or a sensitivity or scenario analysis (described in Topic 4 of this chapter) for making business and financial decisions such as whether or not to out-source, or use of one or more of the quality tools discussed in the prior topic to analyze the best way to improve processes, products, or services.

SWOT analysis

The SWOT analysis is revisited here as an example of a method of decision analysis, summarizing "Application of SWOT and Principal Component Analysis in a Textile Company—A Case Study" by Jeyaraj et al. (See bibliography.) As a precursor to strategy development for a textile company, the researchers created preliminary lists of SWOT items using a combination of experience, brainstorming, and research. The researchers started with 33 items in their SWOT table and then sent out a rating questionnaire to managers to gather reactions from the organization. A principal component analysis (PCA) analysis of results was used to reduce the list to 24 items. PCA is a form of multivariate analysis (which is yet another type of decision analysis) that combines or removes items that are found to be correlated, reducing the set to just those uncorrelated items that are the principal components or distinct factors.

Exhibit V-18 paraphrases the results of the textile company SWOT analysis. The research presented an SO and a WO strategy for each opportunity identified and an ST and a WT strategy for each threat identified. The exhibit shows just one of these opportunities and one of the threats along with the proposed strategies for the sake of brevity. The strengths and weaknesses are all shown in the left column as they all may contribute to the strategy formation.

Exhibit V-18: SWOT Analysis for a Textile Company

SWOT Matrix	**Opportunities** (external analysis) Huge export market and local market	**Threats** (external analysis) Requirement for an ecological textile product and competitors with shorter product lead times
Strengths (internal analysis) Cost-aware, mass production, low-cost labor, low-cost raw materials, strong R&D for finishing/dyeing, capital available	***SO strategies*** Capitalize on internal strengths to maximize opportunities. Maximize production line output by optimizing product mix. Develop own retail sales operations to expand local market.	***ST strategies*** Draw on internal strengths to reduce external threats. Research and develop a fast dyeing technology that reduces electricity, fuel, and water use and wastewater discharge.
Weaknesses (internal analysis) Water shortages, limited waste treatment capacity, textile machine upkeep, fragmented organization, worker fatigue	***WO strategies*** Overcome internal weaknesses to maximize opportunities. Implement Occupational Safety and Health Assessment Series (OHSAS) 18001 and an environmental management system (EMS) to reduce water consumption and improve waste treatment efficiency.	***WT strategies*** Reduce internal weaknesses to guard against external threats. Integrate the value chain to reduce product lead times and invest in worker training and skill development to enhance production effectiveness.

Notice that this SWOT analysis uses techniques from decision analysis to reduce the number of variables being considered to just those that have a differentiating effect from a statistical basis. This allows the strategic planning processes that follow to be more focused on what might create a real difference for this organization.

The full textile company case study can be viewed at www.ijerd.com/paper/vol1-issue9/I0194654.pdf.

Decision tree

A more complex tool for decision analysis is a decision tree. Decision trees are ways of mapping out probabilities and costs of various decisions over time. They include decision nodes (represented by squares) and chance nodes (represented by circles) to indicate states of nature or variable results. For example, the first decision point will have two or more options, each of which is a branch of the tree shown by a line. Each of these lines will lead either to another decision with two or more choices to make (further branches) or to a chance node where a range of possibilities that are not controllable can occur. Each branch from this point will be weighted based on probability of occurrence, such as 40% chance of A or 60% chance of B. Such a tree would be built by an analyst with statistical and programming skills or by use of a specialized computer application. It is important to ensure that all possible outcomes are mapped out. When complete, the cost, profit, or other measured result is multiplied by its probability of occurrence. In this way, the optimum result can be easily seen by which final node has the highest positive value.

Uses

Many possible uses of decision analysis have been suggested over the course of these materials as each tool or model was presented. However, here we will only concentrate on three uses that are applicable to most forms of decision analysis. First, it helps build relationships between decision makers and analysts when done correctly so that better decisions can be made. The method promoted here for relationship building is called progressive model building. Second, it helps decision makers make decisions in the face of uncertainty. Since all decisions related to future events are by their nature uncertain, addressing risk and opportunity are the key to any forward-looking rational decision-making process. Third, it helps the organization move from data, to relevant data, to observations, and then to knowledge that can be acted upon.

Relationship building using progressive model building

Decision analysis is an activity that typically occurs between at least two people: a decision maker and an analyst of some sort (business, marketing, financial, and so on). This distinction between analyst and decision maker is important because it is a relationship like any other that requires building up mutual trust and respect over time. If an analyst takes a business problem and develops a detailed computer-based simulation in isolation, the decision maker, who cannot understand the complexities of the model, could choose to trust it blindly or reject it utterly. Blind trust keeps the manager from seeing what a change in assumptions might do and prevents the manager from making a reality check on the results. In other words, it robs the manager of the benefit of his or her experience. Model rejection often happens because of a lack of relationship building: Perhaps the manager thinks that the analyst is unschooled in business and may have been making unrealistic assumptions. In both blind trust in and rejection of analysis, the time and energy of both parties is wasted.

A best practice for decision analysis is for the complexity of analysis to evolve as the relationship evolves. This is called progressive model building or bootstrapping. Analysts start with a very basic model that can be generated quickly and can be understood easily even if admittedly crude. Then if this model is rejected, it will be rejected before significant effort was made. If it makes sense to the decision maker, it can be further refined, complexities can be added, and results improved over time. The decision maker can help the analyst prioritize what factors to add and what weights or probabilities seem realistic when expert judgment must be used. Sometimes progressive model building can keep a model from becoming too complex, because it must always be in line with the decision maker's comfort level. If a simple but fast method gets the decision maker to very close to the right answer, it is still better than a model that gets him or her very precisely to an answer too slowly to be of use or too difficult to comprehend.

Making decisions in the face of uncertainty

Decision makers often must make decisions even though they lack sufficient information. While more information generally helps make better decisions, people can change their minds or may have yet to make a decision, so almost all decisions are made in the face of uncertainty. Statistical analyses and other probability-based decision analysis methods help quantify the gap between what is known and what needs to be known in order to make the best decision. The essence of decision theory is to treat decisions as if they were gambling problems in which the decision maker is playing the best odds so as to achieve the biggest payoff.

Two key elements of decision theory are utility, such as the size of a reward or the impact of a risk, and probability, such as the likelihood of an opportunity or risk. Utility and probability help decision makers visualize the potential consequences of a decision and anticipate other future decisions that will need to be made. This is called seeing the range of options and is another element of decision theory. Seeing the likely outcome several steps in advance is the essence of planning, as any good chess player might tell you.

Exhibit V-19 shows a model for making decisions based on theories of decision analysis. Note that the model starts with understanding stakeholder objectives. Analysts should develop these into criteria that can be expressed objectively and included in any model so that that the alternatives or options that meet more of these criteria can be given more weight or utility. Similarly, the situation, or the environmental context and other constraints, can be deliberately included in modeling so that decisions reflect these realities.

Exhibit V-19: Decision-Making Model from Decision Analysis

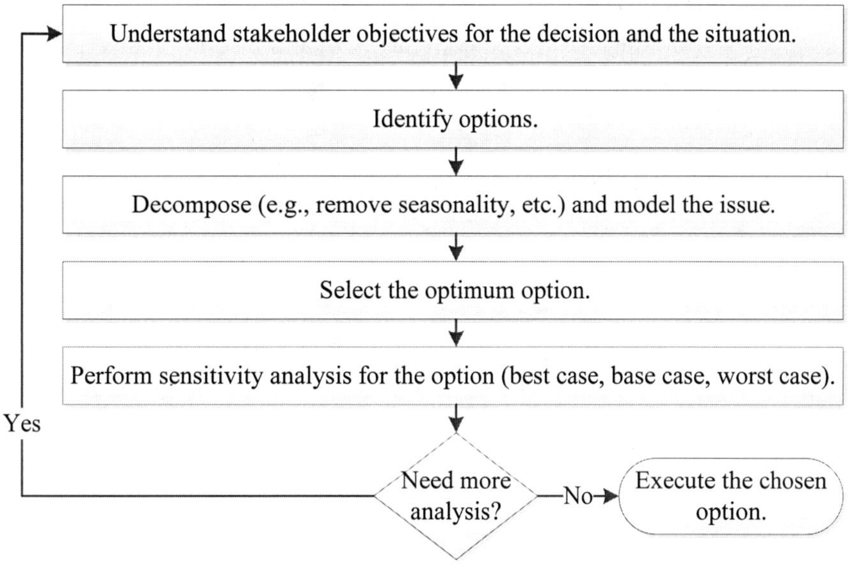

Moving from data to knowledge

Knowledge is more than just collected information. Knowledge is information and observations that have a familiarity due to experience or association with their application and their likely results. Exhibit V-20 shows how increasing the precision and predictive ability of statistical models results in improving the decision-making process itself, thus resulting in a progression from just collecting data, to determining what data is relevant, to then being able to form observations (the facts), and finally creating knowledge or organizational learning. Recall that the dependent variable is the value being forecast and the independent variable is the factor that is assumed to influence or drive the variations seen in the dependent variable.

Exhibit V-20: Better Decision Analysis Improves Decision Making and Creates Knowledge

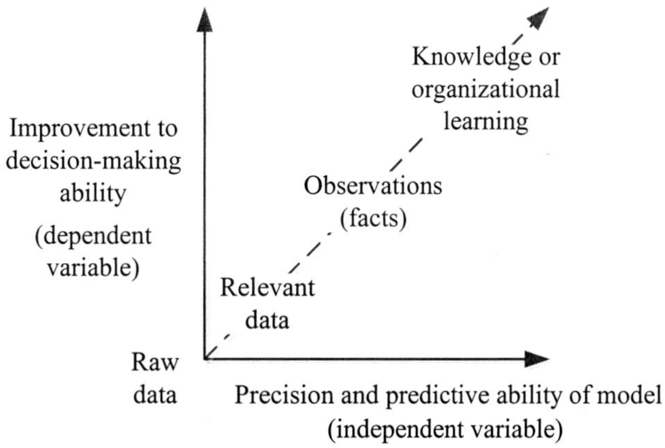

Going back to the discussion of organizational learning in Section III, Chapter B, the knowledge gained could be individual knowledge, but if championed from the top, shared convincingly, and institutionalized through policy and procedure, this knowledge can become organizational learning.

Chapter B: Organizational Behavior

Chapter Introduction

Organizational behavior refers to the way individuals and groups behave in the organizational setting. The organization can be thought of as a system with interdependent parts. The culture and other factors influence the way individuals and groups respond. In turn, individual and group dynamics affect the dynamics of the organization.

Organizations foster certain behaviors by their operational and motivational frameworks. This section touches on factors that affect how motivated and empowered organizations, groups, and individuals feel. These factors include the organizational structure, management style, exertion of power and influence, organizational culture, cultural differences, communication strategies, and employee recognition and reward systems.

Internal auditors need to understand organizational behavior because different methods of control work better in different organizations. Also, the root cause of a control deficiency may lie in dysfunctional organizational behavior. Auditors will benefit from a broader, enterprise-wide view of organizational behavior for the important work done in the organization. The auditing activities become a knowledge source in the overall knowledge management system of the organization.

Topic 1: Describe Structures and Configurations within Organizational Theory (Level A)

Recall the discussion of centralized versus decentralized and other organizational structures presented in Section III, Chapter A. Keep these basic structures in mind along with their benefits and drawbacks (these are summarized in a table at the end of this topic) as we explore some nontraditional configurations developed in response to the drawbacks of one structure or another or as a response to changing business environments. Also keep in mind that, if acceptable to the organization, some business functions could be organized under different organizational structures than others if it makes sense, for example, centralizing procurement even if other parts of the organization are more decentralized. Similarly, some of the nontraditional configurations that follow may have a niche application even if the overall organization uses some other structure.

Nontraditional configurations

Globalization, strong competition, mergers and acquisitions, technology, workforce diversity, and other forces have pushed traditionally structured organizations to reframe and reorganize. These changes allow organizations to more quickly and effectively compete in the marketplace and respond to their stakeholders—consumers, partners, investors, boards of directors, local communities, and others.

Nontraditional organizations tend to exhibit these characteristics:

- **Decentralization.** Organizations are becoming flatter, which means that there is less hierarchy and leaders are closer to the front lines and consumers. Employees are participative and feel more empowered.

- **Organic structures.** Organizations are behaving more like living organisms that evolve and adapt to the environment they live in. Organic structures are flatter, with fewer rules and regulations and high employee participation.

- **Learning organization.** A learning organization can be described as a boundaryless organization with individuals who recognize the value of knowledge creation and sharing. This collaborative team environment helps employees solve problems, learn faster, and contribute to organization effectiveness.

- **Flexibility.** The workplace is becoming more flexible for employees, especially with regard to individual and work team autonomy, work schedules, telecommuting, virtual conferences, international travel, and benefit options.

- **Networks.** Organizations are developing informal and formal relationship networks both inside and outside of the organization. These relationships link separate organizations in a decentralized manner.

While organizations are exhibiting many of these characteristics, changing an organizational structure is an immense effort. The following are a few examples of nontraditional configurations for organizations.

Hourglass organization

An hourglass organization is shaped in the form of an hourglass, as shown in Exhibit V-21, with a wider span of senior management control at the top, a narrower middle management span of control, and a wider lower level of control at the bottom.

Exhibit V-21: Hourglass Organizational Structure

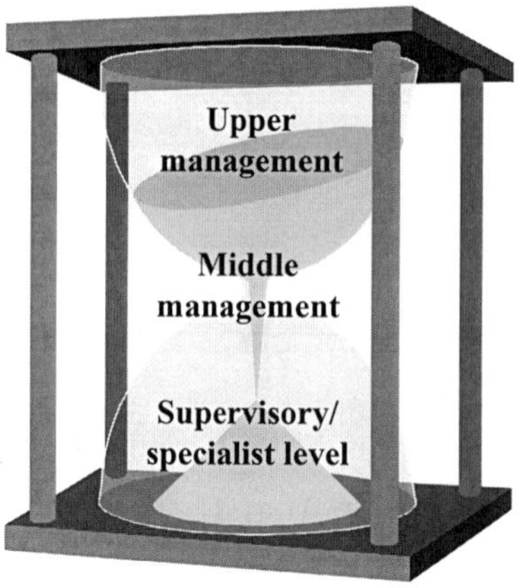

Some organizations have reduced staffing in middle management to save on personnel costs. With this model, routine decisions are more easily made at the lower supervisory/specialist level. However, disadvantages occur when more important approvals stall in the middle or top of the hourglass. In this structure, there are fewer middle managers to respond, and upper-level management may be very bureaucratic.

Network structure

A network structure involves relationships between multiple organizations or separate entities within an organization that perform different aspects of work. Examples of network organizations are joint ventures, licensing arrangements, and owned subsidiaries. Some of the distinguishing features of network structures are:

- Lack of a vertical order with production, marketing, and other functions.
- Management by broker organizations.
- Strong relationships and coordination among the network partners.

Exhibit V-22 shows a simplified version of a network organizational structure. A broker manages the interplay between the various partners. The connecting arrows could also be directed from each partner to another, given the strong communication and reliance that occurs between partners.

Exhibit V-22: Network Organizational Structure

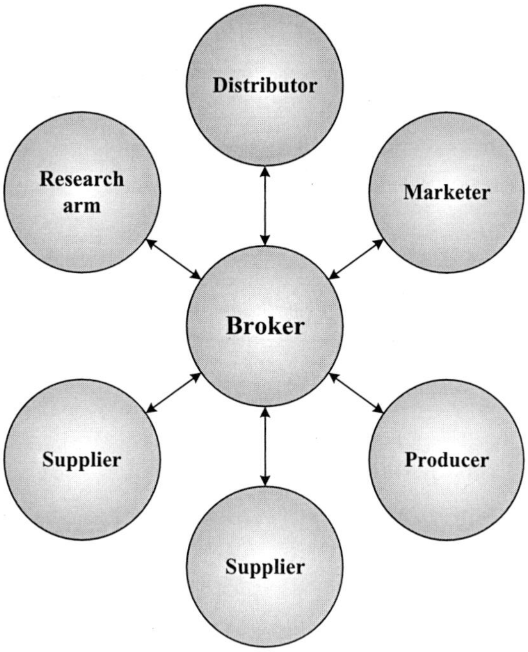

The advantages of a network organization are high flexibility and the ability to respond to change, new combined marketplace strengths, global expansion possibilities, ease of application to organizations that grow through merger and acquisition, and synergy building upon partner strengths. The disadvantages are the difficulty of lateral management across different organizations, sustaining the interest and contribution of the separate organizations, and the vulnerabilities in sharing proprietary information.

Cluster organizations and virtual organizations, to be discussed next, can be considered forms of network structures.

Cluster organizations

A cluster organization refers to an organizational structure with many groups or teams to accomplish organizational objectives. Team-based organizations offer much by way of flexibility. Projects can be approached on a planned or ad hoc basis. Cross-functional teams add creativity and efficiencies in the organization. Team members are chosen for their individual skills that contribute to the collective effort. The team environment fosters organizational learning and high employee participation and keeps its employees motivated. Teams can also produce on a faster basis.

Disadvantages to cluster groups are the fact that teams need strong leaders, coordination of work, and effective group communication skills to perform at a high level.

Clusters have broader business environment application as well. For example, industry clusters are interrelated organizations that band together for competitive advantage in an industry.

Virtual organizations

A virtual organization is a geographically dispersed organization that is linked together through electronic communications. Members primarily communicate via telecommunications, Web-based virtual meetings, Web discussions, and e-mail correspondence.

The structural relationship relies on lateral communication. Boundaries in the organization are blurred. Teams form and disband according to needs.

A virtual organization is typically functionally and culturally diverse, which enables greater adaptability and response times in the global marketplace. Disadvantages are the lack of face-to-face contact, less relationship building, less loyalty to the organization, more organizational conflict, and information overload.

In summary, there are various organizational structure options, each with its own advantages and disadvantages, as described in Exhibit V-23 on the next page. Each organization must seriously consider its industry, type of work, core strengths and business processes, and the optimum ways to interact to foster better decision making, creativity, and innovation for the future.

Topic 2: Demonstrate an Understanding of Organizational Behavior (Level A)

Motivational theories

Basic to human behavior, and thus organizational behavior, is motivation. Motivation is an individual's desire or drive toward a reward or goal. In the workplace, this refers to an individual's self-direction and persistence toward accomplishing work goals and outcomes.

Motivation has to do with people's needs, what they value, and their perceptions and feelings. There are two basic types of motivation:

- **Intrinsic motivation** is internally driven, such as when an action is important or matches personal values.
- **Extrinsic motivation** is externally driven by factors such as money, public recognition, or other rewards.

Exhibit V-23: Organizational Structure Comparisons

Structure	Advantages	Disadvantages
Centralized	• Management consistency and control • Economies of scale	• Slower decision making/responses • Low employee participation
Decentralized	• Higher employee participation and satisfaction • Faster decision making/ responses	• Loss of economies of scale • Less control over productivity and efficiencies
Departmentalization	• Focus on common knowledge and skills	• Possible conflict/inefficiency between departments
Functional	• Specialization by function • More employee participation	• Narrower area perspective • Coordination difficult
Divisional	• Autonomy by division • Specialization	• Narrower perspectives • Loss of economies of scale
Matrix	• Blend of technical and market emphasis • Efficient use of resources	• Dual reporting causes employee confusion and possible manager conflict
Hourglass	• Broader span of control at the bottom for daily decision making	• Slower responses through the channels for important decisions
Network	• High flexibility and adaptability • Combined strengths and synergy • Global possibilities	• Difficulty in lateral management • Difficulty in sustaining interest • Vulnerabilities in sharing knowledge
Cluster	• Team-based and high flexibility • Encourages motivation and learning	• Strong leaders and communication necessary
Virtual	• High adaptability and response times • Team-based with specializations	• Communication conflict • Less loyalty • Information overload

There are several historical theories of motivation that have relevant application for behavior in organizations today. A brief account of some of the primary motivational theories follows.

Hierarchy of needs (Maslow)

Abraham Maslow's hierarchy of needs theory is displayed in a pyramid fashion. There are five levels in the hierarchy, starting with the most basic physiological needs on the bottom. The basic premise is that only after the bottom order of needs are met can the higher need levels be met.

The need levels, listed here from the lowest to the highest with examples, are:

- **Physiological needs**—body functioning such as sleep, food, and water.
- **Safety needs**—safe environment, protection, and financial security.
- **Social/belonging needs**—friends, love, and a sense of belonging.
- **Esteem needs**—internal needs such as self-esteem and self-respect and external needs such as status, reputation, and recognition.
- **Self-actualization**—personal growth and striving to reaching one's full potential.

Maslow's hierarchy of needs has application in organizational settings. Exhibit V-24 lists ways to meet individual needs in the workplace.

Exhibit V-24: Meeting Needs in the Workplace

Maslow's Hierarchy	Workplace Examples
Self-actualization needs	Challenging assignments, professional development opportunities, and leadership responsibilities
Esteem needs	Promotions, job titles, special recognition, and rewards
Social/belonging needs	Employee orientation programs, peer and mentor coaching, work teams, and social functions
Safety needs	Safe physical environment, job security, and job benefits
Physiological needs	A job, sufficient earnings, work breaks, refreshments, and health and wellness programs

Managers have an opportunity to take an interest in those around them and encourage growth toward self-actualization. Understanding where an employee might be in the needs hierarchy helps managers determine what strategies might motivate the employee. It should be noted that needs will vary given current circumstances in an individual's work or personal life. They will also vary depending on the current business cycle or job market.

Motivation-hygiene theory (Herzberg)

Frederick Herzberg developed a "two factor" theory that says that there are factors in a work environment that cause employee satisfaction or dissatisfaction. Herzberg's theory is that people have two important types of needs—survival and personal growth.

In the workplace, survival (or hygiene) factors can be sources of dissatisfaction. Motivator factors are sources of personal growth and satisfaction. Exhibit V-25 provides examples of each.

Exhibit V-25: Hygiene and Motivator Factors

Hygiene (Survival) Factors		Motivator (Personal Growth) Factors	
Organizational policy Manager/ supervisor relationships	Working conditions Salary	Achievement Recognition	Responsibility Advancement

An important part of the theory is that a hygiene factor cannot itself provide job satisfaction but can only prevent dissatisfaction. For example, good working conditions may prevent an employee from being dissatisfied, but they do not in and of themselves provide job satisfaction.

A motivator factor can create job satisfaction. However, if the factor is not there, it does not lead to dissatisfaction. For example, added responsibility may increase an employee's job satisfaction, but if the responsibilities were not added, the employee might not be dissatisfied.

With application to motivation in the workplace, the thrust of Herzberg's theory is that hygiene factors must be provided to prevent dissatisfaction. For job satisfaction, additional motivation factors should be provided. Job enrichment, discussed later in this section, is a key strategy in this regard.

Theory of needs (McClelland)

David McClelland's theory describes three types of motivational needs that are learned and acquired over time:

- **Achievement**—Motivated individuals need accomplishment. They strive toward goals and want feedback on their progress.
- **Affiliation**—Motivated individuals need interaction with others. They seek acceptance, develop friendships, and cooperate well with others.
- **Power**—Motivated individuals need power and authority. They want to lead, influence, and make an impact. Recognition and status are important.

McClelland's theory is that individuals have some degree of each characteristic. In the organizational setting, managers will want to consider need motivation to shape work responsibilities and rewards for individuals.

Theory X and Y (McGregor)

Douglas McGregor developed Theory X and Theory Y, espousing that there are two basic approaches to management based on assumptions about employees.

Theory X supports these assumptions about the average employee:

- Dislikes work and will avoid it when possible
- Must be coerced to achieve organizational goals
- Has little ambition and prefers to be directed
- Seeks security above all else

Theory Y supports these assumptions about the average employee:

- Enjoys work as a natural effort
- Is motivated by rewards
- Seeks responsibility and, when committed, is self-directed
- Has creative and intellectual potential that is underutilized

From a management perspective, Theory X lends itself to an authoritarian management style, where managers and supervisors exert a higher level of authority over employees with regard to decision making and work accomplishment. Theory Y lends itself to a participative management style, where managers and supervisors encourage a high level of employee participation and collaboration in decision making and work accomplishment.

Most organizations' managers and employees fall somewhere in between these two theories. The theories cultivate awareness about motivation. McGregor implied that either theory could motivate employees but that Theory Y is a more positive approach.

Organizational management styles (Likert)

Rensis Likert identified four organizational management styles:

- In the **exploitive-authoritative system,** leaders have authority, decisions are imposed, and threats are made. There is little communication and no teamwork.
- In the **benevolent-authoritative system,** leaders have authority and motivation comes through rewards. There is little communication or teamwork.

- In the **consultative system,** leaders have a good deal of trust in employees and motivation comes through rewards and some involvement. There is some communication and some teamwork.
- In the **participative system,** leaders have full trust in employees and rewards from goals are set together. There is much communication and much teamwork.

Likert's overall thrust is that a high level of participation between leaders and employees fosters a high level of motivation among all.

Expectancy theory (Vroom)

Victor Vroom's expectancy theory is based on the assumption that employees' motivations and actions are choices based on three beliefs:

- **Expectancy** refers to how high an expectation there is that effort will produce successful outcomes and rewards.
- **Instrumentality** is how strong the belief is that rewards will actually be received if effort is exerted.
- **Valence** is how strongly rewards are valued and desired.

In essence, individuals will tend to be more motivated if they have high expectations of success, if they have a high belief that they will receive rewards, and if the intrinsic or extrinsic rewards are highly valued.

The expectancy theory has implications for today's managers. Managers can encourage individuals toward successful outcomes, act on promises to deliver rewards in a timely manner, and discern which rewards are most valued.

Equity theory (Adams)

J. Stacy Adams put forth the equity theory, which refers to employees' expectations that they will be rewarded fairly for their contributions to the organization. Employees want to receive rewards, or "outputs," that align with their contributions, or "inputs," to the organization. Inputs in the equity theory are hard work, dedication, years of service, special skills, flexibility, ambition, and other contributions; outputs are pay, benefits, perquisites, flexible work arrangements, praise, promotions, status, and professional development opportunities.

Individuals seek a fair balance of the inputs and outputs, both by their own estimations and by comparison to others. If the circumstances feel unfair in the reward system, individuals may lose confidence and become demotivated. They may reduce their efforts, cause disruption, or resign.

If the balance of rewards is perceived to be overcompensated, individuals may try to increase their efforts to better match the outputs. Or individuals may become demotivated, given the higher balance of outputs for their current inputs, and consequently decrease their efforts.

If circumstances feel fair, employees are likely to be motivated and content and maintain their contributions. Related to the equity theory, managers and the human resources area need to carefully design reward systems to be as fair and equitable as possible.

Goal-setting theory (Locke and Latham)

Edwin Locke and Gary Latham's goal-setting theory espouses that:

- Setting specific and challenging goals (as opposed to no goals or vague goals) results in improved performance.
- The more challenging the goals, the higher the performance outcomes (unless the goal is unrealistic).
- Feedback helps individuals adjust performance and reach goals (unless an individual is not committed to the goals).
- Having an employee participate in goal setting helps as an information exchange rather than as a way to get goal commitment.

Goal setting is important to motivation. It helps employees determine the activities and adjust their level of effort to reach the goal. This encourages persistence until a goal is reached. Managers will want to encourage use of goal-setting techniques to realize organizational objectives.

Reinforcement theory (Skinner)

B. F. Skinner's reinforcement theory says that behavior is a function of its consequences. Behavior modification techniques are involved in trying to "modify" employee behavior:

- **Positive reinforcement** delivers a desirable consequence to encourage repeat behavior in the future.

- **Negative reinforcement** includes an undesirable consequence to encourage desired behavior in the future. A speeding ticket is an example of negative reinforcement. It strengthens a behavior (following the speed limit) because a negative condition is stopped or avoided as a consequence of the behavior.

- **Extinction** removes a reinforcing consequence to discourage repeat behavior in the future. For example, a behavior might be ignored if it seems to be motivated by giving it attention.

- **Punishment** delivers a negative consequence to discourage repeat behavior in the future. It should not be confused with negative reinforcement; punishment weakens a behavior while negative reinforcement encourages a desired behavior.

Reinforcement has much relevance in organizational behavior. There are distinct challenges, however, in recognizing when and how to use behavior modification techniques. The techniques can be applied on a scheduled basis, such as yearly bonuses, or on an intermittent basis, such as periodic rewards for work well done.

Environmental factors

Motivated and engaged employees help organizations become more productive and reach overall organizational goals. One may well understand theories of motivation, but they need to be understood in the context of the organizational environment. Strictly speaking, employee motivation and empowerment must come from within each individual. However, the organizational environment has much to do with shaping employee motivation and outcomes. There are influences in the organizational culture that may work for or against employee motivation and performance improvement.

For purposes of this discussion, the environmental factors that directly influence an employee and his or her motivations follow:

Organizational structure and culture

The organizational structure and culture are the foundation for organizational behavior. As described previously, an exploitive-authoritative organizational management system will look very different in practice than a participative system. There are many ways that organizations can provide a supportive environment:

- Communicate organizational goals and expectations widely.
- Develop a culture that welcomes employee participation.
- Provide necessary resources and remove system or process barriers.
- Provide for physical needs such as a clean, safe, and ergonomic work environment.
- Provide flexibility with options such as flexible work schedules and choices in health plans.
- Support continuing education and professional development activities.

Managers and supervisors

Managers and supervisors interact with employees on a daily basis. Several studies have indicated that the relationship an employee has with his or her supervisor is very important to workplace attitudes and employee retention.

When managers set high expectations and create a positive work environment, employees are more likely to reach those expectations. Goal setting is an effective means to encourage achievement. It is important to provide the resources and feedback necessary to propel employees toward the established goals.

Managers should understand the basic concepts of motivational theories and the application to the workplace. However, managers will want to first examine their own beliefs about motivation and consequences. An atmosphere of trust is built by delegating and exhibiting confidence in employees' abilities to succeed. That, in turn, builds employee confidence and empowers work groups.

Performance feedback is a vital component in motivational behavior. Constructive feedback should be given on a continual basis so that employees will learn, grow, and take corrective measures. Opportunities should be taken to praise, recognize, and celebrate successes and to otherwise utilize appropriate reward systems.

Work group design

The way an organization organizes work affects employee attitudes and behaviors. Work groups and teams are increasingly used to achieve organizational objectives. Work groups also support employee affiliation and social needs in the workplace setting.

Groups have work designs as well. Teams have goals to achieve, and rewards are based on team outcomes.

Team members are behavior influencers in an organization. Group norms, dynamics, communication, and other issues may affect individual motivations and outcomes. For example, "groupthink" causes members to conform without considering a range of alternatives.

Group dynamics are further discussed in Chapter C, "Management Skills/ Leadership Styles."

Job design

Job motivation in the workplace really begins with the selection process. An individual who is a good fit for a role is likely to be more motivated from the start. Appropriate selection and promotion decisions are important to the organizational framework.

The way that work is organized and the ways in which jobs are designed also impacts employee motivation. A person's job can be a source of reward in and of itself.

Job design is the way a job and its tasks are organized. The design includes what the tasks are, what order they are done in, and how they are done. The job design also includes how the job relates to other jobs in the organization.

The workplace design for the job is important as well. Employees need certain resources in their work environment to be able to physically do a job, whether that be an ergonomic office arrangement or specific equipment or tools.

Factors to consider in job design include:
- Proper orientation and training.
- Variety in task type and level of challenge.
- Clear links from tasks to organizational outcomes.
- Solicitation of employee input for arrangements.
- Autonomy to complete the work.
- Work schedule balance, including breaks and vacations.
- Mental and physical exertion requirements balance.
- Performance feedback opportunities.
- Sense of accomplishment.

An important concept in job design is that adjustments can be made over time to help increase employee satisfaction. These adjustments include job enlargement, job rotation, and job enrichment:

- **Job enlargement** broadens the scope of a job with an expansion of similar or different tasks. A person's responsibilities in the organization are not necessarily increased. Job enlargement reduces the risk of boredom and encourages employees to learn and grow.
- **Job rotation** is a method of job enlargement where employees move between different tasks and jobs.
- **Job enrichment** is when more depth is added to a job by adding responsibilities. Employee participation increases with more responsibility, accountability, and independence.

Reward systems

Employee behavior is influenced by intrinsic and extrinsic rewards. Organizations will want to develop effective reward systems based on guidelines such as these:

- Communicate the organization's reward systems widely.
- Provide reward options that are meaningful to individuals.
- Ensure that rewards are consistent with levels of accomplishment.
- Ensure that rewards are readily available for distribution.
- Distribute rewards close to the time of accomplishment.
- Clearly communicate reasons for individual or team rewards.
- Make rewards as long-lasting as possible.
- Set policies that are equitable when compared internally and externally.
- Praise publicly but reward privately to reduce perceptions of unfairness.

Performance appraisals

Many organizations use performance appraisals to encourage desired behaviors and link job performance to the reward system. Traditionally, performance appraisals were done on a set schedule and followed a formal process. Alternative methods are often the result of motivational theories discussed earlier and the need for employees and organizations to include frequent performance feedback.

In either case, the best use of performance appraisals focuses on communication between managers and employees.

Traditionally, input for the appraisal came from management; however, it can also come from various sources including the employee's peers, customers, the employee (self), or a combination, as in 360-degree feedback. In this case, feedback is received from everyone, including peers, self-ratings, upward assessment, and management.

Performance appraisal is also covered in Topic 4.

Topic 3: Describe Traits, Stages, and Implications of Group Dynamics (Level A)

Group traits

A group is characterized as several individuals working toward a common purpose who connect with one another on a regular basis. A group may form on its own or be intentionally formed as a means for sharing workload or gathering multiple perspectives. Groups are goal-oriented. In order to achieve their goals, they must be open to change, be creative, and be flexible enough to adapt to changing circumstances.

An understanding of group dynamics is essential to management because in a workplace where people interact on a regular basis groups are a natural phenomenon. Group dynamics is the way groups and individuals act and react. It plays a role in an organization's effectiveness. The organization's culture and politics in turn affect group dynamics.

Group types

There are different types of groups:

- **Structural.** A structural group is one dictated by the organization's formal organizational chart or governance structure, typically with an appointed supervisor and subordinates. An administrative department reporting to a director or vice president is one example of this type of group.

- **Functional.** A functional group is established to accomplish a specific ongoing purpose. A finance or customer service department are examples of functional groups.

- **Task.** A task group is charged with the completion of a task. The group's formal existence is expected to end with the completion of the assigned task.

- **Informal.** Informal groups often develop on their own, without a formal decision by management. They may form spontaneously in response to a function or task or from a sense of shared experiences or interests.

Group roles

As covered in the Topic 2 discussion of motivational and leadership theories, when work is to be done there are tasks and relationships involved. There needs to be a balance of attention to tasks and people relationships so that work gets accomplished and people feel positive about working together.

While groups are usually self-managing, a group leader or facilitator plays an important role in balancing the task and people relationships. The role of group leader emerges in any group. This is true in informal groups, where there is no formal leader position, as well as in groups with a designated leader. In groups with a designated leader, another group member may emerge as the person to whom the group turns for guidance. A group facilitator is someone who keeps the group on task and uses effective meeting management techniques. The group facilitator may or may not be the group leader.

It is also typical for group members to settle into informal roles. Whether they realize it or not, group members play specific roles when working together. In the group context, roles can be classified as functional roles, which are task- or relationship-oriented and facilitate work accomplishment, or as nonfunctional roles, which are dysfunctional and hinder work progress.

Group role dynamics have been a topic of study by Benne and Sheats and several other researchers over time. Some of the common functional roles identified are these:

- Harmonizer, who tries to resolve tension and conflict
- Encourager, who is positive and supportive of others
- Compromiser, who yields or suggests alternatives
- Initiator or contributor, who initiates new ideas and strategies
- Elaborator, who clarifies thinking and gives examples
- Evaluator, who challenges thinking and asks good questions
- Gatekeeper, who facilitates communication within the group and with other groups in the organization

The following are examples of nonfunctional roles that impede progress:

- Dominator, who contributes too much or too forcefully
- Blocker, who shuts out ideas of others
- Aggressor, who is overly aggressive about opinions and ideas

Group norms

As groups work through conflicts and competition for roles, they begin to establish norms of behavior. Norms are based on values and are the standards for which behaviors are acceptable and which are not. In some cases, norms are formalized into group policies and procedures. More commonly, norms are informal and unstated, enforced by group reactions to behaviors that fall outside these norms. Norms dictate many aspects of individual behavior such as dress, timeliness in arriving at meetings, or choice of language.

Group norms are also applied to aspects of task performance and contribution to the workplace. These norms apply positive pressure, encouraging group members to raise their performance to meet the group's expectations.

Work groups may develop performance norms that allow all group members to feel comfortable about their level of productivity. For example, norms may also create a "lowest common denominator" effect, with top performers pressured to reduce their efforts.

Cohesiveness

Cohesiveness describes the degree to which members of the group feel a sense of belonging and loyalty and are willing to make personal sacrifices in support of the group's goals and norms of behavior.

Some of the advantages of cohesive groups are:

- A high degree of trust between members, which encourages honest communication and disagreement without feeling threatened.
- High morale, which leads to higher productivity and less absenteeism and employee turnover.
- Motivation to work toward achieving the organization's goals when the group's objectives are aligned with the organization's goals.
- Greater tolerance for different personalities and cultural perspectives, which enables the group to come up with innovative approaches.
- Acceptance and support of group decisions that allow the group to move more quickly to carry out its initiatives in the organization.

Cohesive groups also have disadvantages:

- When the group's objectives are not aligned with the organization's goals, the group becomes a negative force.
- Group pressure can cause conformity and too much decision making by consensus. Over time, groups may lose their perspective in the organization.

Communication and influence

Informal group communication processes are usually much simpler and more efficient than the formal organizational processes. Each group develops its own group personality based on the styles of the individuals who compose the group. The highest-functioning groups are able to accept and utilize the strengths of these individual styles. Over time, group decisions become well balanced between impacts on people, appropriate information, and timely decision making.

Group size

It is suggested that groups communicate better and are more satisfied when the number of group members is ten or fewer. Groups also tend to process decisions more efficiently with an odd number of participants. An odd number means that when the group members are divided on an issue, one coalition will always have more support.

Group conflict

Group conflict is natural and can be a source of energy, clarity, creativity, and better decisions. In fact, too much consensus in groups can cause "groupthink" (discussed below). Group leaders and facilitators should monitor disagreements and employ effective communication and conflict management principles. Conflict management is further discussed in Chapter D.

Groupthink

Irving Janis developed the theory about decision making called "groupthink." Groupthink occurs when group members agree on a course of action too quickly and without sufficient attention to risks or alternatives.

Groupthink is the result of a combination of forces:

- Group norms that value consensus
- Consideration of few alternatives
- Disregard for negative alternatives
- Lack of thorough alternative discussion
- Dominant group members imposing opinions
- Homogeneous member perspectives
- Isolation from outside points of view
- Overconfidence with no backup plans

The following are strategies for preventing groupthink:

- Develop evaluation criteria to guide group decision making.
- Encourage ideas from all members and do not discount ideas.
- Use techniques such as brainstorming, and work in smaller groups to encourage ideas.
- Discourage leaders or dominant group members from pressuring others.
- Collect information from individuals outside the group.
- Challenge solutions and develop at least one good alternative.

Decision making

While some aspects of decision making are information-driven, many others are largely subjective, with more than one acceptable outcome. These are circumstances in which the likelihood of adopting any particular option is largely a function of who has been granted the most power by the group.

There are a number of decision-making methods that are used to encourage groups to explore innovative ways in which to solve complex and ambiguous challenges:

- Brainstorming is used to generate a large number of ideas from a group without making value judgments about each idea.
- Lateral thinking is used to encourage the group to move away from entrenched or predictable thinking to new or unexpected ideas.
- Nominal group methods are used when the group wants to make a decision quickly, by voting, but wants all members' opinions taken into account.

Group decision making has advantages such as increased acceptance of the decision. However, arriving at a decision may take longer, and it is not always clear who is responsible for the decisions made.

Development stages

Bruce Tuckman developed a model that describes the stages that groups and teams naturally move through. The level of leader or facilitator direction varies with each stage.

- **Forming.** The first stage is an orientation stage that is more formal. Members get acquainted with one another, set goals, are polite, and act independently. Group members feel anxious and awkward in this stage. The group needs strong direction in the beginning.

- **Storming.** In this stage, group members address issues, disagree, and compete with one another. There is role confusion and interpersonal conflict. The group needs strong guidance and coaching with an emphasis on being tolerant.

- **Norming.** In the norming stage, the group settles down. Members adapt to each other's communication and work styles, agree on values and rules, and become more motivated. The group becomes more autonomous, and a participative management style is used.

- **Performing.** This is the stage where the group is cooperative, effective, competent, and autonomous. There is still conflict, but it is handled well. A participative management style is used.

- **Adjourning.** In this stage, the group has completed its tasks and disassembles. The group feels a sense of loss. Group leaders or sponsors may look for a new purpose for the group.

These developmental stages may be called different names in different theories of group development, but the basic patterns are similar. It is helpful for the group leader or facilitator to point out these developmental stages during the forming stage. That way, group members know what to expect and they understand that these types of behaviors are normal.

It is important to note that some groups never reach a high-performing stage. Some groups may reach the performing stage and revert to a former stage if circumstances change for them.

Organizational politics

Whether the formation of a group is intentional or unintentional, groups display similar behaviors and stages of development. When the goals of a group are consistent with the organization's best interests, group cohesiveness and norms are assets that help achieve organizational goals. Groups can also serve to reinforce ideas or behaviors that work against organizational goals. In either case, understanding group dynamics helps an organization get the most from group synergies while appropriately responding to counterproductive group attitudes and behaviors.

Work teams, such as cross-functional teams, are becoming more ingrained in organizational cultures. Organizations are realizing the value that high-performance teams can bring, producing innovation and effectiveness that is better attained in a collaborative rather than individual fashion.

There are, however, organizational politics that may impede the development of a team-based culture:

- Group members may feel pressure from their functional areas and feel divided loyalty.
- Groups must seek information from other areas in the organization and may or may not get cooperation.
- There may not be an organizational sponsor, or the sponsor may not be committed to helping the group.

- A cohesive and performing team may become a strong influence on some part of the organization. Exerting influence and changes in the environment will naturally be met with resistance.
- Broader organizational norms about open communication, innovation, performance improvement, and other areas directly impact how the norms of the small group form and how much influence the small group can have in the organization.

Group effectiveness

Now let's review the characteristics of an effective group:

- The group has clear goals and is enthused about its purpose.
- The group understands how its role aligns with the organization's goals.
- The group is comfortable with shared values and norms.
- There are strong bonds with a high level of trust and respect.
- There is honest communication and encouragement of ideas. Ongoing communication and networking are strong.
- Effective problem solving and decision making are exhibited.
- Alternatives are discussed and groupthink is avoided.
- The group reaches consensus and members are supportive.
- Members of the group are interdependent and motivated to achieve group goals.
- The group leader avoids undue pressure and influence.
- Group members strongly influence one another and the leader.
- The group leader fosters a cooperative and supportive atmosphere.
- Group members support one another with skill and knowledge development.
- The group is open to new ideas and develops creative approaches.
- There is strong participation and autonomy.
- The group is confident of its decisions and influence.

Some of the factors that support the development of effective groups are these:

- The right group members are selected to enhance productivity.
- The group leader is committed and trained in group facilitation.
- The group members have the maturity to move through development stages.
- The group members use effective interpersonal skills.
- The group members use effective conflict management skills.
- The group members put aside personal agendas for the good of the group.
- There is a task focus and high performance outcomes.

Topic 4: Demonstrate an Understanding of Human Resource Processes (Level A)

Human resource management

Every goal in an organization is affected by people. Therefore, an effective human resource (HR) strategy and an effective workforce are essential components of a successful organization. Strategic human resource management includes the processes and activities within an organization that ensure the effective and efficient use of human capital to accomplish organizational goals. These activities include:

- Helping the organization prepare for change.
- Restructuring the organization.
- Managing employee training, hiring, and compliance needs.
- Administering employee compensation and benefit programs.
- Developing performance management systems that support an organization's short- and long-term business goals, objectives, and strategies.

Performance management

An effective performance management system consists of the processes used to identify, encourage, measure, evaluate, improve, and reward employee performance. It links organizational strategy to results. A successful performance management system:

- Provides information to employees about their performance.
- Clarifies organizational expectations.
- Identifies development needs.
- Documents employee performance for personnel records.

Performance management is concerned with the four key functions of management: planning, organizing, directing, and controlling. Internal auditors can be very useful in evaluating the internal operating controls necessary to help managers establish criteria for acceptable employee performance in each of these key functions which, if met, can provide reasonable assurance that specific management objectives are being achieved.

Individual performance management involves setting goals, communicating the goals to employees, and giving employees feedback on how they performed. It gives employees and supervisors (or managers) an opportunity to set and discuss goals and to jointly create a performance plan for achieving those goals.

Although the format and contents of performance plans vary from organization to organization, generally they:

- Identify company values and goals.
- Identify and measure desired work behavior.
- Encourage personal growth and motivate employees.
- Set and communicate performance standards (expected behavior and results).
- Measure results and provide feedback through performance appraisals.

Effective performance measurement depends on a job being well defined so that employees know what tasks are necessary for a satisfactory appraisal. Employers should establish and fairly apply a minimal acceptable performance level for each task. Job descriptions are often too vague or general to be helpful in assessing performance. Managers should develop specific performance standards for measuring employee performance.

Performance standards should be:

- Written.
- Brief.
- Realistic.
- Precise.
- Consistent.

Performance measurement (appraisals)

A performance appraisal is a process that measures the degree to which an employee accomplishes the work requirements stated in the performance standards and then communicates that information to the employee. Appraisals are used by organizations in two very different ways: 1) to measure performance for the purpose of making pay and other compensation and administrative decisions about an employee and 2) to offer employees developmental feedback.

In addition, performance appraisals:

- Help determine employee aspirations.
- Determine employment status.
- Identify training needs.
- Communicate expectations.
- Provide necessary documentation to defend employer and management actions against potential employee claims or lawsuits.

Performance appraisals can be administered on an individual or group basis. Exhibit V-26 shows the steps that are often part of a performance appraisal.

Exhibit V-26: Common Appraisal Steps

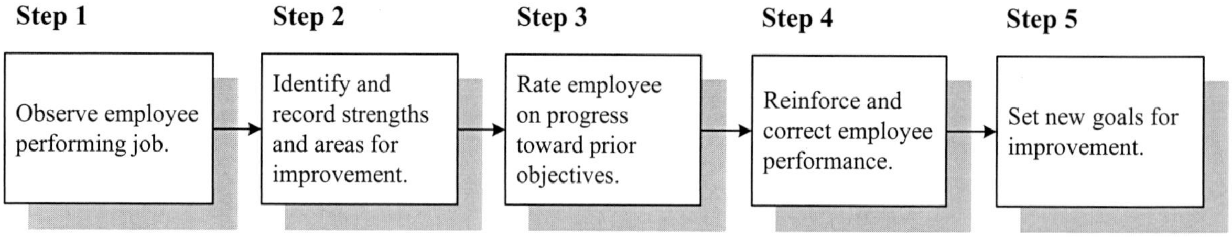

Common appraisal methods

Appraisers may include the employee, the supervisor or manager, peers, outside sources, or a subordinate. There are a variety of methods available for conducting an appraisal, including:

- Category rating.
- 360-degree feedback.
- Comparative methods.
- Narrative methods.
- Behaviorally anchored rating scale.

Category rating

Category rating is the least complex method of appraising performance. It requires the appraiser to mark an employee's level of performance on a form. There are several common category rating methods.

- The **graphic scale** is the most common category rating method. The appraiser checks the appropriate place on the scale for each task listed. The appraiser must avoid grouping separate activities together and rating them as a unit rather than individually.

- With the **checklist,** the appraiser is given a list of statements or words and checks the items on the list that describe the employee's characteristics and performance. A limitation of this method is that it could be subjective.

- **Forced choice** is a variation of the checklist in which the appraiser is required to check two of four statements. The statements require an appraiser to choose one that the employee is most like and one that the employee is least like. Constructing valid statements can be difficult.

360-degree feedback

As noted earlier in this chapter, the 360-degree feedback approach, or multisource rating, is an appraisal method that solicits evaluation feedback from virtually everyone an employee interacts with, including subordinates, superiors, and internal and external customers as well as the employee. The goal is to provide a more complete evaluation of an employee from a variety of vantage points.

Comparative methods

With comparative appraisal methods, the appraiser directly compares the performance of each employee with that of others. Comparative performance appraisal includes the following methods.

- With the **ranking** method, the appraiser lists all employees from highest to lowest. This method is limited by appraiser bias and varying performance standards as well as the fact that the amount of difference between ranks may be much wider at different parts of the scale.

- In **paired comparison,** each employee is paired with every other employee and compared using the same scale for performance. This method yields much information about employees but is time-intensive.

- In **forced distribution,** employees are rated and placed at different percentage points along a bell-shaped curve with sections such as poor, standard, or excellent. The drawback is that regardless of their abilities some employees must be placed in the lowest and highest sections.

Narrative methods

Narrative methods require appraisers to submit written performance appraisals. The following are narrative methods.

- With the **essay** method, the appraiser writes a short essay describing the performance of each employee during the rating period. Quality depends on the appraiser's writing abilities. The method is slow and hard to quantify.

- The **critical incidents** method uses a record of positive and negative employee actions in addition to ratings. It can be slow and subjective.

- With **field review,** an HR professional interviews the manager regarding each employee's performance and compiles comparison ratings for each employee. The ratings are submitted to the supervisor for approval or changes. HR may lack control over the ratings, and it can be slow.

Behaviorally anchored rating scale

The **behaviorally anchored rating scale (BARS)** method clearly indicates examples of desirable and undesirable behavior and then associates the examples with different performance levels. BARS works best when many employees are performing the same tasks. This method is time-consuming to develop and maintain, and it requires an organization to develop different BARS for different jobs.

However, the following are advantages of BARS:

- It provides a more accurate gauge than other methods.
- It presents clearer performance standards.
- It provides valuable feedback.
- It provides options for being developed specifically for different jobs.
- It provides a consistent method.

Document employee performance

Performance documentation is a critical part of the appraisal process and provides evidence for a manager's comments and actions. Specific, objective, accurate, and consistent documentation is crucial from a legal perspective in protecting an organization from lawsuits. Performance documentation commonly takes two forms:

- Performance diary/log—an anecdotal record of critical incidents or tasks performed by the employee
- Performance records—notes that include measures (accounting, quantity, and quality) that relate to the employee

It is important that managers document situations as they happen and that observations are job-related and objective. Observations should focus on behavior and be supported with facts. Managers should avoid drawing conclusions or voicing opinions in performance documentation. Documentation is not only a valuable tool for protecting an organization from litigation; it is also used to improve employee communication and to reward and recognize good performance. It can also be used when auditing human resource effectiveness.

Appraisal errors

There are many possible sources of error in the performance appraisal process, and the most common involve appraiser mistakes. Completely eliminating appraiser error may be impossible, but training can reduce errors significantly. Possible errors can stem from:

- **Varying standards.** The appraiser may apply different standards and expectations for employees performing similar jobs.
- **Recency/primacy effect.** The appraiser may give greater weight to either recent events or the first information reviewed.

- **Central tendency, leniency, strictness.** The appraiser may rate all employees within a narrow range or may be too strict or too lenient.
- **Bias.** The appraiser's own values or prejudices may distort the assessment.
- **Halo/horn effect.** The appraiser may rate a person high (halo) or low (horn) in all areas because of performance in one area or due to past performance.
- **Contrast error.** The appraiser may rate an employee against others rather than against performance standards.

Legal considerations

Performance appraisals are included among the employment practices covered under Title VII of the Civil Rights Act, which prohibits discrimination in employment practices based on gender, race, color, religion, or national origin. A performance appraisal process that meets legal requirements must be job-related and must include:

- An absence of evidence that might imply discrimination.
- Evidence that proves the validity of the appraisal.
- Formal evaluation criteria that limit subjectivity of the appraiser.
- Personal knowledge of and contact with the employee being rated.
- An appraisal process that prevents one manager from having too much influence over an employee's career.
- Equitable treatment of all employees.
- Training of appraisers.
- Counseling to help poor performers improve.

Managers decide which appraisal tools are appropriate to specific situations by weighing their advantages and disadvantages. These methods must consider the potential for appraisal errors and the overall goals of a performance management system. Performance appraisals should be:

- Consistent with the strategic mission of the organization.
- A beneficial development tool.
- A useful administrative tool.
- Legal and job-related.
- Viewed as fair by employees.
- Effective in documenting employee performance.

Supervisory responsibilities in performance management and evaluation

After completing appraisals, managers must communicate the results to employees. Employees need to know how they have been rated so they understand how the manager and the organization perceive them. Organizations commonly require managers to conduct an appraisal feedback interview. Handled well, a performance appraisal interview can provide both the appraiser and the employee with a sense of accomplishment, understanding, and clear priorities for the future.

Give feedback

When giving feedback to employees, appraisers should keep the following guidelines in mind:

- Describe the employee's behavior impersonally; don't judge it.
- Use a helpful attitude rather than a domineering or forceful approach.
- Empathize with the employee and understand his or her position.
- Give specific examples of good and poor performance.
- Focus on future behavior.
- Discuss the employee's training and developmental needs.
- Be specific about reasons for ratings.
- Decide on specific steps for improvement.

Develop an action plan

For feedback to result in change, an action plan should be created with input from both the supervisor or manager and the employee. The objective of the action plan is to help the employee meet organizational, departmental, and individual performance goals.

The action plan should:

- Outline specific objectives to be met by the employee before the next appraisal period.
- Describe a concrete plan for how the employee will achieve the agreed-upon objectives.

Reward good performance

While performance appraisals are a formal method of evaluating and giving feedback, managers can also give daily or weekly informal feedback. Good performance should be recognized and rewarded promptly. Rewards include salary increases, additional vacation time, bonuses, or other monetary rewards. Rewards can also include:

- Plaques and trophies.
- Recognition ceremonies.
- Organization-wide announcements.
- Team awards.
- Merit awards.

Employees appreciate such rewards. However, well-timed praise, recognition in a department newsletter, and a simple thank-you are also welcome.

Factors that affect performance

The effective performance of an organization's human capital largely determines an organization's success. Organizations can maximize the effectiveness of their human capital by making improvements in three key areas: individual performance, motivation, and employee retention.

Individual performance factors

There are three primary factors that affect how an employee will perform on the job: the individual's ability to do the work, how much effort the employee expends (motivation), and how well the organization supports the employee.

The relationship of these factors is expressed in the following formula.

$$\text{Performance (P)} = \text{Ability (A)} \times \text{Effort (E)} \times \text{Support (S)}$$

If all these factors are present and interacting, an employee's performance will be enhanced. If one or more is absent, performance will be diminished.

Motivation

Motivation is the desire within a person that causes that individual to act. It typically relates to achieving a goal and is affected by the person's work ethic, their ability to do the job, and how interesting a particular job is to them. Motivation was discussed previously in Topic 2.

Job satisfaction is a critical success factor in employee motivation and productivity. It often depends on managing the relationship between the individual employee and the organization through what is called the psychological contract. The psychological contract refers to the unwritten expectations employees and employers have about the nature of their work relationships. This contract includes tangible items like wages, benefits, productivity, and attendance. It also includes intangible items like loyalty, fair treatment, and job security. During times of downsizing and shifting allegiances, skepticism on the part of employees and new economic realities facing employers can change the contract for both parties.

Under the psychological contract, employers might offer competitive compensation and benefits, career development opportunities, and work/life flexibility in exchange for employees with continuous skill improvement and increased productivity, extra effort when necessary, and a reasonable time commitment to the organization. It is important for internal auditors to be aware of how changes in the psychological contract can have a significant impact on morale and the control posture of an organization.

Job dissatisfaction occurs when an employee's expectations under the psychological contract are not met. The relationship between productivity, motivation, and job satisfaction is not entirely clear. However, what is clear is the impact job dissatisfaction can have on an organization's bottom line:

- Absenteeism costs an estimated US $600 per employee per year and more than US $12 billion annually in total employer productivity losses.
- Turnover, the process of having to replace employees who leave, can exceed US $10,000 per person depending on the industry. The hotel industry reports that typical annual turnover costs a single hotel more than US $600,000 each year. For higher-level executives and professionals, the costs can run as much as two times their annual salary.

Employee retention

Retention of employees is a primary concern for many reasons, including:

- Fewer employees have to be recruited, selected, and trained.
- As mentioned above, turnover is costly, in terms of both expense and diminished productivity.
- Organizational and individual performance is enhanced by employee continuity.
- Retaining high performers helps an organization achieve its strategic goals.
- Continuity of employees helps attract and retain other individuals.

Surveys of employees consistently show that career opportunities and rewards are two important determinants of retention. Tuition aid programs, career planning, mentoring, competitive benefits, recognition, and linking compensation to performance can enhance employee retention. Other important factors influencing retention include:

- Employee-supervisor relationships (clear expectations, fair and nondiscriminatory treatment, support from supervisors, open coworker communications).
- Organizational components (values and culture, strategies and opportunities, well-managed company or department, job security).
- Job design and work (autonomy in job responsibilities, flexibility, working conditions, work/life balance).

When evaluating the human resource management efforts of a particular organization, internal auditors should assess the consequences of employee absenteeism and turnover and whether appropriate controls and measures are in place to aid employee retention.

Personnel sourcing/ staffing

Human resource planning supports an organization's mission, goals, and objectives by anticipating employee skill and labor needs. The HR planning process includes a detailed internal and external assessment of an organization's HR needs and supply sources. HR professionals use a variety of quantitative and qualitative tools to forecast staffing needs, including trend and ratio analysis, turnover analysis, judgmental forecasts, and statistical forecasts. (See Chapter A, Topic 4, in this section for a discussion of forecasting techniques.) Accurate forecasts account for movement into and inside the organization (new hires, promotions, and transfers) and out of the organization (resignations, layoffs, retirements, and discharges).

Job analysis

An important part of determining the labor needs of an organization is to systematically gather and analyze information about the content, context, and human requirements of jobs within an organization. This process is known as job analysis.

Job analysis is the basic building block of HR management and the foundation of staffing. It identifies the activities and responsibilities of a job (not the person doing the job), the job's relative importance and relationship to other jobs, the personnel qualifications necessary to perform the job, and the conditions under which the work is performed.

Job analysis gathers various differentiating characteristics, including:

- Work activities and behaviors.
- Interactions with others.
- Performance standards.
- Machines and equipment used.
- Working conditions.
- KSAs—the knowledge, skills, and abilities needed to perform the job.

Job analysis is not only important in staffing an organization. The legal defensibility of an organization's recruiting and selection procedures, performance appraisal system, employee disciplinary actions, and pay practices also rests in part on job analysis.

In addition, job analysis is used in:

- Organizational design.
- Establishing performance standards.
- Time management/goal setting.
- Training.
- Establishing career paths/succession planning.

Job analysis methods

Determining what employees actually do on the job can be challenging, since even direct observation is a subjective experience. Job analysis is typically conducted by someone from HR, an outside consultant, or a supervisor or manager, depending on the complexity of the analysis.

The following are common job analysis methods.

- **Observation.** The observer records the tasks and duties performed while watching an individual perform the job. Observation may be continuous or based on intermittent sampling. This method is limited because many jobs do not have easily observed job duties or complete job cycles. It is best used for repetitive jobs.

- **Interview.** The observer visits each job site and talks with the employee performing the job using a standardized interview form. This method is appropriate for difficult-to-define jobs and often requires interviewing both the employee and the supervisor.

- **Questionnaires.** This widely used method allows information to be collected inexpensively about a large number of jobs in a short period of time. However, it assumes that employees can accurately analyze and communicate information about their jobs. Questionnaires are best used in combination with other methods.

- **Work diary or log.** The employee "observes" his or her own performance and keeps a log of job duties, how frequently they are performed, and the time required for each duty. This method is time-consuming and can be a burden.

Internal auditors can help HR managers determine which combination of these methods is the most appropriate depending on the situation and the specific needs of the organization.

Job analysis outcomes
The output from a job analysis is used to develop a job description and its job specifications.

A **job description** summarizes the most important features of a job:
- Job title and location
- Organizational relationships
- Primary tasks, duties, and responsibilities
- Working conditions
- Level of financial accountability

Job specifications list KSAs necessary to perform the job satisfactorily:
- Education
- Experience
- Work skill requirements
- Personal abilities
- Mental and physical requirements
- Judgment

Job specifications can be a separate section of a job description or a separate document. Both the job description and job specifications must be carefully worded to meet legal requirements under equal employment opportunity (EEO)/affirmative action legislation and the Americans with Disabilities Act (ADA) as well as to ensure legal defensibility. It is critical to avoid asking for any KSAs that are not truly needed for job success. For example, if a college degree is not truly needed, it should be omitted from the specifications. Together, the job description and job specifications create a written document or documents that serve a variety of HR functions, including job evaluation, selection, and recruitment.

Recruitment

Recruitment is the process of generating a pool of qualified applicants for an organization's jobs. A strategic approach to recruiting is critical as labor markets shift and become more competitive.

The following are some strategic recruiting decisions facing organizations:
- **Organizational-based recruiting vs. out-sourcing.** Can recruitment be out-sourced (e.g., employment agencies), freeing up HR staff to handle other matters?
- **Regular vs. flexible staffing.** Should an organization hire full-time, part-time, temporary, or contract workers?

- **Diversity and EEO considerations.** Recruiting practices must comply with legal requirements and serve the best interests of an organization.
- **Recruiting internally vs. externally.** Hiring from within an organization (e.g., promotions, transfers, and referrals) can lower recruitment costs, lower training costs and time, provide a morale boost, and provide greater knowledge of past performance. Hiring from outside (through the Internet, media, colleges, job fairs, etc.) can provide sources of new ideas, increase the breadth and depth of an organization's labor pool, avoid organizational politics, and promote needed change.

Analyzing recruitment efforts

Evaluating the success of an organization's recruitment efforts is critical to its financial health and competitive advantage. Both short- and long-term considerations should be analyzed, including:

- Average time required to recruit applicants.
- Selection and acceptance rate of applicants.
- Cost per applicant hired.
- Quantity and quality of applicants.
- EEO implications.
- Absenteeism and turnover rates among hires.
- Training costs.

When analyzing recruiting efforts, it is important to take into account both direct and indirect expenses as compared to the benefits. Yield ratios can determine which recruitment source or method produces the greatest yield and can also identify areas that may need improvement. It is also important to weigh costs against both short- and long-term consequences. Continuous recruiting may be more expensive and time-consuming in the short run, but in the long run it may pay off by providing a ready pool of qualified applicants.

No matter which method or source is used, effective recruiting hinges on how well an organization's recruitment efforts are strategically aligned to its overall goals and priorities.

Employee selection

Choosing qualified individuals with appropriate capabilities to fill jobs within an organization can make the most of any training, career development, and performance improvement efforts already underway.

The ultimate purpose of selection is placement, or fitting a person to the right job. How well an employee is matched to a job directly affects the quality of an employee's work. Selection activities focus on matching an applicant's KSAs with the job characteristics. A good match increases the likelihood of higher employee performance, lower turnover, and lower absenteeism.

The selection process in organizations can vary depending on size, industry, nature of jobs to be filled, and number of open positions. Selection must be carried out subject to a variety of legal concerns, in particular EEO regulations and laws.

The selection process can be perceived as a series of filters designed to narrow the field of applicants. Although not all organizations handle the selection process in the same way, a typical process includes:

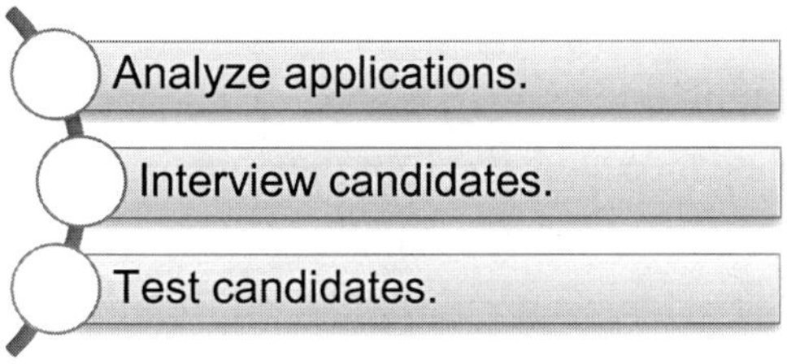

Analyze applications

Analyzing the candidates' application forms, and/or résumés to see which fit the minimum selection criteria can narrow the field significantly. Efficient prescreening at this stage can ensure that line management's time is spent interviewing only qualified candidates.

Organizations use a variety of application forms, including short forms, in-depth long forms, and targeted forms designed to gather specific information. The most important factor is that the application used must request information from candidates that is critical to job success. Once the applications have been reviewed, chosen candidates can be called and prescreened and the more formal interviewing process can begin.

The process of selecting applicants for interviews should include checking information they have provided in the application process. Employers may be somewhat hampered in their efforts by restrictions on what previous employers can say legally, but a great deal of information can be obtained by simply calling former employers, institutions, and references. Many employers now add Internet searches to their usual process of checking applications. When a position provides an opportunity for the commission of fraud, employers should be especially diligent and check criminal backgrounds and credit ratings in addition to application information.

Information on the application and gathered through follow-up should be assessed in the same way that evidence is considered during an audit. It should be sufficient, reliable, and relevant:

- An applicant's statement that he or she possesses a certain skill is not as sufficient as witnessing the performance of the skill (e.g., a writing test).
- A copy of a transcript provided by an applicant would not be reliable since it is not original and could have been falsified.
- Verified employment attendance at a summer job on a construction site would not be relevant to selecting a good candidate for a laboratory assistant job, unless reliable attendance is a significant aspect of the lab job.

Interview candidates

Selection interviews are designed to help the interviewer determine how well a candidate meets the needs of the organization. The validity of the selection process can often be substantially improved by training managers and supervisors in interviewing skills and techniques.

Interviews range from very structured to very unstructured, with structured interviews being the most effective.

A structured interview uses a set of standardized questions asked of all applicants so that comparisons among candidates can be made easily. This type of interview is especially helpful in an initial screening. It allows the interviewer to prepare questions in advance and then to complete an evaluation form after each interview documenting why one applicant was selected over another. Structured interviews tend to be more reliable and valid than other approaches.

Examples of structured interviews include:

- Behavioral interviews, in which applicants give specific examples of how they have performed a specific task or handled a problem in the past.
- Situational interviews, in which applicants are asked about how they might handle specific job situations.

Less-structured interviews are relatively unplanned and are typically conducted by managers or supervisors with little interview training. These interviews include questions like "Tell me about yourself," which have no identified direct purpose.

Examples of unstructured interviews include:

- Nondirective interviews, in which applicants are asked general questions and the interviewer develops additional questions based on the applicant's answers. For example, if the applicant mentions that he or she enjoyed working with a former supervisor, the interviewer might ask, "What type of supervisor do you enjoy working with?" It is difficult to obtain comparable data among applicants. Comparing and ranking candidates is more open to subjective judgments and legal challenges.

- Stress interviews, in which the interviewer assumes an aggressive and insulting demeanor designed to create anxiety and put pressure on the applicant to see how he or she responds. The risk with this approach is that it generates a poor image of the interviewer and the employer.

The most important factor in the interviewing process is that consistent interviewing practices must be maintained. Interviewers must also be careful not to violate an individual's privacy or other rights. Questions that are not necessary to judge an applicant's qualifications, skills, and overall competence to perform a specific job should be avoided.

Test candidates

Some organizations use different tests during the selection process to identify superior candidates. However, because of legal concerns, it is critical that any preemployment testing be nondiscriminatory and a valid, reliable, job-related predictor. Great care must be taken that selection tests comply with Title VII and the Civil Rights Act of 1991 as well as ADA and international laws that restrict preemployment tests.

The following are types of selection tests:

- Ability tests, including cognitive ability tests, which measure an applicant's memory, reasoning, and verbal and math skills; physical ability tests, which test strength and endurance; work sample tests, which require applicants to perform a simulated job task; and psychomotor tests, which measure a person's dexterity and hand-eye coordination.
- Personality tests, such as the Minnesota Multiphasic Personality Inventory (MMPI) and the Myers-Briggs test.
- Honesty/integrity tests, including polygraphs; these are controversial.

Selection testing can provide useful insights about the abilities and characteristics of applicants that may not be determined by other methods. However, organizations must keep in mind that tests represent only one data source. The use of selection tests must be carefully evaluated to ensure that the tests are both appropriate and legal.

Training and development

Continuous training to update employees' knowledge, skills, and abilities is essential. For many employers, training expenditures average 2% of payroll expenses. Although costly, organizations recognize that training efforts are integral to organizational success and that gains in productivity can more than offset training expenses.

Training is defined as the process in which people acquire the capabilities to help them achieve organizational goals and objectives. Development is often understood in a broader context, focusing on employees gaining new capabilities that are useful for both present and future jobs. For ease of discussion, only the word "training" is used in this section. However, the information presented applies equally to both training and development.

Strategic training focuses on efforts that develop competencies, value, and competitive advantages for the organization. Strategic training:

- Helps retain employees.
- Must be linked to enhancing organizational performance by identifying root causes of performance problems.
- Recognizes the interaction of individual and organizational factors.
- Documents the gap between high and low performers.
- Develops employee capabilities.
- Encourages change.
- Promotes continuous learning.
- Creates and disseminates organizational learning.
- Facilitates communication.
- Supports the organization's business strategy.

Training process

Effective training requires the use of a systematic training process that improves the chances that training will be planned, coordinated, and successful. Such a process can be described as having four phases:

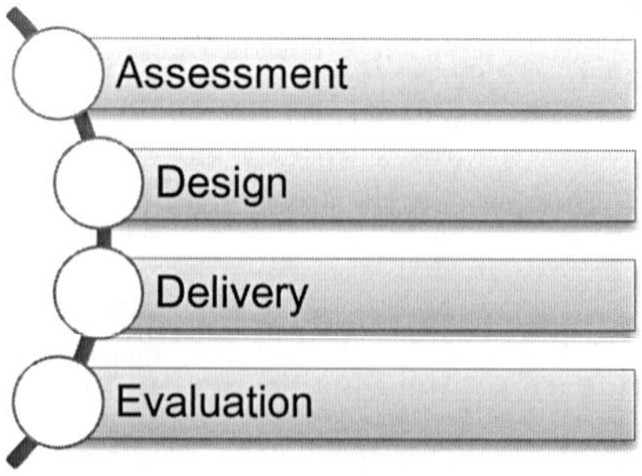

Assessment

During the assessment phase, organizational training needs are analyzed and specific training objectives and criteria are identified. Different assessment tools include:

- Organizational analyses—reviewing operational KPIs and HR data to find weaknesses (e.g., high turnover or absenteeism, low performance).
- Job/task analysis—comparing the requirements of jobs with the KSAs of the employees performing the jobs.
- Individual analyses—using performance appraisal data and training need surveys to diagnose individual employee training needs.

Once training needs have been identified, gap analysis can be used to establish training objectives and priorities. Gap analysis can illustrate where employee capabilities are presently and where they need to be. Training objectives should be measurable, and training needs should be prioritized.

Design

Effective training design considers how individuals learn, legal issues related to training, and appropriate training methods. In designing a training program, it is important to assess the level of motivation and confidence of trainees. Trainers should also consider individual learning styles and diversity issues. Training can be designed to meet a variety of objectives.

Common training types include:

- Required and regular training—complies with mandated legal requirements and serves as training for all employees (new employee orientation).
- Job/technical training—enables employees to perform their jobs, tasks, and responsibilities.
- Interpersonal and problem-solving training—addresses interpersonal communication, conflict resolution, and managerial skill building.
- Developmental and innovative training—long-term focus on building capabilities such as executive development and organizational change.

Any training design must consider the legal issues affecting the criteria and practices used for selecting individuals to be included in training programs. Selection must be based on job-related needs and must not unfairly restrict protected classes of employees such as people with disabilities.

Delivery

Common training methods mix classroom training and on-the-job experiences. Instructor-led classroom and conference training is still the most prevalent method of training, although e-learning is a close second. When choosing appropriate training methods, organizations should consider factors such as:

- Nature of training.
- Subject matter.
- Number of trainees.
- Individual vs. team.
- Self-paced vs. guided.
- Training resources.
- Costs.
- Geographic locations.
- Completion time line.

Organizations must also consider whether to conduct internal or external training.

Internal training is popular because it is less costly and reduces the need to send employees away or bring in outside trainers.

Internal training methods include:

- Informal training, which occurs through employee interactions and feedback. Informal training includes apprenticeship, coaching, and mentoring.
- On-the-job training (OJT), which is the most common type of training. A supervisor or manager shows an employee what to do. It is critical that the trainer has experience in training and that OJT does not disrupt regular work.

External training is used extensively by organizations where there are no internal training capabilities or when many people need to be trained quickly. In organizations where human resource staffs are small and training resources are limited, external training may be the most cost-effective method.

External training methods include:

- Out-sourcing—outside trainers, vendors, and suppliers are brought in to provide training.
- Computer-assisted/e-learning—using the Internet or intranet to conduct training online. This includes distance learning/training and computer-supported simulations and is the most explosive growth area of training. It can be very effective if implemented properly, trainees are self-motivated, and the content is updated continuously. Limitations include cost, the fact that it may not be appropriate for all learners or content, and the possibility that managers and employees may be resistant to it.

Evaluation

No matter what training methods are used, it is critical that organizations compare post-training results to the objectives expected by managers, trainers, and trainees. Too often, training is conducted without a means to measure or evaluate its success. Evaluations should consider the effect of training on trainee learning levels, their behaviors and reactions, and the achievement of organizational objectives.

Different evaluation methods include:

- Post-training interviews, tests, and questionnaires of employees, supervisors, and trainers.
- Performance appraisals.
- Cost-benefit analyses.
- Return on investment (ROI).
- Benchmarking.

To evaluate the effectiveness of any training program, both pre- and post-training evaluation measures should be used to determine whether trainees can now perform according to intended training objectives.

Safety

Employees expect their employers to provide a safe and healthy work environment. Organizations are required to comply with a variety of federal and local laws and to have safety programs in place to prevent work-related accidents and injuries.

US health and safety laws

The following are some of the most significant US federal laws affecting safety and employer responsibilities.

Workers' compensation

Currently all states have workers' compensation laws in some form. Under these laws, employers contribute to an insurance fund to compensate employees for injuries on the job. These laws also provide payments to injured workers to cover lost wages, medical bills, and, when necessary, retraining.

Americans with Disabilities Act

This law affects the type of work an injured employee can be asked to do and also requires specific security procedures, access restrictions, and storage measures to be followed as it relates to employee medical information.

Child labor laws

These laws set the minimum age for employment (16 for most employment and 18 for "hazardous" occupations).

Occupational Safety and Health Act

This law is administered by the Occupational Safety and Health Administration (OSHA). OSHA provisions are implemented through specific standards that regulate equipment and working environments.

With a few exceptions, most US employers conducting business with one or more employees are covered under the OSHA standards. These standards fall into four major categories: general industry, maritime, construction, and agriculture. There are many different provisions under OSHA that different employers must comply with, but there are two basic provisions that are key to OSHA compliance for most organizations:

- **General duty.** Employers have a "general duty" to provide safe and healthy working conditions, even in areas where OSHA standards have not been set. Employers who know or should reasonably know that working conditions are unsafe or unhealthy can be cited.
- **Notification and posters.** Employers are required to inform their employees of safety and health standards established by OSHA. OSHA posters must be displayed in prominent locations in the workplace.

OSHA rules and standards are frequently complicated and technical and are beyond the scope of this text. It is important that organizations have systems in place to ensure compliance with a wide range of regulatory issues, inspections, and record-keeping requirements.

International health and safety laws

The following are examples of international laws protecting the health and well-being of employees.

- The **Canadian Environmental Protection Act (CEPA)** protects the environment and the health of Canadian citizens from the risks associated with pollution, dangerous substances, and products of biotechnology in the home and the workplace.

- The **Canada Labour Code** applies to employees who work under federal jurisdiction. It includes provisions covering standard hours, wages, holidays, and vacation. It also includes occupational health and safety legislation and requires employees and employers to observe specific mandates in order to prevent occupation-related injuries and diseases.

- The **Health and Safety at Work Act** requires UK employers to ensure the health, safety, and welfare at work of all their employees.

- Numerous directives from the EU's **Amsterdam Treaty** also specifically prohibit practices that will endanger the health and well-being of EU citizens at home and in the workplace.

Safety management programs

In addition to legal compliance requirements, effective safety management programs can reduce employee accidents and their costs such as workers' compensation and possible fines. A comprehensive safety program includes:

- Designing jobs, work settings, and equipment with safety in mind.
- Using ergonomic principles (designing the work environment so that it addresses physiological and physical demands on workers).
- Developing and implementing safety policies and disciplining violators.
- Using safety committees to disseminate information in the workplace.
- Reinforcing safety motivation and attitudes through safety training.
- Rewarding safety through incentive programs.

Organizations should audit their safety efforts periodically and compare current and past accident and injury records to identify significant changes and to measure progress in safety management.

Creating a positive work environment

A "sustainable" workforce—one in which employee turnover is in line with the organization's goals and needs and in which employees continue to develop new and valuable skills throughout their employment—requires:

- Fulfilling employee expectations' of consistency and fairness.
- Providing the means to resolving employee disputes or grievances quickly, fairly, and without retribution.
- Developing managers who can train, correct, coach, and discipline employees appropriately.
- Providing employees with opportunities to contribute and to develop new skills.
- Ensuring work/life balance through programs that address employee needs (e.g., flex time, employee assistance/support programs).

Topic 5: Express the Risk/Control Implications of Different Leadership Styles (Level A)

Specific leadership styles are beyond the scope of this discussion. But as leadership pertains to risk and control, two considerations that have important implications are authoritarianism and empowerment.

Authoritarianism refers to the rigidity of a leader's beliefs. Attributes of a leader high in authoritarianism include:

- Top-down management style, with the leader making the decisions and the subordinates carrying them out.
- Rigid adherence to conventional values and recognized authority.
- Toughness and power as opposed to subjective feelings.
- Ideas accepted/rejected based on accepted authority.

Empowerment implies that employees have the authority to make decisions and take actions in their areas without prior approval. In an empowered environment, a leader:

- Is committed to empowerment and promotes the concept.
- Shifts knowledge, responsibility, and authority to the people who actually perform the business processes.
- Ensures that management and employees have access to critical business information.
- Ensures that management and employees have the authority and discretion to take appropriate action and the opportunity to make valuable contributions.

To successfully implement empowerment in an organization, leaders must balance their need for personal control with providing freedom for others to act on their own authority. This transfer of authority requires working with subordinates to establish clear expectations, responsibilities, and boundaries for empowerment throughout the organization. People must clearly understand their responsibilities and limits of authority pertaining to risk management and related controls and how all actions ultimately are linked to organizational goals and objectives.

Whether a leader is authoritarian or supports empowerment will affect not only the way the organization is managed but also the kinds of business risks accepted. For example, authoritarian leaders may be more reluctant to take risks tied to harsh economic or regulatory consequences. The authoritarian leader will typically institute a culture with more written policies, performance indicators, exception reports, and similar documentation. In an empowered environment, risk decisions are made at lower levels. Control is achieved more by vision, values, general guidelines, and face-to-face interactions with key personnel than by written documents. In an empowered culture, it is very important that employees be well trained and understand the limits of their risk-taking authority.

Either leadership style can be effective if it fits the situation. The authoritarian leader is well suited to a staff performing repetitive tasks that require little judgment and whose members are not self-motivated or self-disciplined. The same style might cause resentment leading to control breakdowns in a professional staff who will be frustrated if they are not able to make decisions for themselves.

Consider, too, the implications these two leadership distinctions have for internal auditing. The internal audit function should have unrestricted access to senior management and the audit committee. Some highly authoritarian individuals may pose special challenges. It is possible to envision scenarios where rigid adherence to authority could block access and promulgate unethical behavior.

Implications of different management styles

Four distinct models of management have evolved over the years, as shown in Exhibit V-27.

Exhibit V-27: Models of Management

Model	Description
Autocratic	The autocratic model was the result of military authority and the classical school. It was almost universal up to the mid 1900s. It is based on pure power. It has given way to more behavioral management styles, but for some organizations it is still effective. People are motivated by a call for obedience.
Custodial	The custodial model took form in the 1930s. It was founded on the proposition that happy people are productive people. Custodial programs depended on material rewards for the worker. The workers were oriented toward the security blanket. Although people seemed happy, they were not fulfilled, nor were they necessarily productive. Rather, they found a relaxed way to earn a living. People are motivated by material rewards and the offer of happiness and security.
Supportive	The supportive model sought to avoid the shortcomings of both the autocratic and the custodial models. Instead of obedience and happiness, the workers are pointed toward performance. They can feel participation and involvement as drives are awakened—drives they were not aware of. This model depends on leaders who have positive feelings toward their people and on people who want to work, grow, and achieve. People are motivated by opportunities for growth and achievement.
Collegial	The collegial model is more likely to be encountered among professional groups. It is founded on the feelings of mutual contribution among its members. The manager is oriented toward teamwork instead of a superior/subordinate relationship. Each contributes to common goals. The results can be self-discipline, responsibility, self-fulfillment, and enthusiasm. People are motivated by teamwork and contribution.

Source: *Operational Auditing*, 2006.

The management model or combination of models that internal auditors encounter may have a significant effect on the nature of the audit to be carried out and the nature of the relationship between auditor and management.

Personalities, attitude, and relationships between operational management and internal audit pose challenges and can potentially derail engagements. The organizational continuum shown in Exhibit V-28 provides a closer look at the implications of different management styles that internal auditors need to understand to facilitate successful engagements.

Exhibit V-28: The Organizational Continuum

Autocratic **Decisions and creativity at top; many procedures to follow.**	**Collegial** **Decisions and creativity at all levels.**

Management Style	Autocratic Custodial	Supportive Collegial
Governance By	Policies/procedures	Mission, vision, values
View of Auditors	Assuring compliance	Consultants
Audit Focus	Policies/procedures	Control frameworks
Types of Audits	Compliance	CSA

Management sees audit's role as monitoring for compliance with policy and procedures.

Management sees audit's role as business analysts who can identify operational improvements.

Source: *Operational Auditing*, 2006.

Topic 6: Measure Various Aspects of Performance (Level A)

Organizational performance

Many of the themes already discussed in this module affect an organization's performance:

- Trends in the industry and marketplace
- Life cycle of the product and the current demand
- Orientation and skills training for employees
- Cross-cultural communication
- Employee motivation and rewards
- Job design and work group design
- Management styles
- Team effectiveness
- Individual and team communication

- Organizational dynamics such as expectations, organizational structure, politics, workplace ethics, change, and diversity
- Advances in electronic communications technology

An organization's performance is its overall success in accomplishing its performance objectives. Performance objectives are the goals and activities related to the organization's strategy. The performance success factors are the indicators of success, which will look quite different from one organization to another.

We'll now discuss two important concepts in this regard—productivity and effectiveness.

Productivity

Productivity is the ability to produce a good or service. In an organization, it refers to the quantity of the outputs (products and services) in relationship to the inputs (human and physical resources). Productivity is a way to achieve cost and quality advantage over the competition.

Quality refers to an organization's standards of excellence for product or service output. The meaning of quality will vary by the type of organization. Physical product quality factors are features, reliability, durability, serviceability, performance, and conformance. Service quality factors are responsiveness, trust and assurance, reliability, and perceptions of customer care.

Efficiency refers to minimizing the use of resources in a product or service process as compared to standard expectations. It is considered to be the ratio of the resources actually used to the resources that were planned to be used. The efficiency ratio, however, does not indicate the quality level of the outputs.

Productivity is also linked to profitability, but it is only one factor. Profitability refers to making a profit, or achieving financial gain, from an effort. Productivity relates to the short term; profitability relates to the longer term and involves other internal and external factors.

The basic guidelines for improving productivity are to:

- Determine where improvements are needed.
- Select appropriate measurement tools.
- Assess the current level of productivity.

- Identify and analyze the key factors affecting productivity.
- Set new improvement standards and provide resources and support.
- Communicate changes and conduct training if necessary.
- Establish procedures to monitor the new efforts.

Performance measures

Performance measures are used to improve productivity. Simply put, if the quality or quantity of products or services increases, there is an increase in productivity for the organization. Or, if there is the same level or quality of product and service outputs but fewer resources are needed, there is an increase in productivity.

There are several ways to measure productivity, and the methods will depend on the circumstances. A few strategies are noted here:

- **Time and motion studies** are measurement tools to determine how much time is involved in an activity.
- **Sampling techniques** are measurement tools using observation and samples from processes and outputs to assess workflow and quality.
- **Capacity planning** is a measurement tool to identify the capacity for workflow and outputs.
- **Volume analysis** is a measurement tool to analyze product volume and ways to meet product demand.
- **Task analysis** is a measurement tool to analyze the tasks involved in jobs and the appropriateness of job design.
- **Cost analysis** is a measurement tool to study cost allocation, cost-effectiveness, cost-benefits, and the possible effects of changing costs.

There are other systematic ways to monitor quality and make continual improvements:

- **Benchmarking** can be used to compare the organization's practices against the best practices of one or more comparable organizations.
- **Quality approaches** for continual quality improvement, such as total quality management (TQM), can be used.
- **Improvement processes** can be implemented, such as Six Sigma, which seeks to improve processes by eliminating defects, and lean, which seeks to improve processes by reducing waste.

(Note that quality improvement tools are discussed in detail in Topic 5 of Chapter A in this section.)

It is more difficult to measure performance in nonmanufacturing and knowledge-based industries, such as financial or legal services, because the outputs and value creation are harder to measure. In these cases, it is important to use more than one performance measure.

Effectiveness

Effectiveness relates to outputs and the degree to which an organization's goals and objectives are achieved. Productivity, quality, efficiency, and profitability are all part of the overall effectiveness of the organization.

Today's organizations need to be adaptive and innovative to respond to unexpected internal or external events. Organizational learning and knowledge management are important. Organizations that learn from their mistakes, formulate best practices, and share knowledge are more likely to be successful.

The organization's structure and its work systems, procedures, and processes make a difference in employee motivation, adaptability, and creativity.

The interrelation of the organization's physical location, external environment, management style, resources, and other considerations directly impact organizational effectiveness.

Organizations strive to be high-performing. In a high-performance culture, employees not only contribute to the success of the organization but are in a mindset to continually assist the organization with improvements. They are encouraged and rewarded for thinking smarter, making new suggestions, and being innovative.

The use of work teams is a strategy in high-performance cultures. Collaborative efforts often produce better problem-solving and decision-making results. Others in the organization are also more likely to accept the outcomes from a team.

Improving effectiveness

Some other ways that an organization might improve effectiveness are to:

- Foster organizational learning and knowledge sharing.
- Encourage improvement on a continual basis.
- Develop a culture of trust, which is critical to individual and team work.
- Provide adequate physical space and workspace flexibility.
- Restructure management and reporting lines.
- Redesign jobs to reflect changes in the internal or external environment.
- Form strategic alliances or out-source.
- Make technology and equipment improvements.

These strategies help measure and monitor organizational effectiveness:

- Determine critical success factors that align with performance objectives.
- Determine ways to measure the critical success factors.
- Use sound data for measurement, monitoring, and control processes.
- Capitalize on information technology and knowledge sharing.
- Make ongoing improvements as necessary.

Chapter C: Management Skills/Leadership Styles

Chapter Introduction

Recall from the section introduction that the role of manager encompasses four activities in a cycle: planning, organizing, leading, and controlling.

Management skills refer to managing the people and processes that accomplish specific organizational objectives. These management responsibilities include planning, organizing, and controlling as well as staffing, directing, and monitoring. Management responsibilities also involve managing group processes, building effective teams, giving constructive feedback, providing a motivating and supportive work environment, and shaping developmental opportunities.

Leadership skills relate to leading—imparting the vision and mission of the organization, setting strategy and direction, ensuring the overall financial stability of the organization, minimizing organizational risk, and inspiring others to achieve the goals. Leaders positively influence behaviors and results in the organization on a daily basis. Here we will examine leadership theories, leadership styles, and the important role of coaching and mentoring others.

The information in this chapter serves as a resource for chief audit executives and others who lead auditing activities. Management skills are important for participation in teams and leading projects. This information is good background as well for the auditing group as it reviews the leadership and management practices that impact performance and internal audit outcomes. Control weaknesses are often the result of poor application of management skills.

Topic 1: Lead, Inspire, Mentor, and Guide People, Building Organizational Commitment and Entrepreneurial Orientation (Level A)

Management defined

As noted above, management is the conduct of business to achieve business objectives by planning, organizing, staffing, leading, and controlling activities in an organization. A manager implements the organization's strategy and provides the necessary structure for people and operations on a day-to-day basis. Managers judiciously allocate and control resources and subordinates to effectively and efficiently accomplish goals. Other than providing leadership, which is addressed separately below, the manager's primary activities of planning, organizing, and controlling can be defined as follows:

- **Planning** is setting the organization's course by specifying expectations, goals, and performance objectives for the long, medium, and short term. Planning includes strategic planning, tactical and operational planning, short-term planning and forecasting, and planning for project management.

- **Organizing** is developing an appropriate organizational structure, process flow, and policies, procedures, and practices so as to coordinate the organization's components into an interdependent system. Organizing activities include staffing, resource gathering, and team building.

- **Controlling** is the use of formal authority in an organizational hierarchy to direct or restrain inputs, processes, or outputs and people by using evidence or experiment to observe, measure, or verify actions and results.

In addition to formal authority or legitimate power, management tools include the power to reward and promote, the power to coerce (either by threatening punishment or threatening to withhold rewards or promotions), the power to control who gets what information, and the power to control the steps and order of processes or tasks—not just controlling the results. These are called bases of power and are defined more formally later in this topic. A key point is that all of these powers could be abused, to the detriment of the organization's effectiveness. Good managers use these powers sparingly.

Note that these management powers help define the employer-employee relationship. By contrast, a manager's relationship with an independent contractor differs. For example, managers have the power to direct the end result only, not the means of accomplishing tasks. Organizations can face significant liability if employees are misclassified as independent contractors to avoid paying benefits and so on. In the US, classification is based in part on whether management directs and controls the process as well as the result.

Having formal authority and a few management powers is necessary but not sufficient for management success. Great managers get their subordinates to take on organizational goals as their goals and to do so voluntarily and with enthusiasm. They get there by exhibiting leadership.

Leadership defined

A leader is a person who influences others to accomplish organizational goals and objectives. Leaders hope to inspire employees to follow them on a voluntary basis. Leaders are responsible for communicating the organization's vision and for providing a motivating environment to gain followers.

An effective organization needs both strong leaders and strong managers. One person can, and should be, both manager and leader. A manager needs to be an effective leader, and a leader needs some task focus in the organization, but the balance differs.

Inspiration defined

Inspiration is from a Latin root that means "to breathe in." As it relates to leadership, inspiration refers to breathing life into or enlivening the way people think, feel, act, and dream so that they are motivated and enthusiastic to accomplish the goals that the leader sets.

Leadership skills

Inspiring followers requires a different skill set than being a good planner, organizer, or controller. It requires building personal influence with others. Personal influence is power that is associated with the individual rather than that person's position. Personal influence may be easier to develop for a person with a certain level of formal authority, but organizational position does not guarantee personal influence. Personal influence can be built up in different ways, such as by making wise and fair decisions over time based on knowledge and experience and by using rational persuasion, which is the use of rhetoric to make goals seem both desirable and achievable.

Also quite critical to leadership and its related qualities of influence and inspiration is relationship building. Building dynamic relationships involves treating subordinates with respect, living by the organizational and social values that one espouses, and following through on promises. It requires communication skills such as active listening, empathizing with others' points of view, and empowering and collaborating with subordinates.

Other ways to develop into a leader who can influence and inspire followers is to study leadership theories and find methods that work well. What works well will differ for different personality types and work environments.

Leadership theories

Many leadership theories have evolved over time to form a foundation for organizational leadership and management. A limited number of theories are highlighted here under key classifications.

Trait theory

Trait theory, developed in the 1930s, is one of the earliest approaches to leadership. Trait theory asserts that some people are born with certain traits or characteristics that naturally make them good leaders. Such characteristics are decisiveness, energy, intelligence, persistence, and self-confidence.

Over time, the research showed that while traits are important, traits alone do not make effective leaders. Eventually, the research shifted to focus more on what effective leaders do, and thus behavior theories emerged.

Behavior theory

Behavior theory, developed in the 1940s and 1950s, focuses on how effective leaders behave. Key studies in this regard are the University of Michigan studies, the Ohio State studies, and the leadership grid.

University of Michigan research

This research identified two forms of leadership behavior, one focused on the job and the other on the employee. Job-centered leader behavior is when a leader concentrates on the work being done and coaches employees to complete tasks. Employee-centered leader behavior focuses on the person and group performance.

Ohio State research

Two types of leader behaviors were identified in these studies. Consideration behavior is when a leader is considerate of employees' feelings and shows a caring attitude. Initiating structure is when a leader uses schedules, rules, and other means to ensure that employees complete their work. Leaders can be high on one behavior and low on the other, high on both, or low on both.

Leadership Grid

The "Managerial Grid," developed by Robert Blake and Jane Mouton in the 1960s, is frequently referenced in discussions about management in organizations. The model was modified and renamed the "Leadership Grid" in the 1990s by Robert Blake and A. Adams McCanse. The basic premise is that a leader has a management style that relates to his or her concern for people and their concern for production, or tasks, as depicted in Exhibit V-29.

Exhibit V-29: Leadership Grid

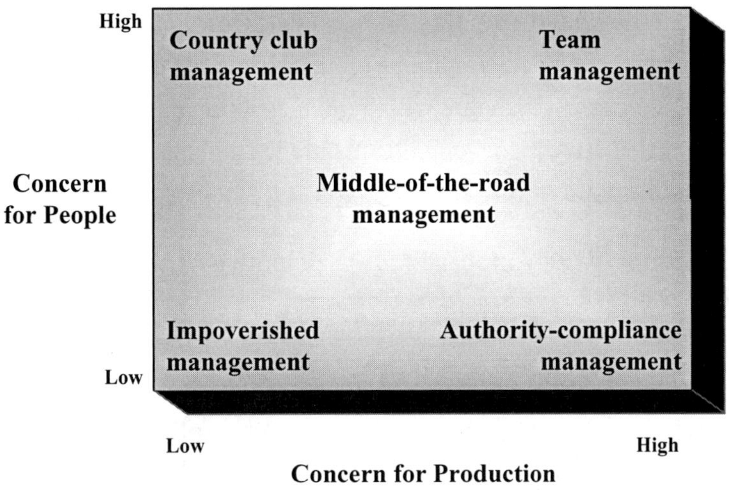

This grid is used to characterize leader styles:

- **Country club management** is low concern for tasks and high concern for people. The environment is friendly, but there is a lack of attention to tasks.
- **Impoverished management** is low concern for people and low concern for tasks. Here, the work is done with minimal effort and minimal direction to people.
- **Authority-compliance management** is high on tasks and low on concern for people. The style is authoritarian and task-oriented and not very collaborative.
- **Team management** is high concern for people and high concern for tasks. The work is productive, and a supportive individual and team environment is encouraged.
- **Middle-of-the-road management** is a halfway balance that falls in the middle of the grid. There is middle-level concern for the tasks and the people.

This theory helps managers see themselves and how they attend to the work and to the individuals and teams in the environment. In this theory, the team management style is said to be the most ideal to strive for, although it may not be ideal in all situations.

Participative leadership

Participative leadership is an approach that encourages employees to be involved in the decision-making efforts of the organization. When leaders delegate problem solving and decisions to others, employees feel more empowered about their work in the organization and their ability to influence organizational outcomes.

There are several variations on this theme. At one end of the spectrum is the authoritarian manager with high decision-making power; on the other end is a participative manager who encourages high participation in decision making to the point of full delegation to the team. This is shown in Exhibit V-30.

Exhibit V-30: Autocratic to Participative Spectrum

The following are theories that describe leadership styles along this spectrum.

Likert leadership styles
As previously described (in the discussion of motivational theories in Chapter B), Rensis Likert categorized exploitive-authoritative, benevolent-authoritative, consultative, and participative leadership styles that are based around decision-making involvement.

Lewin leadership styles
Kurt Lewin identified three leadership styles:

- **Authoritarian.** Makes all decisions, selects team members, selects task, does not participate in groups.
- **Democratic.** Encourages team decision making, allows team to manage its own tasks, shares options and ideas with team.
- **Laissez-faire.** Allows team complete freedom for decision-making tasks, assists only by request.

Likert selects the participative style and Lewin the democratic style as the most effective. The basic assumption is that participation in decision making makes for better decisions and fosters employee commitment and empowerment.

Ouchi's Theory Z

William Ouchi introduced the Theory Z management approach in the 1980s. Theory Z modified American individualistic management practices with aspects of the Japanese collectivistic management practices. Theory Z applies to the organizational level and relates to corporate culture.

Some of the characteristics of a Theory Z organization are:

- Common cultural values.
- Collaborative environment.
- Consensus decision making.
- Stable and longer-term employment.
- Promotion from within and slower promotions.
- Downplay of titles and rank.
- Work team environment with more participation.
- High level of trust and employee loyalty.
- Recognition of individual contributions.
- Concern for employee well-being.

Contingency and situational theory

Contingency models of leadership are yet another way to discuss effective leadership. Contingency models take into account the context or situation that the leader is in. A leader who is effective in one environment or set of circumstances may not necessarily be effective in a different environment.

Fiedler's LPC model

Fred Fiedler's least-preferred-coworker (LPC) model asserts that leadership effectiveness is based on the leader's personality (task or relationship orientation) and how favorable the situation is.

Leaders who are task-oriented are similar to the job-centered or initiating structure leader, who values tasks and work completion. Relationship-oriented leaders are similar to the employee-centered or consideration leaders, in that developing interpersonal relationships is highly valued.

Fiedler developed an exercise for managers that asked them to think about past work relationships and to identify the coworker they least liked to work with. They were then asked to rate this least-preferred coworker on a scale of 1 through 8 with descriptors at opposing poles. Such factors were unfriendly (1) to friendly (8), disagreeable (1) to agreeable (8), closed (1) to open (8), and so forth.

Fiedler asserted that leaders who scored high on the LPC scale tended to rate more positively and were more relationship-oriented. Leaders who scored low on the LPC scale tended to rate more negatively and were more task-oriented. The premise is that either relationship- or task-oriented leaders can be effective, but their orientation must fit the situation.

Fiedler suggested that there are three factors that determine how favorable, or how easy, it is to manage in a situation:

- **Leader-member relations** refers to how good the trust and relationships are with employees. The better the relationships, the more favorable the situation.
- **Task structure** refers to how structured tasks are. Structured tasks are favorable because unstructured tasks require more direction.
- **Leader position power** refers to the manager's power because of his or her position. Stronger position power is a more favorable situation.

The theory describes a way to match leader styles and situations for optimal relationships and performance. Fiedler asserted that a leader's style does not change, so managers should be put in situations that are a good fit for their style, or the situation should be changed.

Path-goal theory

Developed by Martin Evans and Robert House, the path-goal theory suggests that effective leaders can motivate employees to achieve goals by:

- Clearly identifying outcomes and paths to the outcomes.
- Removing obstacles that stand in the way.
- Offering incentives and rewards along the way.

The path-goal theory says that leaders can adapt their behavior according to situations. Four leader behaviors are identified:

- **Directive leadership.** Conveys expectations, gives specific guidance, and helps subordinates improve performance.
- **Supportive leadership.** Shows concern for subordinates and provides a friendly climate.

- **Participative leadership.** Consults with subordinates and takes opinions into account.
- **Achievement-oriented leadership.** Sets challenging goals and shows confidence in subordinates' abilities.

A theme in this theory is that leader behaviors can be adapted to the employee situation for increased efficiency and effectiveness. This theory also relates to the expectancy theory (discussed in Chapter B). Individuals are more motivated if their efforts lead to certain outcomes, if they desire the outcomes, and if they believe they will actually get the rewards.

Hersey-Blanchard situational leadership theory

The situational leadership theory says that leaders should adapt their style to the maturity level of followers. There are four leadership styles placed on a leadership matrix. One axis shows how much relationship and supportive behavior is needed, and the other axis shows how much task and directive behavior is needed.

The four leader behaviors are:

- **Telling/directing.** Used for followers who have a low level of readiness and maturity and need guidance. This is a high task and low relationship focus.
- **Selling/coaching.** Appropriate when a follower has a low to moderate level of readiness and needs information, explanation, and encouragement. This is a high task and high relationship focus.
- **Participating/supporting.** Applies in cases where the follower has a medium to high level of readiness and can share in decision making. This is a low task and high relationship focus.
- **Delegating/observing.** Appropriate when followers have a high level of readiness to work independently. This is a low task and low relationship focus.

The premise in this theory is that the readiness, or maturity, of an employee will change over time. Managers can adapt their strategies for communicating according to the four leader behaviors to meet the employee's situation. This approach encourages the employee in a way that fosters self-confidence and motivation.

Influence and power theories

An effective leader influences others in the organization to accept changes, make decisions, and implement the results of decisions. Influence is the ability to affect thinking, attitudes, and behavior change in the organization.

Power is the ability to influence others. Power and influence theories are more people-oriented.

Transformational leadership

Transformational leadership involves influencing, or transforming, change in employees and the work environment. Leaders who have a strong vision and inspire others toward that vision are better able to move the organization forward. Employees are more likely to follow leaders who are enthusiastic and can sell their vision.

Transformational leadership also helps employees see the larger picture for the organization, inspires individual contributions toward organizational goals, and promotes collaboration for the greater good.

Charismatic leadership

Charismatic leadership usually goes hand-in-hand with transformational leadership. It describes leaders who possess charisma in the interpersonal way they enthusiastically and energetically communicate the organization's vision. A leader who is seen as having charisma is more likely to influence others in the organization.

Transactional leadership

As opposed to transformational leadership, transactional leadership focuses more on accomplishing the work in the organization through structures and reward systems. This type of leader uses rewards, takes corrective action, and reprimands as necessary.

Bases of power

J. French and B. H. Raven developed a theory involving the following bases of social power, which are useful for considering relationships in an organization. Note that the terms "managers" and "employees" are used for illustration purposes.

- **Legitimate power.** This is the power that managers have because of their authority and position in an organization. Employees may comply but may not necessarily feel committed.

- **Reward power.** This is the power that a manager has over resources and rewards in the organization, including promotions. Rewards will need to be of interest and value to employees.

- **Coercive power.** This is the power that a manager has to force an employee to comply or to administer noncompliance punishments. It can involve threats to punish or to withhold rewards or promotions. Coercive power is a last resort because it typically results in only short-term compliance and can generate resentment.

- **Expert power.** This is the power a manager or other individual has because of his or her special knowledge or abilities. Managers may choose how much they are willing to share their expertise.

- **Referent power.** This is the power a manager has because the employee respects and admires him or her. Referent power develops over time as trust and respect grow.

There are various theories about the types of power, sources of power, and political behavior. The primary points to remember are that leaders wield influence in a number of ways and those ways affect the motivation, attitudes, and participation of others in the organization.

Mentoring and coaching

Mentoring and coaching are techniques to encourage learning, career growth, and participation in the organization. These techniques are useful in developing learning organizations.

Mentoring

Mentoring is a process whereby a mentor who has developed certain expertise shares that expertise with a protégé. Mentoring programs can be formally established or accomplished through informal networks and communication. Formal mentor-protégé relationships are usually short-term in nature.

Some of the benefits of mentoring programs are:

- Organizational intelligence and best practices are shared.
- Mentors demonstrate and model for the protégé.
- Protégés are groomed to take on higher-level responsibilities and positions.
- Protégés are given challenging assignments.
- Protégés find encouragement for personal career growth and direction.
- Mentors find new perspectives and a sense of accomplishment.
- Mentors from other countries provide cultural insights.
- Mentors serve as models for behavior in the organization.
- Lifelong friendships are often formed.

The key in mentoring arrangements is to find or make good matches between individuals.

Once the agreement is made, both the mentor and the protégé have duties to uphold:

- Mentors need to be patient, be available, adapt their communication style, share personal experiences, provide challenging learning experiences, assess progress, reflect with the protégé on an ongoing basis, and treat communication confidentially.
- Protégés need to accept opinions and advice, show respect, keep appointments, express appreciation, keep the mentor informed, take on challenging assignments, learn from successes and failures, and treat communication confidentially.

Mentor-protégé relationships go through development stages similar to group development. In the end, there is a separation stage, but individuals may keep in contact on an infrequent basis. In some cases, it is determined that there is not a good personality or skill competency match, and the relationship separates early on.

As organizations become more networked, the environment naturally encourages the spontaneous development of mentor-protégé relationships.

Coaching

Coaching in the organizational setting refers to specific advising for new learning and improved work performance. While individuals are responsible for their own learning, guidance facilitates faster and smarter learning.

Managers and supervisors need to develop good coaching skills to make a positive difference in the performance of individuals and teams. Many of the principles discussed in motivational theory and leadership theory apply in coaching.

Effective coaching involves:

- Assisting with goal setting and the path to get there.
- Questioning and listening skills.
- Trusting and empowering.
- Demonstrating how to perform tasks.
- Giving positive reinforcement.
- Providing resources and removing obstacles.
- Designing challenging learning opportunities.

Supervisors have a responsibility to help employees succeed. Employees benefit from coaching and feedback on a regular basis, not just in weekly meetings or at the time of performance reviews.

Specific benefits of coaching are that it:

- Facilitates self-directed learning.
- Provides information and techniques for problem solving.
- Pulls people out of their comfort zones.
- Encourages and helps motivate.
- Builds confidence and trust.
- Brings about organizational results.

Other coaching situations include executive leadership assessment and coaching programs, peer coaching such as matching a new hire with a seasoned colleague, and subject matter coaching by internal or external experts.

One cautionary note is that coaching in the business environment is not to be seen as a dependent counseling or therapy relationship. Individuals who need psychological counseling should be referred to professional help for their situation.

Topic 2: Create Group Synergy in Pursuing Collective Goals (Level A)

Organizations do well to foster intra-organizational synergy, which involves sharing information and resources across the organization. Synergy is when informal or formal cooperative efforts bring about a result that is much stronger and more advantageous than the sum of the individual parts alone.

Since this topic relates to management and leadership of groups, it picks up where Topic 3 of Chapter B ("Describe Traits, Stages, and Implications of Group Dynamics") left off. In that topic, the basics of group dynamics are presented. In this topic, we discuss how to foster group synergy so that collective goals are not only achieved but the process of achieving those goals is itself a competitive advantage for the organization. Theories related to organizational synergy stress that an organization's competitive advantage comes as much from how the organization's resources are mobilized as the nature of those resources. Mobilizing resources is a job for a leader.

Put more simply, business is like a team sport. In high-performing sports teams, team members trust each other to do their part and therefore do their own part with more confidence and selflessness, putting the needs of the team above their personal aspirations.

So how do leaders create group synergy? Let's look at it from the perspective of the four management activities: planning, organizing, leading, and controlling. From a planning perspective, it involves developing strategies that are likely to improve teamwork and reduce barriers to collaboration. From an organizing perspective, it may be creating a culture of empowerment or hiring staff who have complementary rather than identical skill sets. From a leading perspective, it may involve providing individuals with empowerment opportunities by delegating some decision-making authority. From a controlling perspective, it may involve transferring or terminating staff that continue to act in counterproductive ways.

Let's look at two specific case studies in which leaders promote group synergy: promoting selfless behavior by diffusing organizational politics and promoting collaboration by developing a plan to move an organization toward empowerment.

Diffusing organizational politics

Organizational politics can limit or destroy synergy. Organizational politics is the pursuit of self-interest in the workplace in reaction to actual or imagined opposition. For example, a worker might set unchallenging goals so as to be able to easily report that he not only met but always exceeded goals. Sabotaging other employees verbally, perhaps by taking credit for others' work, or making others look bad to make oneself look good are other examples.

To promote selfless behavior in such an environment, organizational leaders start with planning. They develop a vision of an organization that has a climate of trust and openness. They set the "tone at the top" as one that will not permit executives to engage in organizational politics in order to ensure that lower-level managers will not imitate this negative behavior.

Then they organize. They integrate their organizational goals with employees' individual goals by instituting career planning and redesign of jobs to provide more meaningful work. This process includes participative review of goals so that they are challenging while producing buy-in because the employee is still allowed input. They also develop a job rotation system that includes rotation of appropriate staff through the internal audit activity to promote understanding of the pains and perspectives of other organizational areas.

Throughout, they lead by example. They promote their vision formally and informally. They set clear expectations and encourage open communications so as to diffuse conflict. They provide verbal discipline to employees who try to engage in organizational politics such as deriding others.

Finally, they control the process. They measure the results of training. They measure individual performance based on objective results rather than allowing managers to measure based on subjective assessments of personality. They discipline employees who fail to adapt to the program.

Developing empowerment

Empowerment implies that employees have the authority to make decisions and take actions in their areas without prior approval. The organization goes about developing this capability starting with planning. They develop a vision of what empowerment can do: "Delegating empowers you" is their slogan, referring to the concept that the more power one gives away, the more power one has since there is no finite amount of power to go around. They develop a two-part strategy:

- Provide training to selected employees to prepare them for self-management.
- Develop a system of oversight that can ensure that managers are comfortable with the risks employees can take and can exercise control when needed.

From an organizing perspective, they roll out the training plan, starting by assessing the maturity level of all employees who might qualify for the program. They select or hire individuals who have good team and communication skills as well as technical skills. They also look for candidates who have good character development and are mature emotionally, such as exhibiting honesty, trustworthiness, a drive to learn, an ability to admit to mistakes, and a commitment to the organization. These employees receive training on self-management skills and on the policies, procedures, and controls developed for the self-management system.

From a leadership perspective, they start by developing a culture of empowerment. They promote open communications and work to develop mutual trust between employees and the managers responsible for delegating to them. They devise ways to make these relationships win/win, for example, designing rewards to be based on showing initiative or cooperation. They also provide freer access to information across business functions within the boundaries of protecting privacy and intellectual property. They encourage managers who delegate to provide frequent and diverse empowerment opportunities, from simple delegation to more advanced self-managed teams. They also provide mentoring, which focuses on character development such as willingness to adapt to new situations.

From a controlling perspective, they stress personal accountability and responsibility. Self-managed individuals are assessed based on their results. Failure to achieve results may not always be penalized: Bad news presented in a timely fashion is treated more favorably than bad news presented too late to do anything about it. However, assessments are also made of each individual's ability to live up to the challenges of self-management, and some individuals may need to be moved back into a situation with more direction and control.

Topic 3: Demonstrate an Understanding of Team Building and Assessing Team Performance (Level A)

A team is a smaller group of individuals that has been organized to accomplish a common purpose and performance objectives. Work groups collaborate together but do not have a purpose toward express performance objectives and results. Teams are an effective way to get work done in the organization because they allow flexibility in membership, experience levels, size, specialization, longevity, output, and leadership requirements.

Types of teams

The most common types of teams are listed in Exhibit V-31 on the next page.

As previously mentioned, entire organizational philosophies and structures can be built with a team-based approach—such as a learning organization or a virtual organization. Teams are also incorporated on an informal or ad hoc approach as is beneficial.

Team building

Team building is an important responsibility for leaders and managers. Work teams benefit the organization and allow employees more participation to influence organizational outcomes.

Supportive culture

The foundation for successful work teams is a supportive culture. This includes acceptance of teams in the organizational structure and management philosophy, equipped and supportive team leaders, and motivated team members.

Exhibit V-31: Types of Teams

Type	Description
Formal team	A formal team is one that is appointed in the organization for an express purpose. Team members are carefully selected based on their expertise. There is typically a sponsor who will develop the team's charge and help the team move forward.
Informal team	An informal team is usually less structured in terms of the number of meetings and communication, the deadlines for results, and the specific outcomes. Members are not necessarily appointed by the organization and may have volunteered for the special project.
Ad hoc team	An ad hoc team is a team that is formed "just in time" based on a need that has arisen.
Cross-functional team	A cross-functional team, such as a product development team, is made up of subject matter experts from different functions in the organization to provide expertise and different perspectives.
Problem-solving team	Problem-solving teams focus on researching and bringing resolution to a specific problem, such as a customer service issue, and are usually temporary.
Action learning team	An action learning team fills a need in the organization and provides a professional development opportunity for members. For example, a team may be formulated to prepare a departmental proposal. During the process, team members develop interview questions, learn about conducting effective interviews, and conduct interviews to collect data for the proposal.
Quality control team	Organizations with continuous quality improvement programs may assign teams to monitor quality assurance efforts. These teams are called quality circles or other quality-related names.
Virtual team	Virtual team members are distributed across organizational boundaries and across the globe. Virtual teams may have a set duration and often involve diverse team backgrounds. They communicate via telecommunications and electronic methods.
Self-managed team	Self-managed or self-directed teams manage their own resources, processes, schedules, communication, and outcomes. Team members are usually trained in problem-solving and decision-making techniques.
High-performing team	High-performing teams have all the features of a well-functioning team and are highly committed to each other and to the results they bring to the organization.

If an organization is just shifting to a team-based culture, there may a lack of understanding and support for team development. Employees may see teams as "different," and team purposes may not be clearly understood. There also may be jealousies over why certain members were chosen to participate. Managers may disregard teams as not "official" if they are not under their supervision and may communicate with these teams only minimally. Managers may also have a hard time understanding and empowering self-managed teams.

Team members must be carefully selected, both in terms of their expertise and their motivation levels. Some individuals are less motivated to participate in teams due to the responsibilities, the collaborative work nature, or the potential rewards. Attitudes heavily influence team participation.

Managers must set a culture of support that includes delegation, trust, and empowerment. Motivated teams welcome the freedom and control to accomplish their objectives and influence organizational decisions.

Team requirements

Teams need proper direction and resources from the start. Organizational sponsors should see that teams have:

- Clear purpose, goals, and measurable outcomes. (This is described in the team's charter and work design.)
- The right people on the team who are qualified, motivated, and will work cooperatively in a diverse group.
- Adequate resources, including necessary training, information, and a good working environment.
- Processes and time frames for getting work done.
- An effective team leader or rotating leaders.
- Open communication within the team and organizational channels.
- A coach or quality advisor to encourage the team.
- Accountability methods for individuals and the team as a whole.
- Measurements based on the team objectives and meaningful rewards.

Team leadership

The team leader is responsible for developing open communication and trust within the team, which is critical to success. The leader must also have good facilitation skills, help the team move through the stages of group development, as discussed earlier, and resolve team conflict. Conflict resolution is further discussed in Chapter D, "Conflict Management."

There are special considerations to be aware of regarding diverse teams and virtual teams:

- **Diverse teams.** Leaders will want to recognize, not avoid, team diversity. They can help individuals develop global mindsets and become culturally sensitive. Guidelines for developing multicultural teams are found in Section VIII, "Global Business Environment."

- **Virtual teams.** These teams are typically global or regional teams with members widely dispersed. The team leader must be a virtual coach and help the team:
  - Create cohesiveness given geographic separation.
  - Be sensitive to cultural communication differences.
  - Learn to use new electronic communication/collaboration methods.
  - Use appropriate communication channels.
  - Be accountable to one another.

The team leader acts as a general coach to the team, but an outside coach or special advisor may also be useful to improve team knowledge or team communication dynamics.

Team-building techniques

Team building starts with a supportive culture, a good work team design, an effective leader, and open communication. There are certain techniques that help teams develop problem-solving skills, communication skills, and strong working relationships:

- **Introductory activities.** When the team first forms, introductory activities help the team get acquainted with each other and the team charge. Activities might involve simple questions, problem-solving activities, or games.

- **Experiential learning.** These activities are structured team experiences. Examples may be physical game challenges, travel outings, or adventure-based team-building experiences in a higher-risk environment. The goal is for teams to have an experience together that challenges them and then allows them to reflect on the experience together.

- **Team assessments.** Another way to build awareness, enhance skills, and encourage team cooperation is through the use of team assessments. There are a number of tools that can be used, such as cultural awareness, communication style, and team assessment instruments.

- **Case studies.** These are carefully written situations that call for problem solving and decisions. The case is presented and teams work through the example and possible alternatives for action. This type of activity encourages critical thinking and group discussion.

- **Simulations.** These are replications of the work environment that are used as a learning tool. Simulations can be staged, or they can be arranged in the actual work environment if the exercise is not too disruptive. Team members work through the simulation exercises as a learning experience.

- **Multimedia presentations.** Video, CD-ROM, or Web-based presentations are used to convey relationship and work principles. Team members react to the scenarios and discuss the principles learned.

- **Post-activity reflection.** Post-activity discussion is important to understanding each other and building trust. The team debriefs and shares how they approached the situations, what they observed, and what they learned from the experiences.

High-performing teams

Organizations hope to foster high-performing teams that contribute to high organizational performance. High-performing teams have all of the features of a well-functioning team, plus they are highly committed to each other and to the results they bring to the organization.

The primary characteristics of high-performing team members are that they:

- Share the team's purpose and goals.
- Show commitment to the group.
- Use effective communication and conflict resolution skills.
- Balance tasks and processes.
- Use effective problem-solving and decision-making skills.
- Show trust and respect for team diversity, placing value in complementary skills.
- Have a strong focus and plan toward outcomes.
- Are accountable.
- Continuously evaluate and improve their skills.
- Celebrate successes.

Performance assessment

Team performance is directly linked to the original team charter, which should be linked to goals and objectives of the organization. An assessment of performance needs to be customized to the type of team and the specific outcomes desired.

Performance criteria that apply for any work team are:

- Were the critical milestones and deadlines met?
- Were effective decision-making and problem-solving skills applied?
- Was there open and honest communication?
- Was there healthy conflict and conflict resolution?
- Was there trust among team members?
- Were there continual improvement efforts?
- Have quality outcomes been achieved?
- Overall, were team objectives successfully met?
- Are there follow-up activities and, if so, are responsibilities assigned?

When assessing performance, there are two aspects to consider: collective team performance and individual performance. With respect to individuals, team participation can be linked as an additional aspect of the standard performance appraisal process. Individuals are also held accountable in the team environment, usually by pressures from the group members and the group leader.

Team rewards

Team motivation and rewards are an important part of building a successful team. Rewards should be of value to the team members.

Autonomy, ownership of work, and challenging responsibilities in a team effort are intrinsic rewards. Members enjoy getting support, feeling empowered, accomplishing tasks, learning something new, and having fun together. Training to learn new skills, trips, prizes, and money are all extrinsic rewards.

A diverse team will have cultural value differences. The key to providing team rewards is to make sure that the rewards are of value and are flexible enough for everyone on the team regardless of his or her background. For example, an individual who values family time over work time is not likely to appreciate a weekend away from family as a reward. An individual who values close interpersonal relationships, socializing, and status would value a celebratory occasion to visit with organizational leaders about the team successes.

Fairness in team rewards is an issue because each team member contributes differently to the team effort. A way to help resolve this is to involve the team in selecting the rewards and determining up front how they will be distributed when team objectives are met.

Chapter D: Conflict Management

Chapter Introduction

Conflict management and resolution, value-added negotiating, and relationship management skills are key business management skills. They are especially applicable to the internal auditing role.

The internal auditing group has the distinct challenge of developing good relationships and building trust in all areas of the organization while at the same time evaluating the effectiveness of the organization. Clients are keenly aware that the auditing group is looking for inefficiencies, defects, and fraud and may tend to view the auditing group in an adversarial way.

Internal auditing involves change, and there will be auditor-client conflicts. However, when a cooperative approach is used, clients are more apt to recognize the value that is brought by the auditing group. Conflict management skills are especially useful when presenting the results of audits, making recommendations, and developing action plans to correct weaknesses.

Topic 1: Demonstrate an Understanding of Conflict Management (Level A)

Causes of conflict

Conflict is a disagreement about interests, ideas, opinions, beliefs, values, behaviors, or other things. There will always be conflict in the environment, and having some conflict is healthy. Conflict surfaces underlying issues, energizes individuals and teams, brings out new perspectives, and may result in positive win/win situations.

Functional conflict is conflict that is constructive and fosters positive outcomes and improved performance. Dysfunctional conflict is destructive and negatively impacts the achievement of group or organizational goals.

Understanding what causes conflict and ways to manage conflict is essential to business management skills. Conflict occurs between individuals, within groups, between groups, and systemically within an organization.

There are many conflict triggers, which are prompters that cause conflict in an organization:

- Personal value differences
- Unethical behavior
- Poor communication
- Small- or large-scale change efforts
- Different goals and objectives
- Allocation of resources
- Lack of information
- Stressors in the environment
- Group incompatibility
- Cultural background differences
- Questionable motives for actions
- Incorrect assumptions
- Leadership and management approaches
- Status differences
- Lack of trust
- Reward systems
- Short-sighted problem solving

Conflict management

There are different levels of conflict, and many disagreements are managed effectively without high escalation. A typical conflict pattern involves the stages of disagreement, confrontation, escalation, de-escalation, and finally resolution. There are times when involving a neutral third party is an appropriate resolution strategy.

Mediation is a process where a neutral third party intervenes to help parties in a dispute negotiate their differences. Arbitration is a process where the parties in a dispute agree in advance that they will abide by the decision of an arbitrator who is chosen to hear both sides and make a judgment.

Conflict can be categorized in low-level, mid-level, and high-level stages:

- **Low-level conflict** involves some disagreement, anger, and discomfort. Resolution is usually found by examining the facts, considering alternatives, and coming to agreement.

- **Mid-level conflict** involves a win/lose situation. Individuals take sides, and disagreement is more personal and emotional. Mid-level conflict takes more time to resolve. A facilitator may be needed to create a neutral environment and help bring the parties to agreement.

- **High-level conflict** involves intense emotions with sides drawn. Much effort is expended, and winning is important. A mediator is most likely required to bring resolution. If the conflict permeates more widely in the organization, an external mediator would be required. If mediation does not work, the last resort is arbitration.

Topic 2: Describe Different Methods of Conflict Resolution (Level A)

Conflict resolution steps

Strategies for conflict resolution will differ based on the interests of the parties and the situation.

Steps to resolution usually include:

- Select an appropriate time and place.
- Consider what your goal is.
- Have a set agenda for discussion.
- Focus on facts and the real issues.
- Try to understand the other party's point of view.
- Express the other party's point of view back to them as well as possible to demonstrate your understanding.
- Separate the people from the problems.
- Openly discuss disagreements in a respectful manner.
- Use good communication skills (questioning, active listening).
- Remain calm.
- Try to find common ground.
- Consider the consequences of winning or losing.
- Use a facilitator or mediator if necessary.
- Develop alternatives.
- Come to an agreement.

Competitive/ cooperative approaches

Individuals may tend to handle conflict in either a competitive or a cooperative stance. The circumstances and issues will also dictate the approach a person uses.

Typical ways that people manage and resolve conflict are noted here:

- Competing is focusing on winning and less on the issues at hand.
- Accommodating is giving in to others even if not convinced.
- Avoiding is ignoring the conflict and hoping it will go away.

- Compromising is giving in some to gain resolution.
- Collaborating is working together to gain a win/win solution.

When managing conflict in the organization, there are five conflict management styles managers can use:

- Withdrawing is when managers avoid or ignore conflict because it is unimportant; the timing isn't right or there may be some other reason. This is a legitimate choice, but the conflict may continue to grow.
- Smoothing is when a manager tries to reach common ground and will give in to the other party if necessary. The relationship is more important than winning.
- Forcing is when one side dominates and forces a win/lose situation. This is the opposite of smoothing.
- Compromising is when both sides reach a less-than-ideal solution.
- Collaborating is when both sides look for a solution acceptable to all.

Topic 3: Demonstrate an Understanding of Negotiation Skills (Level A)

Negotiation is a process of bargaining between two or more parties to try to reach a mutually acceptable outcome.

Principled negotiation

Principled negotiation, described in the book *Getting to Yes* by Roger Fisher and William Ury, is an approach developed through the Harvard Negotiation Project. Principled negotiation is a method to decide issues based on their merits rather than on competitive or cooperative negotiating tactics. It is based on several criteria for long-term gain that all negotiations must be judged against to determine if they are a success:

- If agreement is reachable, results should meet the needs of both parties to the extent possible and should be fair, long lasting, and in the public good.
- The negotiation process should be efficient at finding a solution.
- The negotiation process should increase or maintain good relationships between parties.

Important negotiation skills in this method are:

- Separate the people from the problem.
- Focus on interests, not positions.
- Generate a variety of possibilities before deciding what to do.
- Insist that the result be based on some objective standard.

The first negotiation skill to develop is to see yourself and the other party as problem solvers—neither adversaries nor friends. Attack the problem rather than one another, and leave emotions out of it.

Establishing a position, such as the highest rent you will pay or a recommendation that just cannot be ignored, is an emotional investment. Egos require defending the position. Therefore, the next negotiation skill to develop is to avoid taking positions at all and instead start by generating mutual understanding of each party's interests. Instead of making offers or threats, or disclosing or obfuscating a bottom line, identify interests: a stable renting situation or ensuring that a control weakness is repaired in some way.

The third negotiation skill is to invent options for mutual advantage. Rather than putting pressure on the other party to compromise quickly, which results in poor decision making, first negotiate a time period in which parties can come to an agreement with less pressure. Spend the time to devise as many alternatives as possible that can satisfy both parties' interests. The goal is to make the other party's choice easier, not harder. If your recommendation solves their problem while solving yours too, the other party will be more likely to negotiate.

The last negotiation skill to learn is to insist on using objective criteria. The terms of a decision should be based on something other than one or the other party's opinion. Instead, make the negotiations all about finding a reasonable standard for the agreement. This could be the law, fair market value, expert opinion, a risk assessment, ethical standards, or organizational culture.

Next we'll look at a different but complementary negotiating theory.

Added-value negotiating

Added-value negotiating, as described by Albrecht and Albrecht, is a cooperative negotiation approach based on shared interests and objectives. The difference from other negotiating processes is the focus on presenting exchanges of value for each party rather than each party just presenting what they want. It is not about trying to get the other party to concede.

In order to consider value exchanges, this process involves a good deal of study and preparation about why the other party wants an agreement. This takes effort because the end result is still a win/win circumstance.

Another point of difference from other processes is that several alternatives, or deals, are presented for discussion. Other negotiation processes typically present one offer, wait for a response or counteroffer, and then again make an offer until agreement is reached.

Specific steps

The following are specific steps in added-value negotiating:

- **Clarify interests.** The first step is for each party to identify his or her own interests and research the interests of the other party. Both subjective interests, like a long-term relationship, and objective interests, like money, are listed. The more interests that can be listed, the more possibilities for alternatives of mutual interest.

- **Identify value options.** The next step is for each party to list what kinds of values he or she has and what kinds of values the other party has. A value includes money, property, actions to take or refrain from, certain rights, risks, and other value factors.

- **Create several offers.** Again, a distinction from other negotiation processes is in this step of creating more than one offer to present. The offers will hold advantages for both parties. Each offer has a different combination and balance of the value options identified. Presenting several offers allows parties to pick an option, if one is agreeable, or pick elements of options and put together a new agreeable option.

- **Select the best offer.** Parties then work together to review offers and narrow the choices down to the closest offer. Both parties need to study the proposal for value and fair balance. If there is not a satisfactory offer, the parties back up and create more offers.

- **Perfect the deal.** The last step is to fine-tune the offer to make sure both parties are comfortable with the final agreement. The offer needs careful review to smooth out any questions or problems.

To recap, the added-value negotiation process provides a more collaborative approach than position-based methods. The process usually takes less time than other processes because of the multiple offers presented at the beginning. This approach avoids many of the tactics (sometimes negative or deceitful) used in traditional approaches.

Global deal making

Global deal making and negotiation processes require additional attention. As organizations compete in the global marketplace, they want to negotiate creative and forward-looking business arrangements.

However, there are cultural background differences to consider. Methods and acceptable practices for negotiation will vary by country. There are also language, culture, time, distance, and cross-border legal issues that make offers more difficult.

The use of cultural informants and interpretation services are a way for organizations to interpret behavior, prepare written proposals, and resolve conflicts. In many cases, a cultural mediator will need to be officially engaged to assist the negotiation process.

Chapter E: Project Management/Change Management

Chapter Introduction

Project management and change management are related concepts. Project management requires a fair dose of change management to succeed, and change management must use the organizing tactics of project management to succeed. Furthermore, both are critical methods for internal auditors to master. Internal auditing is a project-based discipline. Each assurance or consulting engagement is a project that needs to be run through the plan-do-check-act cycle to minimize the amount of work and expense needed while maximizing the achievement of audit and stakeholder objectives. Change management is also a necessary element of internal auditing, since internal auditors are change agents.

Topic 1: Demonstrate an Understanding of Change Management (Level A)

It is generally accepted today that the future success—even the survival—of an organization can depend on how well it anticipates and responds to both unexpected and foreseeable change. Change management is the continuous process of planning and directing changes that occur within an organization to achieve an intended result. It implies that it is possible to introduce change deliberately and steer the initiative rather than allowing change to happen on its own accord, often unpredictably. An organization committed to continuous improvement needs to have effective change management practices in place.

To a degree, change management is an art and a science. It incorporates aspects of thinking, learning, acuity, agility, tenacity, and innovativeness. The ability to respond quickly to customer and market demands and other types of change pressures and do it more responsively and effectively than competitors is often what differentiates winners from losers.

Changing procedures, formulas, physical flows, production specifications, etc., is often done routinely and can be easily planned and accomplished. Changing behaviors, thought processes, and attitudes must also be planned but takes longer to achieve, and it may be harder to measure outcomes.

Change management techniques

Successful organizations have a proactive approach in place that allows them to anticipate and respond to change. They literally get out in front of change and do not just sit back and allow change to happen. They also have mechanisms in place to help everyone in the organization efficiently and effectively assimilate change.

Many tried and true change management models exist. Through various means, they all tend to:

- Create an environment for change.
- Help facilitate change.
- Monitor progress against the plan to see if desired results are obtained.
- Communicate updates about progress and results.

Ultimately, an effective change management model is one that leads an organization from its current state through a transition state to an improved state of operations.

Depending on the specific nature of the change, different levels of management should be involved. For example, with major change events (e.g., mergers or acquisitions), senior executives are in a unique position to sanction and legitimize the change. They can be a part of setting the organization's change management strategy, lead by example, and assume overall accountability for its success. Middle and front-line managers who are closer to daily operations can help employees make the change, monitor progress against the plan, revise incentives and penalties to be in alignment with new objectives, and work at removing process barriers.

Organizational roadblocks to change

Managing change has been compared to a balancing act—the key being not just attending to individual pieces and processes in the initiative in isolation but rather taking a holistic view of how the pieces fit together, how changing one element changes the rest, and how sequencing and pace affect the whole initiative.

Successful change management is not like driving on a well-groomed racetrack. In spite of suggested processes, insights, and lessons learned from others, there are many potholes in change management approaches—often rooted in conventional wisdom—that can derail a change initiative. A critical part of any change initiative is identifying such barriers, evaluating their significance and risk, and planning how to best address them. The most significant barriers to change are often inherent in an organization's culture and structure.

Cultural barriers are often rooted in reactionary attitudes and beliefs. Change is a disturbance in the status quo, and therefore it creates strong emotional responses. Distrust, fear of change, fear of loss such as job loss or loss of job relevance, and even management's failure to create a shared vision can undermine a change effort. The following are basic cultural barriers and general solutions.

- **Physical tasks cannot solely be equated to change; "mental work" needs to be a part of the process and a sense of urgency created.** Change is often intensely personal and, fundamentally, it involves feelings. Organizations that want to get their employees on board have to accept that managing emotions is often a big part of the process. In most successful change initiatives, organizations clearly communicate the need for change and connect with their employees through values.

- **Trust is essential but often hardest to establish when needed the most; a guiding vision must be in place.** Trust can make or break a change effort. But if new processes are aligned to a vision to help direct the change effort and there are strategies and objectives put in place, resistance can be overcome. If employees see how risk management and controls are in place to support the change, the desired results will often follow. Further, employees need to understand their roles and responsibilities.

Organizational structures have the potential to introduce structural barriers to change efforts. For example, hierarchical or vertical structures may foster a "silo" mentality, where each department focuses on its own interests, procedures, and people rather than cooperating with other groups and supporting a change effort. While this structural isolation may increase the efficiency of individual groups, it ultimately detracts from the organization's ability to successfully implement change.

Flattened horizontal structures may produce communication barriers between management levels. For example, potentially negative information at one level may be distorted and filtered before being passed up to higher management. Or management plans may not be communicated to front-line employees at all.

The best way to overcome structural barriers is to promote shared priorities and an open flow of information across the organization.

Topic 2: Describe Project Management Techniques and Best Practices (Level A)

Project management is the process of planning, organizing, directing, and controlling an organization's resources (people, equipment, time, and money) for a temporary endeavor so that project objectives can be met within defined scope, time, and cost constraints.

Why use project management techniques? It takes time to set up a project and develop a project plan. Why not just get started on all the work that needs to be done? Project management requires much up-front work to define the problem that needs to be solved and then form a plan to achieve it. However, without such a plan, the total effort (including cost) and project duration may end up being far greater overall because of problems such as scope creep and/or rework. Scope creep is when project objectives are extended by external influences, resulting in unplanned additions to a project's scope or time, cost, and quality constraints. It is a common cause of missed deadlines and budgets or unnecessary project features. While project change is necessary to keep it responsive to changes in the situation and environment, such changes must be controlled using the project objectives as a gatekeeper. Rework may also be needed because the wrong tasks were being executed such as the wrong audit tests. Exhibit V-32 shows how more up-front "pain" or effort can reduce total effort, thus reducing risks of uncertain achievement of goals or failure.

Exhibit V-32: More Up-Front Planning Effort Reduces Total Effort Required

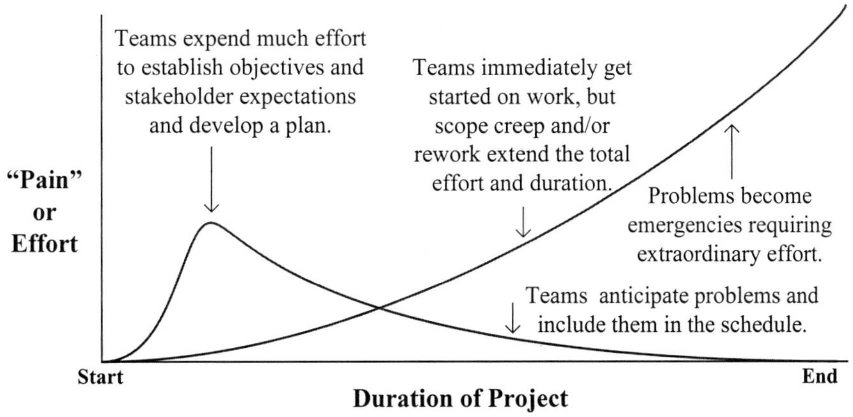

Project management basics

The basic challenges of successful project management include delivering a project:

- Within defined constraints.
- At a desired performance/quality level.
- By effectively optimizing allocation and integration of the inputs needed to meet the predefined objectives.

Projects can vary in duration and complexity, but the majority of projects share the characteristics listed below:

- A project is a series of tasks and activities with a stated goal and objective.
- It fulfills some need or requirement in an organization.
- It has objectives that outline a path for achieving the goal.
- It has a defined start date, time line, and target completion date.
- It has funding or budget limits and dedicated resources (which also include materials, energy, space, provisions, communication, quality, risk, etc.).

Project life cycle

Most projects cycle through similar stages from beginning to end. Although the terms and specifics of the cycles vary from industry to industry, they generally include these stages:

- **Conception or project initiation** is where the project is born and the project goals and objectives are established. Stakeholder expectations must be discovered and guided. It is vital to acquire support from senior management at this stage. During this stage, the nature and scope of the project are determined in a project charter and the project manager and project team are selected.

- The **planning, design, and scheduling** stage is where the project schedule is outlined and resources are assigned.

- The **execution and production** stage is when the work takes place.

- During **monitoring and control,** the project manager is responsible for overseeing the quality of the work being produced, the progress against the schedule, and the use of resources necessary to complete the project. Project control systems keep a project on track, on time, and within budget.

Each project is assessed for the appropriate level of control needed. Internal auditors can help determine how important specific projects are to an organization's bottom line, the types of controls that exist, and any additional controls necessary.

- The **completion and evaluation** stage typically involves some culminating event, for example, the launching of a new line of software. Evaluation often includes assessing the project's effectiveness at the end of the process. Administrative activities include archiving files and documenting the lessons learned.

Exhibit V-33 on the next page shows the project life cycle and tasks associated with each phase.

Project team

Project plans and their execution are only as successful as the manager and team who implement them. Building effective teams is critical to the success of any project.

Projects commonly include the following project roles and team members:

- **Project stakeholders** are individuals and organizations (both internal and external) who are actively involved in the project or whose interests may be affected as a result of project execution or completion. Key stakeholders can include the project manager, the customer or end user (e.g., the board for internal audit projects), the people executing the project, and many others.

- The **project sponsor** is the person or group that provides the financial resources, in cash or in kind, for the project.

- The **project manager** is the leader of the project. He or she is responsible for coordinating and integrating activities across multiple functional lines in order to reduce the risk of overall failure or scope creep. A project manager is often a client representative who must determine and implement the client's needs.

- The **project team** is the core group of people who come together for a specific project and then disband when the project is over.

Exhibit V-33: Project Life Cycle

Project Phase	Project Tasks
Conception or project initiation	• Analyze project and spell out organizational needs in measurable goals. • Conduct review of current operations. • Complete conceptual design of finished project. • Prepare financial analysis, cost and benefits, budget. • Prepare list of assumptions, risks, and obstacles. • Select stakeholders, including users and support personnel, and develop an understanding of their expectations. • Develop project charter, including costs, objectives, tasks, deliverables, and schedules. • Gain approval for the project charter and acquire funding.
Planning, design, and scheduling	• Define work requirements. • Determine quantity and quality of work. • Determine and allocate resources needed. • Establish major timetable milestones. • Define deliverables (can include feasibility study, scope statement, project plan, communications plan, issue log, resource management plan, project schedule, status report). • Establish basis for performance measurement. • Generate a project management plan and get formal approval for it, including approval for the required resources.
Execution and production	• Launch the project management plan. • Confirm availability of adequate and appropriate project resources. • Document work teams. • Teams do work, provide status updates, and produce deliverables. • Project managers lead, direct, and control. • Managers and stakeholders receive progress reports and review action plans for correcting differences between plan and actual.
Monitoring and control	• Track progress, especially during execution but also during planning. • Compare actual and predicted outcomes. • Analyze impact. • Make adjustments to meet project objectives and acceptance criteria.
Completion and evaluation	• Obtain client acceptance based on acceptance criteria. • Install project deliverables. • Complete project documentation such as lessons learned. • Complete evaluation/post-implementation audit such as measuring stakeholder satisfaction. • Issue final project report and communicate lessons learned.

Constraints

Projects need to be performed and delivered under what has traditionally been known as the "project management triangle," as shown in Exhibit V-34. One side of the triangle cannot be changed without impacting the others. As continuous quality and performance initiatives like TQM have become increasingly important in performance management, quality and performance are sometimes separated from scope, turning quality into a fourth constraint.

Exhibit V-34: Project Management Triangle

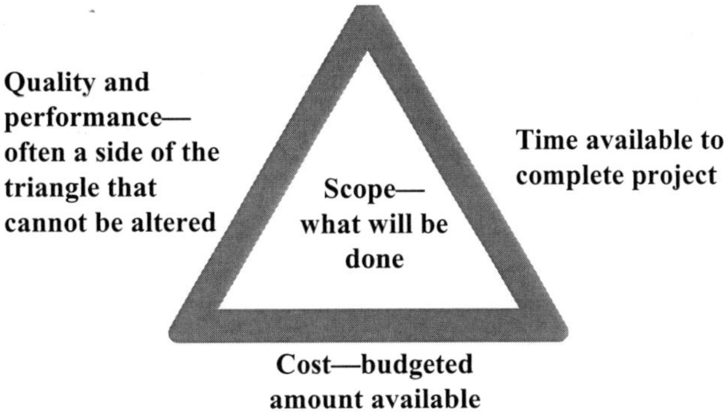

- **Time** is the amount of time available to complete the project. It is broken down into the time required to complete each component of the project, which is then broken down further into the time required to complete each task that contributes to the completion of each component.
- **Cost** refers to the budgeted amount available for the project. It depends on variables such as labor rates, material rates, risk management, plant, consultant rates, equipment, and profit.
- **Quality and performance** of the final product are major components of scope. The amount of time put into individual tasks and the amount of cost expended on resources influence the overall quality of the results. Over the course of a large project, meeting a defined quality level can have a significant impact on time and cost. Often, organizations define what quality should be from the start, thus fixing the size of this side of the triangle and requiring juggling of the other constraints to meet this requirement as defined by customer acceptance criteria.
- **Scope** means what must be done to produce the project's end result. It is sometimes represented as the area of the triangle to show that scope is strongly affected by the time, cost, and quality inputs. This is the overall definition of what the project is supposed to accomplish and a specific description of what the end result is supposed to be or accomplish.

These constraints often compete with each other. Increased scope or quality typically means increased time and increased cost. A tight time constraint might mean increased costs and reduced scope. A tight budget can mean increased time and reduced scope. Quality project management is about providing the tools and techniques that enable the entire project team to organize their work and meet these constraints.

Project management techniques

Project managers and their team members can use a variety of tools and techniques to plan, schedule, and manage their projects. The three tools most commonly associated with project management are Gantt charts and two types of network analysis: the critical path method and the program evaluation review technique.

The essential concept behind all of these tools is that during a project, some activities, known as "sequential" or "linear" activities, need to be completed in a particular sequence, with each stage being completed before the next activity or task can begin. Other activities are not dependent on the completion of any other tasks and can be completed at any stage during the time line. These are known as nondependent or "parallel" tasks.

Gantt chart

The Gantt chart (also known as a horizontal bar chart, a milestone chart, or an activity chart) is a project scheduling technique that divides each project into sequential activities with estimated start and completion times. It allows the decision maker to visually review a schematic presentation of the project time budget and allows for subsequent comparison with actual times.

To create a Gantt chart, the project manager plots the steps of the project and their sequence and duration. The list includes the earliest start date for each task, the estimated length of time it will take, and whether it is parallel or sequential. This forms the basis of the scheduling chart shown in Exhibit V-35. A Gantt chart's simplicity allows for easy schedule modifications.

Exhibit V-35: Gantt Chart

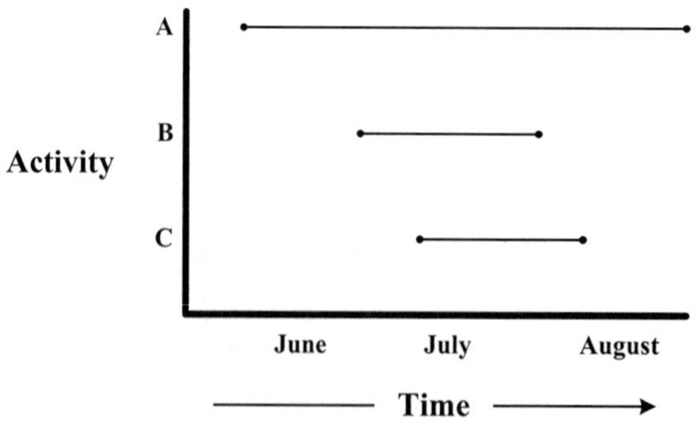

A Gantt chart:

- Helps plan tasks that need to be completed.
- Provides a basis for scheduling when tasks will be executed.
- Helps plan the allocation of resources necessary to complete the project.
- Helps determine the critical path for a project that needs to be completed by a specific date.
- Is appropriate for internal audit scheduling because the audit process does not often require sequence revisions.

Network analysis

A project network is the graphical representation of a project's tasks and schedule. Network analysis involves evaluating the network of tasks and functions that contribute to a project in order to determine the most efficient path for reaching the project goals. Network analysis can help project managers carry out their scheduling activities during projects that consist of many separate jobs or tasks performed by a variety of departments and individuals. It can also help identify possible ways to revise or shorten the sequence of activities to expedite the project and/or lower costs. In industries like construction and aircraft manufacturing, an understanding of networks is critical to an internal auditor. Network analysis computer programs can help complete project scheduling, including tracking resource costs and usage.

Critical path method/program evaluation review technique

Although developed independently, two of the most common types of network analysis, the critical path method (CPM) and the program evaluation review technique (PERT) are so similar as to be nearly synonymous. This type of network analysis is now often referred to as some variant of PERT/CPM. Internal auditors may be called on to use these tools in evaluating efficiency and adherence to an organization's policies and procedures.

The critical path method and the program evaluation review technique are project management tools used to schedule, organize, and coordinate tasks. This method is generally used for large, complex projects with a high degree of inter-task dependency.

A PERT/CPM chart illustrates a project flow graphically. A number of circles or rectangles represent project milestones that are linked by arrows that indicate the sequence of tasks. Constructing a PERT/CPM network requires three inputs: the tasks necessary to complete the project, the time required to complete these tasks, and their sequence (i.e., the degree to which one task's completion depends on the completion of a separate task).

The goal of the PERT/CPM chart is to identify the critical path—the sequence of tasks that will take the longest time to complete, without any slack time between activities. All of the activities on the critical path must be completed in order; a delay in any activity will delay the entire project. Tasks that are not dependent on any other tasks, which can be completed simultaneously with other tasks, are referred to as parallel or concurrent tasks.

Generally, the critical path is defined as the path for which the earliest start time (ES) equals the latest start time (LS) and the earliest finish time (EF) equals the latest finish time (LF), where:

- ES is the soonest an activity can start after any necessary preceding steps that must be finished first.
- EF is the ES plus the time needed to finish the activity.
- LF is the longest deadline allowed for an activity without delaying the project.
- LS is the LF less the time needed to finish the activity.

Exhibit V-36 shows an example of a PERT/CPM chart.

Exhibit V-36: PERT/CPM Chart

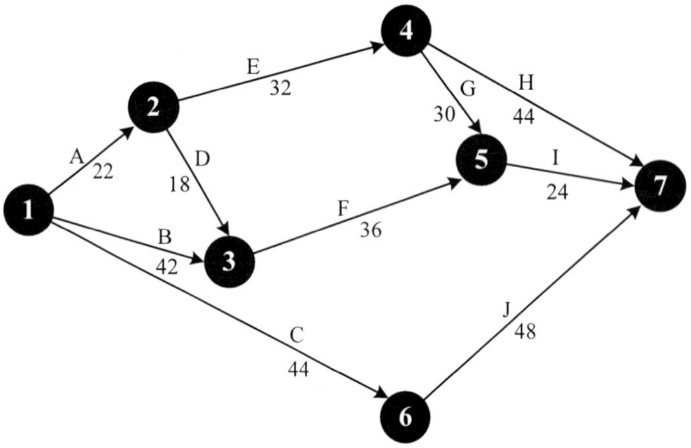

Source: *Sawyer's Internal Auditing,* fifth edition, by Lawrence B. Sawyer, et al. Used with permission.

In Exhibit V-36, there are five possible paths to reach the project endpoint (7):

- 1-2-4-7 (98 days)
- 1-2-3-5-7 (100 days)
- 1-2-4-5-7 (108 days)
- 1-3-5-7 (102 days)
- 1-6-7 (92 days)

Path 1-2-4-5-7, requiring 108 days, is the critical path. It includes all the required activities, in the necessary sequence of completion, without slack time. Activities B and D (which end in node 3) and activity C (which ends in node 6) have slack and could be delayed or durations extended without affecting the total project duration—up to a point.

Due to unexpected delays or tight deadlines, a project manager can use PERT/CPM charts to help identify ways to shorten a project's time line. The project manager can:

- **Allow for lead time.** Lead time is when a scheduled task begins before its predecessor task is completed. For example, the original time line for an advertising brochure may call for the graphics to be completed after the writer finishes the first draft. However, if the illustrator receives the list of necessary graphics two weeks prior to the first draft completion date, the illustrator will have two weeks' lead time to finish the graphics and will be able to deliver them at the same time the writer completes the first draft.
- **Identify slack time.** Slack time is the amount of additional time that an activity can consume without delaying the project past the expected completion date. Slack is the difference between the earliest expected time and the latest allowable time for each task. By definition, all activities in the critical path have a slack of zero. But other activities not in the critical path will often have slack. In our brochure example, the marketing activities are ancillary to the critical path activities. This means that there is slack in the start date for the marketing activities.
- **Assign additional resources.** Depending on the project, it may be possible to increase the resources committed to a task on the critical path. Assigning two people to write the first draft of the advertising brochure could cut the writing time in half (assuming no learning curve). The process of adding resources to shorten the length of a task on the critical path is called "crashing." The length of the project could also be shortened by "fast tracking," or performing certain tasks simultaneously.
- **Schedule overtime.** Any of the tasks may be shortened by scheduling project members for overtime. If the critical path is shortened, a different sequence of tasks could become the new critical path.

The following are benefits and disadvantages of PERT/CPM:

- They identify and prioritize tasks that must be completed on time for the whole project to be completed on time.
- They identify sequential and parallel tasks.

- They identify which tasks can be delayed or accelerated without jeopardizing the overall timing of a project.
- They assess the shortest time in which a project can be completed.
- They form the basis for all planning and predicting.
- They help schedule and manage complex projects.
- They provide management with the ability to plan for the best possible use of resources to achieve a given goal within time and cost limitations.
- They do not make the relation of tasks to one another as obvious as in Gantt charts. (Gantt charts may still be necessary with CPM/PERT.)
- They can help a project manager determine an approximation of project scheduling. However, there are a number of uncontrollable unknowns that can impact a schedule such as delays in the availability of critical resources.

PERT and CPM are very similar. However, there are a few key differences:

- PERT is a variation of CPM that takes a slightly more conservative view of time estimates for each project stage.
- PERT was developed to address projects with uncertain task times; it allows task times to be forecast based upon a range of possible values, from worst-case to best-case scenarios.
- PERT is appropriate in projects that involve new or unique situations where task times cannot be accurately forecast.
- CPM was developed for factory-type projects where task time was already known.
- CPM is able to relate costs to rewards because task times are known. Rewards for shortening the completion time of a contract, for example, may be substantial. In return, the costs associated with moving up the completion date can be tracked (additional resources, overtime pay, etc.).

Next Steps

You have completed Part 3, Section V, of The IIA's CIA Learning System®. Next, check your understanding by completing the online section-specific test(s) to help you identify any content that needs additional study.

Once you have completed the section-specific test(s) and feel confident that you have mastered the information, you can advance to studying Section VI.

Section VI: IT/Business Continuity

This section is designed to help you:

- *Describe the role of physical and system security in reducing information security vulnerabilities.*
- *Differentiate between specific IT general controls and IT application controls and understand the basic functions of other security measures such as firewalls.*
- *Comprehend threats that information is exposed to and methods of protecting information, including application authentication, encryption, data protection, and backup procedures.*
- *Describe end-user computing.*
- *Describe how change and patch management controls can result in predictable and repeatable application upgrades.*
- *Show that application development or software selection must follow a defined methodology such as the systems development life cycle or an accelerated alternative.*
- *Define and describe application development and related terminology.*
- *Describe various levels of application controls.*
- *Describe the overall process of information systems design and development.*
- *Demonstrate an understanding of workstations.*
- *Have broad knowledge of the functioning of databases and database management systems, specifically relational databases and database controls.*
- *Describe the basic purpose of and tools used within common IT control frameworks.*
- *Show how various functional areas of IT operations should be organized for efficiency and segregation of duties.*
- *Understand the underlying principles of enterprise resource planning (ERP) systems and operating systems.*
- *Interrelate the hardware and software needed to create data, voice, and network communications and connections within and between organizations.*
- *Demonstrate an understanding of servers.*
- *Delineate software licensing laws and regulations from the perspective of both buyer and seller.*
- *Demonstrate an understanding of mainframes.*
- *Describe the Web infrastructure, including basic terminology as well as risks and responses to e-mail and browser threats.*
- *Explain the role of the internal audit activity in business continuity planning/ implementation.*
- *Describe how an IT contingency plan uses risk-based objectives to set priorities and the importance of documenting and testing the plan.*

The Certified Internal Auditor (CIA) exam questions based on content from this section make up approximately 15% to 25% of the total number of questions for Part 3. Topics are covered at the "A—Awareness" level, meaning that you are responsible for comprehension and recall of information

Section Introduction

Access to relevant and reliable information is key to business decision making. Relevance includes timeliness of information and an appropriate level of detail. Successfully applied information technology (IT) speeds the availability of information, automates aggregation and sorting of data, and ensures information accuracy. Unsuccessfully applied IT gives away a business's competitive advantage to better-informed competitors. IT is successfully applied when the organization is able to use it to fulfill business objectives, measure and address risks appropriately, grow and adapt fluidly, communicate effectively internally and externally, and react quickly to business opportunities as they arise.

IT and auditing are primarily concerned with information risk, which is the risk that inaccurate information is used to make a business decision. However, widespread use of IT for all business processes has led auditing away from a focus on assurance regarding historical data at a specific point in time to assurance about the reliability of processes. This is because IT generates the historical data almost automatically, so if the process is wrong, the data will be too, and vice versa. Therefore, auditing can have an effect on mitigating information risk.

Risks specific to IT environment

IT can potentially remove risks from a manual system but introduces its own risks. In addition, because of the nature of IT activities, these risks may also affect each other.

- **Physical audit trail replaced by data trail.** Many physical documents are eliminated for audits, and controls must be used to compensate.
- **Hardware/software failure.** Permanent loss of data, e.g., from environmental damage, outages, civil disruption, and disasters, is costly.
- **Systematic errors.** IT reduces random errors such as in data entry, but automated systems can uniformly duplicate errors, e.g., via faulty code.
- **Fewer human inputs/less segregation of duties.** Many IT systems reduce labor costs through automation. Mitigating controls include reviewing segregation of duties and requiring end users to review their output at a low enough level of aggregation to catch problems.
- **Access authorization.** Increased ability to access sensitive information remotely also increases the risk of unauthorized access.

- **Automated transaction authorization.** Transactions that formerly required review and authorization, such as credit decisions, can be entirely regulated by a computer application. Authorization assurance rests on software controls and master file integrity.

- **Deliberate harmful acts.** Dishonest or disgruntled employees with proper access as well as outside individuals with profit or destructive motives can cause significant harm to an organization. Trusted insiders are the more significant risk.

The Institute of Internal Auditors' GTAG 4, "Management of IT Auditing," states that IT risks may be divided into two general categories:

- **Pervasive risks** are not limited to one system or activity but affect the enterprise as a whole. For example, when a new operating system is not tested adequately and causes total system shutdown upon implementation, all aspects of an operation are affected.

- **Specific risks** can be attributed to specific processes. For example, a malfunction that prevents vendors from accessing current inventory levels affects only inventory management and production.

Both types of risks must be addressed in an IT audit, although to different degrees, since pervasive risks are potentially more costly to the enterprise.

Challenges of IT auditing

To identify and assess the control of IT risks properly, an internal auditor must:

- Understand the purpose of an IT control, what type of control it is, and what it is meant to accomplish.
- Appreciate the significance of the control to the enterprise—both the benefits that accrue to the enterprise through the control (e.g., legal compliance or competitive advantage) and the damage that a weak or nonexistent control can cause.
- Identify which individuals or positions are responsible for performing what tasks.
- Balance the risk posed with the requirements of creating a control.
- Implement an appropriate control framework and auditing plan.
- Remain current with methodologies and business objectives.

Exhibit VI-1 summarizes the challenges internal auditors must master in conducting IT audits.

Exhibit VI-1: The Challenges of IT Auditing

Assessing IT Controls	
Understanding IT controls (covered in Chapter C, Topic 3)	• Governance, management, technical • General, application • Preventive, detective, corrective • Information security
Importance of IT controls	• Reliability and effectiveness • Competitive advantage • Legislation and regulation
Roles and responsibilities (see Chapter C, Topic 4)	• Governance • Management • Audit
Based on risk	• Risk analysis • Risk response • Baseline controls
Monitoring and techniques (covered in Chapter C, Topic 3)	• Control framework • Frequency
Assessment	• Methodologies • Audit committee interface

Source: GTAG 1, "Information Technology Controls."

Guidance

Exhibit VI-2 on the next page identifies International Professional Practices Framework guidance related to IT auditing.

Role of CAE in IT auditing

The chief audit executive is responsible for ensuring a good fit between the enterprise and its IT controls and proper implementation of a control framework. This involves:

- Understanding the organization's IT control environment.
- Being aware of all legal and regulatory requirements.
- Defining and assigning appropriate roles related to IT controls for the entire organization.
- Developing and implementing an appropriate risk assessment process.
- Identifying all internal and external monitoring processes.
- Establishing appropriate metrics for control success and policies for communicating with management.
- Communicating IT risks and controls to the board and executives in an understandable manner.

Exhibit VI-2: IT Auditing Guidance

Type of Guidance	Description
Standards	Standard 1210.A3 Internal auditors must have sufficient knowledge of key information technology risks and controls and available technology-based audit techniques to perform their assigned work. However, not all internal auditors are expected to have the expertise of an internal auditor whose primary responsibility is information technology auditing.
	Standard 1220.A2 In exercising due professional care internal auditors must consider the use of technology-based audit and other data analysis techniques.
	Standard 2110.A2 The internal audit activity must assess whether the information technology governance of the organization supports the organization's strategies and objectives.
Practice Advisories	Practice Advisory 2130.A1-1, "Information Reliability and Integrity"
Practice Guides	"Auditing Privacy Risks," second edition
Global Technology Audit Guides (GTAG)	GTAG-1, "Information Technology Controls"
	GTAG-2, "Change and Patch Management Controls: Critical for Organizational Success"
	GTAG-3, "Continuous Auditing: Implications for Assurance, Monitoring, and Risk Assessment"
	GTAG-4, "Management of IT Auditing"
	GTAG-6, "Managing and Auditing IT Vulnerabilities"
	GTAG-7, "Information Technology Outsourcing"
	GTAG-8, "Auditing Application Controls"
	GTAG-9, "Identity and Access Management"
	GTAG-10, "Business Continuity Management"
	GTAG-11, "Developing the IT Audit Plan"
	GTAG-12, "Auditing IT Projects"
	GTAG-13, "Fraud Prevention and Detection in an Automated World"
Guide to the Assessment of IT Risk (GAIT)	"The GAIT Methodology"
	"GAIT for IT General Control Deficiency Assessment"
	"GAIT for Business and IT Risk"

Ethics in IT

There is also an ethical dimension to the design and implementation of an IT control framework. IT systems generate significant information on individuals, making maintaining the privacy of employees and customers an ethical issue. The interests of stakeholders in an organization (e.g., shareholders, communities, governments) pose an additional obligation to ensure that internal controls robust enough to remove the temptation of fraud or management manipulation of financial results are in place. Executives have an ethical obligation to understand IT controls at a high level and to make sure that everyone knows their responsibilities.

Chapter A: Security

Chapter Introduction

The goal of systems security is to maintain the integrity of information assets and processing and mitigate and remediate vulnerabilities. COBIT, formerly known as Control Objectives for Information and Related Technology, is an internationally accepted framework created by ISACA that helps enterprises to achieve their objectives for the governance and management of IT. With the release of COBIT 4.1 in 2008, 11 systems security objectives were identified that reflect the breadth and complexity of the systems security environment:

1. Manage IT security, as aligned with business requirements.
2. Implement an IT security plan that balances organizational goals and risks and compliance requirements with the organization's IT infrastructure and security culture.
3. Implement identity management processes to ensure that all users are identified and have appropriate access rights.
4. Manage user accounts through appropriate policies and processes for establishing, modifying, and closing accounts.
5. Ensure security testing, surveillance, and monitoring to achieve a baseline level of system security and to prevent, identify, and report unusual activity.
6. Provide sufficient security incident definition to allow problems to be classified and treated.
7. Protect security technology by preventing tampering and ensuring the confidential nature of security system documentation.
8. Manage cryptographic keys to ensure their protection against modification and unauthorized disclosure. Prevent, detect, and correct malicious software across the organization in both information systems and technology.

9. Implement network security to ensure authorized access and flow of information into and from the enterprise.
10. Ensure that sensitive data is exchanged only over trusted paths or through reliable media with adequate controls to ensure authenticity of content, proof of submission, proof of receipt, and nonrepudiation of origin.

(COBIT 5 is the current version of the framework, released in 2012, and it is addressed in more detail later in the section.)

Systems security is made up of controls general to the organization and specific to IT systems and physical security systems. Because a system is only as strong as its weakest link, systems security must start with use of a control framework such as COSO's *Internal Control—Integrated Framework.* While this section covers only the general controls specific to IT, other controls such as segregation of check signing from check printing are a prerequisite for IT systems security.

When auditors find a weakness in general or application controls, pointing out the issue is only part of the task. Auditors also need to explain to management the risk exposure that the deficiency is causing. Finally, the auditor should recommend the best system that can address the control given the particulars of the organization. Continual monitoring is required for controls to be effective. For example, whenever a software application is reviewed for controls, the security administration procedures and password controls around it should be reviewed, including whether the right people have the right authority.

When auditing for computer-related fraud, auditors trained in computer controls should try to think like a thief or hacker in determining areas of greatest vulnerability and considering how they could be exploited, how the trail might be covered up, what level of authority would be needed to enact the cover-up, and what explanations could be used if the issue were detected. Such activities can help design the audit for maximum impact.

This chapter starts with a discussion of physical/system security, which is founded on a strong set of IT general controls. Topic 2 addresses threats, vulnerabilities, and malicious software such as viruses. Topic 3 covers application authentication, and Topic 4 provides an overview of encryption.

Topic 1: Demonstrate an Understanding of Physical/System Security (Level A)

Physical security

Security involves the physical and procedural measures used to protect an organization's buildings, the occupants, and the building contents. The goal in workplace security is to eliminate or reduce the risk of loss of organizational assets—tangible and intangible—from human and natural disasters.

Physical security vulnerabilities

There are many sources of physical security vulnerabilities. Examples include:

- Natural disasters (e.g., fires, floods, or earthquakes).
- Service disruptions (e.g., telephone, Internet, electrical power, or equipment failures).
- Human error.
- Theft and vandalism.
- Terrorism.
- Sabotage.

Ideally, physical security begins with workspace design. A few obvious examples are:

- Smoke alarms.
- Adequate lighting throughout a facility.
- The installation of an electronic security system for building entry.
- A reception area with staff or a security guard, sign-in sheets, and visitor badges.
- Restricted areas.

Preemployment background reference checks, postemployment security clearances, and separation of job duties are additional measures that can help mitigate physical security risks.

Security risk management process

It is not possible to mitigate all information or physical security risks. An organization needs to ensure that it has a risk management process in place to manage its exposure to potential information or physical losses.

Security risk management encompasses the processes an organization puts into place so that security controls and expenditures are fully commensurate with the risks to which the organization is exposed. Typical security risk management steps include identification, probability determination, quantification of potential loss, and selection.

Exhibit VI-3 provides an overview of these steps.

Exhibit VI-3: Risk Management Steps

Step	Description
Identification	Identifies the exposure to loss in terms of threats (an object, a person, or another entity that represents a risk of loss to an asset) and vulnerabilities (a weakness or fault in a system or protection mechanism that exposes information to an attack or damage).
Probability determination	Determines the probability that a threat or vulnerability will materialize; includes a spectrum from high to low such as: • Virtually certain. • Highly probable. • Moderately probable. • Improbable.
Quantification of potential loss	Quantifies the potential loss in terms of financial and nonfinancial impact; involves cost factors such as: • Temporary replacement of lost or damaged assets. • Permanent replacement of lost or damaged assets. • Related losses due to inability to conduct normal business operations. • Loss of investment income due to short-term expenses incurred to meet the replacement costs or restore normal operations. • Loss/damage to reputation due to the inability to conduct business.
Selection	Evaluates the feasibility of alternative risk management techniques; results in the selection of the best technique(s).

These steps are not cast in bronze. Organizations often adapt the steps and nomenclature.

The internal audit activity can ensure a thorough assessment of security risks by employing the following techniques and tools:

- **Analysis of reported incidents.** Records can provide valuable information about potential and actual losses.
- **Review of exposure statistics.** Statistics from insurance carriers, industry associations, and regulatory agencies can provide guidance about where to look for potential risk exposures.
- **Mapping key processes.** Developing process maps and identifying potential risk points provides helpful insights.
- **Periodic inspections.** Health and safety inspections can surface compliance lapses and also uncover opportunities to decrease risks.
- **Periodic process and product audits.** Such internal audits can incorporate specific questions to identify potential risks.

- **Assessments of management system effectiveness.** Beyond internal audits conducted to verify compliance and conformance to one or more standards or to assess continual improvement, this technique can identify gaps in management systems that expose the organization to potential losses.
- **Scenario analysis.** Tools such as brainstorming and mind mapping are effective to identify all the consequences that could occur in a worst-case scenario.

This list is not all-inclusive. The point is to do whatever is necessary to identify and prioritize risks.

Special information security considerations

Practice Advisory 2130.A1-1 notes that the chief audit executive "determines whether the internal audit activity possesses, or has access to, competent audit resources to evaluate information reliability and integrity and associated risk exposures. This includes both internal and external risk exposures, and exposures relating to the organization's relationships with outside entities." If specialized knowledge and skills are required, the organization may need to secure external service providers.

Guidance endorsed and strongly recommended by The IIA includes specific responsibilities for the internal audit activity. According to Practice Advisory 2130.A1-1:

> The CAE determines whether information reliability and integrity breaches and conditions that might represent a threat to the organization will promptly be made known to senior management, the board, and the internal audit activity.
>
> Internal auditors assess the effectiveness of preventive, detective, and mitigation measures against past attacks, as appropriate, and future attempts or incidents deemed likely to occur. Internal auditors determine whether the board has been appropriately informed of threats, incidents, vulnerabilities exploited, and corrective measures.
>
> Internal auditors periodically assess the organization's information reliability and integrity practices and recommend, as appropriate, enhancements to, or implementation of, new controls and safeguards. Such assessments can either be conducted as separate stand-alone engagements or integrated into other audits or engagements conducted as part of the annual audit plan. The nature of the engagement will determine the most appropriate reporting process to senior management and the board.

Determine disposition of security violations

It is reasonable to expect that the internal audit activity monitor whether and how well security violations are corrected when they are discovered (similar to corrective action plans in response to internal audits). In doing so, the focus of the internal auditor should be to ensure that the root cause of the security violations is addressed.

Disposition of all security violations should be reported to the board periodically, including the number and type of violations as well as management's actions to resolve the root cause.

Report on compliance

The internal audit activity can report to management and the board on the level of compliance with security rules, significant violations, and their disposition.

With regard to information security, high-level compliance can be achieved through the implementation of codes of practice for information security compliance.

An example is ISO/IEC 27002:2005, which establishes guidelines and general principles for initiating, implementing, maintaining, and improving information security management in an organization. The focus of ISO/IEC 27002 is information security controls. It contains best practices of control objectives and controls that can be applied by any organization, regardless of size or industry. Organizations adopt ISO/IEC 27002 to develop organizational security standards and effective security management practices, address legal and regulatory concerns, and better manage compliance.

Systems security: IT general controls

According to COBIT, ensuring systems security involves both creating security policies and continuously monitoring and responding to security threats. Security policies are part of IT general controls. IT general controls (ITGCs) apply to all system components, processes, and data in the organization or the system environment.

Effective ITGCs are measured by the number of:

- Incidents that damage the enterprise's public reputation.
- Systems that do not meet security criteria.
- Violations in segregation of duties.

ITGCs are classified in the *Global Technology Audit Guide* as:

- Logical access controls
  (See Topic 3, "Describe Application Authentication.")
- Systems development life cycle controls
  (See Chapter B, Topic 3.)
- Program change management controls
  (See Chapter B, Topic 2.)
- Physical security controls
- System and data backup and recovery controls
- IT operational controls

The first three of these controls are addressed later. The last three are addressed next.

Physical security controls

Physical security controls include physical access controls, environmental hazard controls, and fire and flood protection. Physical access controls are the real-world means of preventing access to an asset such as locks and/or key cards preventing access to the building, to data centers, and to key operational areas. Key cards use swipe or radio frequency identifiers to identify a particular user badge. A security computer checks the badge against a list for access and also maintains an access log (an audit trail).

All areas of a building should be covered by a general security system, including motion sensors and cameras in key areas as well as devices to detect break-ins. Physical security can also be role-based, with certain areas more secure than others, even to IT staff. Very high security can use biometric devices, which check a user's identity through iris scans and the like.

Hardware not in a data center such as laptops or PCs can be physically secured with locks and have their own small uninterruptible power supplies (UPSs) and surge suppressors. Exposed wiring should be minimized using wiring closets or patch panels.

Data centers should not be located along an exterior wall but should be in an inconspicuous location with as few doors as fire codes allow. Media storage should be fire-rated, and backup and disaster contingency measures should be in place. Fire alarms and moisture detectors should be used. If the data is extremely sensitive, slab-to-slab concrete construction can be employed to prevent access through walls or ceiling.

Heating, venting, and air conditioning (HVAC) are vital because servers function better in cool, low-humidity rooms. UPSs and surge suppression should be employed. Devices need to be grounded and the floor covered with static takeoff. The air must be clean and free from smoke and particles, especially metallic particles, which can ruin tapes or CPUs. Other physical risks include electromagnetic interference from outside devices, which can be minimized by proper shielding.

Maintenance and housekeeping schedules for dust removal should be set and adhered to as per manufacturer recommendations. Logs of hardware cleaning and malfunctions should be kept. Internal auditors can check to see if actual maintenance patterns match suggested patterns; they can also check on the lag between when issues are reported and when they are fixed.

Hardware controls

Hardware controls are built-in controls designed to detect and report hardware errors or failures. Hardware is becoming more reliable but is still a possible source of errors. After determining the existence of hardware controls, auditors should put more effort into finding out how the organization reacts to hardware errors than checking the controls themselves. The controls will report the issue but will not fix the resulting output errors, so a process needs to be in place.

The following are types of hardware controls:

- **Redundant character check.** Each transmitted data element receives an additional bit (character) of data mathematically related to the data. Abnormal changes will void the mathematical relationship.
- **Equipment check.** These are circuitry controls that detect hardware errors.
- **Duplicate process check.** A process is done twice and compared.
- **Echo check.** Received data is returned to the sender for comparison.
- **Fault-tolerant components.** Fault-tolerant components have redundancies in hardware or software to allow continued operations if a system fails.

System and data backup and recovery controls

Backup methodologies include the grandfather-father-son concept, in which the son is the most recent backup followed by the father and grandfather backups. As a new backup is made, it becomes the new son, the old son becomes the father, and so on. The old grandfather may be marked for overwriting. The number of generations retained is set by policy. The organization defines a backup period for a particular data set (hourly, daily, monthly), determined by the frequency that the data changes. For example, payroll data that is changed twice a month would need biweekly updates.

Different permanent storage or secondary storage devices exist, but they can be classified generally by how they access data. Sequential access means that the data must be accessed in the order it was recorded, such as for tape storage. Direct or random access means the system can go to any location for faster retrieval, such as for magnetic and optical disks. Another differentiator is whether the system is designed only for full-volume backup or if it allows incremental backup of just the changes.

Off-site storage

Data should be backed up to an off-site storage facility physically distant from primary operations to keep area catastrophes from affecting both sites. Physical controls for an off-site storage facility might include:

- Revealing the location of the facility to as few people as possible.
- Ensuring that the outside of the facility does not reveal its purpose or use.
- Securing all access points and eliminating windows.
- Providing appropriate controls on environmental conditions (e.g., raised platforms, waterproofing, fire alarms, and climate monitoring and control).
- Keeping inventory of the contents.

Cloud backup

The use of cloud-based backup methods satisfies the physical distance and secret location criteria because clouds are a network of distributed databases and servers in which data is placed wherever there is available capacity rather than having designated storage areas. In this method, backups are also electronically transmitted to the cloud, which could be internally owned or a third-party system. Internally owned clouds need to ensure that the physical distance criterion is satisfied for backups.

Electronic vaulting

Electronic vaulting involves electronically transmitting changes to data to an off-site facility and then creating backup long-term storage, eliminating physical transportation. It is a hybrid solution, combining physical off-site vaulting with electronic journaling. Electronic journaling is a log of the transactions or changes that have happened since the last regular backup. The recovery point is the time after the last safe backup up to the point of failure. Traditional daily off-site backups offer, at worst, a recovery point between 24 and 48 hours. For businesses that see this delay as an unacceptable risk, electronic vaulting can provide a shorter recovery point.

Backup data controls

In addition to physical and logical security, backup systems need to have a methodology for labeling and storing backups and application library items if they are in physical form such as tape, CD, or disk. The labels should be internal (digital) and external (physical) and use a logical file-naming convention to prevent files from being deleted accidentally. This will prevent restoration delays or inadvertent restoration to the wrong point. In addition, the methodology should cover rotating the files from the data center to an off-site location. Large data centers may use a tape management system rather than external labels. The tape management catalog itself must be backed up to prevent disruption of the process. If the backup is on permanent disks, the operating system manages the backups. Such systems need to be closely monitored for disk capacity, and files not used for a given period should be purged and stored instead on cheaper tape backups. To safeguard against storage media failure, critical data should be stored on two separate types of media.

Ethics in data storage

Data storage becomes an ethical issue if data needed for audits or other compliance is deleted. Electronic data such as e-mails are considered legal evidence (in the US, this is covered under the Federal Rules of Evidence), and some companies have received large fines for denying access to or deleting such evidence. Other issues include safeguarding data for privacy.

IT operational controls

IT operational controls include planning controls; policies, standards, and procedures; data and program security; insurance and continuity planning; and controls over external providers.

Segregation of IT duties should follow the IAM (identity and access management) principle of allowing access only if the job function requires it. Information on applications also needs to be restricted. Initiation, authorization, input, processing, and validating data should all be done by different individuals and often by different departments. The other basic separation is between systems development and operations. Programming and change deployment should be organizationally and physically separate from users with access to production systems, and neither should be able to do the others' tasks. Neither should have access to file libraries, a function of a system librarian, or input/output controls, a function of the systems controller or security. Other segregations include systems analysis, IT audit, and data entry. Smaller organizations may not have the luxury of so much separation, but if this is the case, combined roles require greater scrutiny. Inadequate segregation of duties could create potential for the commission of fraud, including misappropriation of assets and fraudulent financial statements. It could also result in data tampering and loss of data privacy.

Operational controls might involve:

- Ensuring that audit trails exist.
- Reviewing exception reporting and transaction logs.
- Minimizing the number of users with administrative privileges.
- Using software tools and direct observation by supervisors to monitor the activities of users with administrative privileges.
- Obligating systems controllers and other persons in sensitive positions to take vacations or rotate jobs.
- Separating testing environments and production environments by formal data migration processes.
- Ensuring that employees with physical custody of assets do not have access to the related computer records.

Audit trails are logs of the functions performed and changes made in a system, including who made the change and when. The trail is either kept in a separate file or sent to the system activity log file. The audit trail must be secure from as many users as possible, and access restrictions should be reviewed. For example, an audit log could show repeated incorrect password entries to investigate. Comparisons of users to their activities can highlight unusual activities. Use of sensitive or powerful command codes should be reviewed.

Preventive maintenance should be performed on hardware and software systems and on their controls, because doing so is almost always less expensive than dealing with problems arising from poor maintenance. An operations control group should also be formed to monitor the results of production, including record keeping and balances of input and output.

Operational data security controls

In addition to controls for backup of data, organizations need controls over data as it is being used. In general, data security must be maintained:

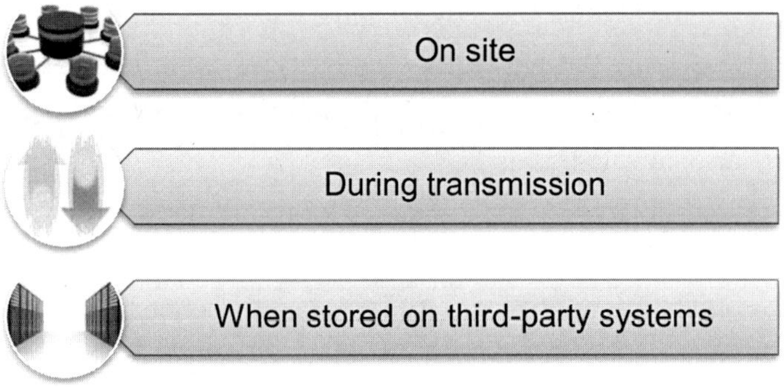

Data policies are enforced through data standards, which define how things need to be done to meet policy objectives. Enforced standards keep systems functioning efficiently and smoothly. Standards should be set for systems development processes (see Chapter B, Topic 3), software configuration, application controls, data structures, and documentation. All of these relate to data security, but only standards for data structures are covered here.

Data structure standards are rules for consistency of data definitions, or the programming tags that define what a data item is used for and its place in a data hierarchy. If all applications use the same data standards, seamless interfaces can be created and security controls will be uniformly applied regarding data privacy and data security.

Some controls over data security have already been mentioned. A few others are covered briefly here. End-user training in the proper use of e-mail and the Internet is important but should be backed up by logical controls such as not allowing end users to install new software. Applications should be safeguarded by keeping them in computer program libraries, which should be restricted by physical and logical access controls. Another example of data security is ensuring that deleted files are really deleted. This can be accomplished through special file deletion software or through physical means, such as electromagnetic wiping. This should be performed on any hard drives or backup tapes being resold.

Security levels

Not every system needs the highest level of security. Like anything, the cost of security should be commensurate with the level of risk mitigation required. To determine appropriate network security levels, first the organization must assess its data repositories and assign security risk levels, either low, medium, or high. This can be done by categories of data, but the highest security data in a database defines the security level. Assessing the availability, integrity, and confidentiality requirements for a group of data is a start. Vital data for key projects such as R&D data is also elevated.

Low security data is data that would have a moderate impact in terms of reputation or productivity losses or lost assets if the data were compromised. Note that even low security data must be safeguarded. Data on public servers such as Web pages fits in this category. Extraordinary measures aren't necessary.

Moderate security levels are used for data that would have a serious impact on the organization's mission and could cause market losses if stolen. Major damage to assets or resources could occur. Most data for an organization fits into this category, including enterprise resource planning (ERP) data, data required to comply with government agency requests, and personal data such as medical records.

High security data is data that if compromised could cause the organization to be in jeopardy of catastrophic losses to reputation, productivity, or market share, for example, contingency plan data listing off-site storage locations, loss of R&D data to a competitor, or accumulated evidence for a court trial.

Once the security level of data is known, a multitiered security system can be designed, including provisions for physical security, software security, program library security, and application level security. Security levels must be customized to the particular organization and its risks. Low security would still have firewalls, hardware locked in a data center, and off-site or cloud backup storage. Moderate security would include all of the low security items plus items such as electronic vaulting or a redundant data center. High security would also include biometric devices, perhaps a physical security checkpoint, and other considerations.

Computer forensics (e-discovery)

Computer forensics is a scientific discovery process applied to computer records, needed for information to be admissible evidence in a court. When fraud or material misstatements are suspected, the organization may need to delegate discovery to computer and physical forensics specialists.

Computer forensics attempts to discover three things: how, why, and who. Finding out how a fraud was committed can lead to determination of motive. Knowing motive plus the required level of access or computer proficiency will lead to a list of suspects.

A mirror image backup, or bit stream backup, is an exact copy of a hard drive, primarily used for forensic auditing, not a way of backing up data for recovery. Properly trained forensic auditors must be used to avoid corrupting the data that needs to be studied.

Role of IT in control self-assessment

Control self-assessment (CSA) presumes that the scope of control for an organization is so broad and continually changing that it takes the efforts of the entire organization to make a timely and adequate assessment. Because CSA takes place in group settings, not in an individual survey form, IT doesn't have a strong role to play. Listening to what people have to say has far more value than any IT aid. However, once CSA teams have met and compiled a list of issues, they can use an intranet survey or electronic voting technology to vote on the issues that they think need to be addressed. The conclusions of the CSA should be reported to participants as soon as possible, so IT can help speed distribution.

Topic 2: Describe Concepts of and Threats to Information Protection (Level A)

Information protection is a management responsibility. Practice Advisory 2130.A1-1, "Information Reliability and Integrity," tells us that this responsibility includes "all critical information of the organization regardless of how the information is stored. Information reliability and integrity includes accuracy, completeness, and security." Auditors must also consider risks for information stored outside IT systems such as in filing cabinets.

The internal audit activity should ensure that:

- Management recognizes this responsibility.
- The information security function cannot be breached.
- Management is aware of any faulty security provisions.
- Corrective measures are taken to resolve any/all information security problems.
- Preventive, detective, and corrective measures are in place to ensure information security.

Elements of information protection

An organization's data can be one of its most important assets. As such, information security is a critical control.

There are three universally accepted elements of information security:

- **Confidentiality.** Policies and practices for privacy and safeguarding confidential information and protections against unauthorized interceptions.
- **Integrity.** Provisions to ensure that data is complete and correct, including how it relates to financial reporting.
- **Availability.** Actions to ensure that there is very little downtime and to enhance recovery of data after disruptions, disasters, and corruptions of data/services.

IT general controls and application controls such as passwords and privileges are the basis for information protection. Information security is the foundation for most other IT controls and has two aspects: data and infrastructure.

Data security should ensure that only authorized users can access a system, their access is restricted by user role, unauthorized access is denied, and all changes to computer systems are logged to provide an audit trail.

Security infrastructure can be part of end-user applications, and/or it can be integral to servers and mainframes, called security software. When security is available only at the application level, such as for small environments, user access and role-based access controls are generally strong but controls over expert programmers are weak.

Security software resides at the server, client, or mainframe level and provides enhanced security for key applications. One typical control provided by security software is allowing only certain transactions to be entered at specific terminals, such as being able to change the list of authorized employees only from within the payroll department. Such terminals can also be set to be available only during normal business hours, automatically time out, or require reentry of a password for each transaction. Finally, such systems can tell users when they last accessed the system so they can know if their user ID is being used illicitly.

Errors introduced into a computer system can be just as costly as malicious attacks. One key control that will help is setting a clear policy on the use of hardware and software and training personnel to address the most common errors. The policy should also address ethics, such as computers being used for personal goals or even illegal acts.

Internal auditing and vulnerability management

Part of the IT internal audit is an assessment of information vulnerabilities and recommendations for improvement. Internal auditors should assess the effectiveness of preventive, detective, and mitigation measures against past attacks, as deemed appropriate, and future attempts or incidents deemed likely to occur. Internal auditors should confirm that the board has been appropriately informed of threats, incidents, vulnerabilities exploited, and corrective measures.

GTAG 6, "Managing and Auditing IT Vulnerabilities," lists six indicators of poor vulnerability management:

- A higher than acceptable number of security incidents within a given time period
- An inability to identify IT vulnerabilities systematically, resulting in exposing critical assets
- An inability to assess risks associated with vulnerabilities and to prioritize mitigation efforts
- Poor working relationships between IT management and IT security
- Lack of an asset management system
- Lack of a configuration management process integrated with vulnerability mitigation efforts

To improve management of vulnerabilities, GTAG 6 recommends:

- Enlisting senior management support consistent with the enterprise's risk appetite.
- Inventorying all IT assets and their associated vulnerabilities.
- Prioritizing mitigation/remediation steps according to risk.
- Remediating vulnerabilities by presenting planned work projects to IT management.
- Continually updating asset discovery, vulnerability testing, and remediation processes.
- Using automated patch management and vulnerability discovery tools as much as possible.

These steps are represented in the vulnerability management life cycle, a process for managing IT vulnerabilities, shown in Exhibit VI-4.

Exhibit VI-4: Vulnerability Management Life Cycle

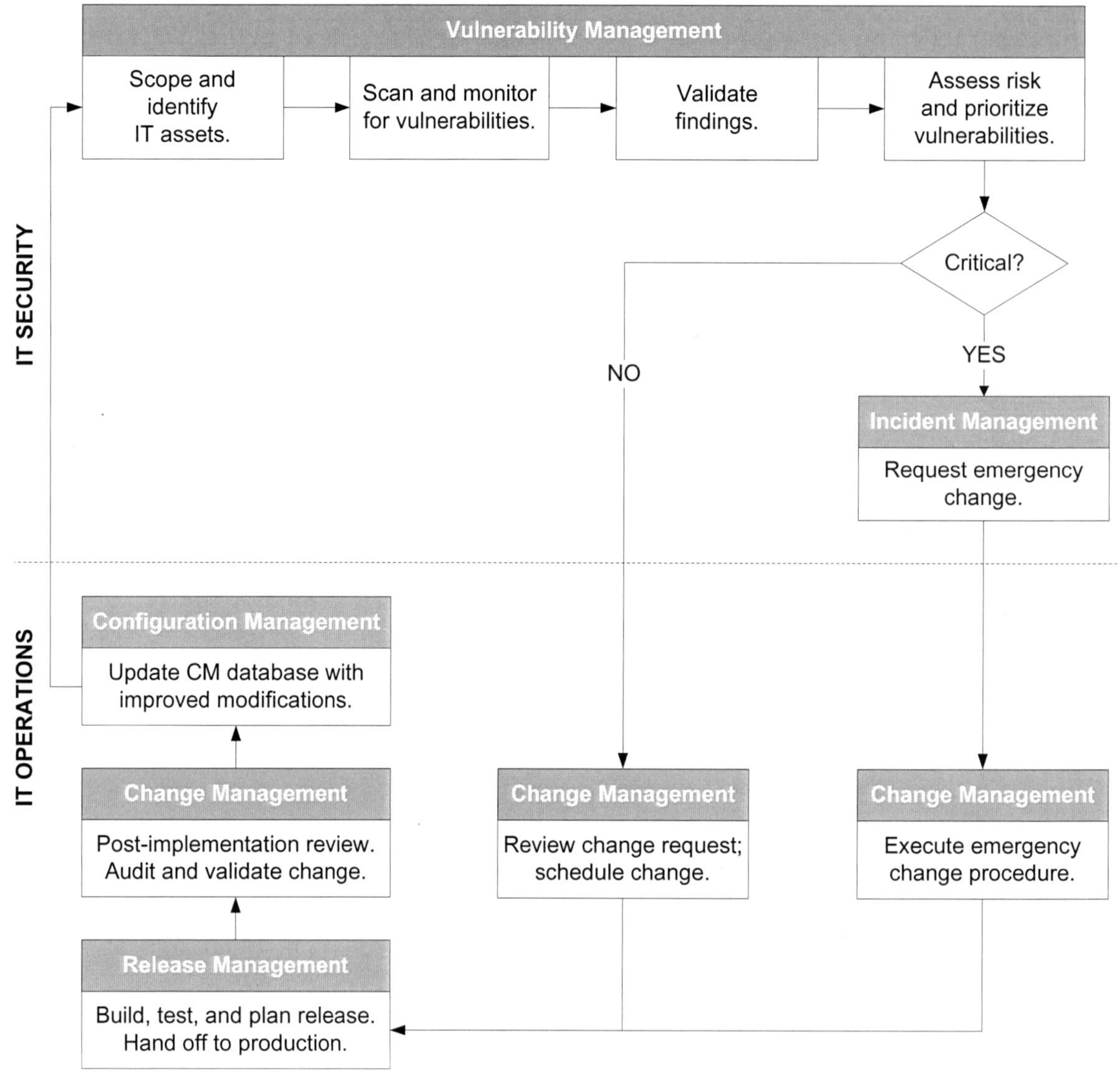

Source: GTAG 6, "Managing and Auditing IT Vulnerabilities."

Malicious software (malware)

Malware is malicious software designed to gain access to a computer system without the owner's permission for the purpose of controlling or damaging the system or stealing data. While the public perception of malware perpetrators is of computer-savvy teens with only mischief as a motive, the actual situation is much worse. Writing malware is a lucrative, organized crime. According to virus analysts at Kaspersky Labs, the professional malware market emerged in 2003 and has been steadily growing. These professional criminals have profit as a motive, and therefore the types of attacks that are increasing are those that gain unrestricted access to user systems and data or gather network passwords and financial data. Purely destructive malware is becoming relatively less common. Also, while malware used to be confined mostly to the Microsoft® platform, the growth in popularity of other platforms such as .NET® and Linux® correlate to growing attacks on these systems.

VirWare

VirWare is a grouping of malware that includes viruses and worms:

- A **virus** is malicious code that attaches itself to storage media, documents, or executable files and is spread when the files are shared with others. One type is a macro virus, which uses the macro function of software such as Microsoft Word® to create executable code. In response, Microsoft created new file extensions to indicate whether a file could contain macros or not (e.g., .xlsx: no macros, .xlsm: macros).
- **Worms** are self-replicating malware that can disrupt networks or computers. Unlike a virus, a worm does not attach itself to an existing program or code. It spreads by sending copies of itself to terminals throughout a network. Worms may act to open holes in network security. They may also trigger a flood of illegitimate denial-of-service data transmissions that take up system bandwidth.

The number of new types of VirWare has been decreasing. Instant message (IM) worms, worms for mobile devices, and net-worms have been increasing, because these are relatively new areas for attack and they don't need to rely on users opening e-mail. E-mail worms have been decreasing, partly due to the rapid response system and improved antivirus software. Cyber criminals have shifted to using more Trojan horses.

Trojan horses

Trojan horses are malicious programs disguised to be innocuous or useful using social engineering. Social engineering is a set of rhetorical techniques used to make fraudulent messages seem inviting and is initiated through deceptive e-mails, instant messages, or phone contact. Trojan horses, once installed, can install more harmful software for long-term use by the writer, such as spyware. Trojan horses are cheaper to develop because writers do not need to create a malicious program capable of self-delivery. They are also smaller and easier to transmit. Therefore, the growth of Trojan horses exceeds that for all other types of malware combined. Trojan horses are defined by how they are initiated. For example, Trojan-clickers require clicking on a hyperlink. Trojan horses include:

- Banker programs, which steal bank account data.
- Backdoors, or trapdoors, which bypass normal authentications for remote access. Backdoors can also be installed by worms.

- Root kits, which are tools installed at the root (administrator) level.
- Trojan-proxies, which use an infected computer as a proxy to send spam.
- Piggyback malware, which allows unauthorized users to enter a network by attaching data to an authorized packet.
- Logic bombs, which are dormant malware activated by a specified variable, such as an action, the attainment of a certain size in a database, or a date. It could also be triggered by a message or a lack of action—for example, failure to log in within a certain period of time. Logic bombs destroy data but can also be used as a threat or for extortion.

Other malware

When criminals have compromised a number of computers, they set up bot nets, which use chat programs to send simultaneous instructions to all systems or upload malware upgrades. SpamTools gather e-mail addresses for future spam mailings. A key logger records keystrokes to steal passwords and anything the user types on his/her keyboard. A dialer automatically dials a 900 number (a high-fee line) to generate huge debts.

Adware creates pop-up advertisements. Spyware gathers information on the user's machine for marketing or illicit purposes. Both are technically legal and are openly developed, but some make use of Trojan horses, infect executables, use root kits, or use other exploits to self-install.

Other external threats

A hacker is anyone who gets into a computer system without authorized access, sometimes called a cracker, or a hacker with criminal intent. Unethical organizations employ hackers to perform industrial espionage. Organized crime uses them for profit. A third reason for hacking is "cyberterrorism" or "cybervandalism," the intentional disruption or destruction of computer data, a Web site, or a network. One example is a denial-of-service attack, in which a system is flooded with false requests or messages from many sources (e.g., via bot nets), crashing the network. Hacktivism is hacking for political purposes.

Phishing, or spoofing, is creating a Web site that appears identical to an organization's site and then luring the organization's users to that site through social engineering, thus capturing IDs and passwords, including social security or other government IDs. Pharming is a more sophisticated attack on the browser bar, using Trojan horses or worms to redirect a valid URL entry to the hacker's site. An evil twin is a Wi-Fi network operated by a cyber criminal that mirrors a legitimate network. Piggybacking is either physically following someone through a secure door or using someone's legitimate password to access a network. A key control is to educate users to initiate all contact themselves (i.e., don't click on an e-mail link; go to the site directly).

Identity theft is the illegal use of sensitive information to impersonate an individual over computer networks in order to defraud the person or commit a crime without the perpetrator's true identity being known. The human-to-browser phase of transactions is where most identity theft occurs, not in the space between browser and Web server. Most of the problem is due to poor password controls and scams that lure users to initiate a compromising transaction. One potential solution is the use of virtual information cards, in which user information is encrypted and hardened against spoofing.

Wireless networks and extensive use of laptop computers have also posed threats to information security. Wardriving software allows intruders to drive through an area and locate vulnerable wireless networks. The intruder can eavesdrop or use overheard data to break encryption codes. Wi-Fi piggybacking refers to the practice of using another's access to enter a network. The practice may be harmless or unintended but may also be malicious.

Internal threats: illegal program alterations

Hackers, or more likely, legitimate users with programming privileges but malicious intent, can alter the code of programs, usually to perpetrate fraud or theft. The following are examples of data manipulation techniques:

- Asynchronous attacks cause an initial system action and then a subsequent system reaction. For example, after a system has been shut down and before it restarts automatically, changes may be made to the restart parameters that weaken security. When the computer restarts, intrusion is now easier.
- Data diddling is intentionally manipulating data in a system.
- Data hiding is manipulation of file names or extensions or other tricks to hide a file from its normal location so that it can be manipulated at leisure (e.g., hiding an audit log).
- Backdoors/trapdoors can be installed by direct code manipulation.
- "Rounding down" and the "salami technique" skim funds by manipulating code to round off the fractional remainder of multiple monetary transactions or alter the final digits of a number, redirecting small amounts to a bank account.

Server/mainframe malware

The percentage of attacks on mainframes is extremely low (almost nonexistent) because of the specific knowledge needed for each particular mainframe. Publicly available servers (servers connected to the Web) are assumed to be under a constant barrage of attacks. When it comes to server attacks, there are two types of hackers: "real" hackers and script kiddies. Real hackers are very knowledgeable about the targeted server system, network, and organization. They collect data on the organization and passively monitor traffic in both directions, probing for a security flaw. Script kiddies are inexperienced hackers who search the Internet for scripts that will do the hacking for them and apply them randomly or to servers that have known flaws. When they fail, they simply move on to easier targets.

Server attacks start by attempting to gain low security access followed by an attempt to elevate the security levels. Once inside, changes include hiding tracks, stealing data, and breaking or taking control of the system.

Microsoft servers have security issues that are regularly patched and publicly announced, but script kiddies will exploit systems that aren't updated. Linux® servers also have flaws that are regularly patched, but the flaws and updates are less publicized and therefore more servers may need updates. Linux servers aren't less prone to attacks and are commonly attacked by real hackers who often have more knowledge about a server configuration than the administrators themselves. In addition to system attacks, publicly available servers can also be attacked through their applications. For example, an intranet server might use a distributed application to allow employees to check customer data. Hackers find flaws in such applications and then publish their findings for use by script kiddies.

The number and frequency of network attacks is increasing, sometimes with several versions of the same type of malware appearing in one day, so much so that antivirus vendors have had to change their update frequencies from several times a day to hourly. The antivirus industry has developed a rapid response system to new threats, but organized criminals have also developed their own structure to scan for and infect vulnerable systems. For example, a network sniffer may detect credit card number formats in streams of data. A packing program is a way of making malware harder to detect.

Protecting systems from malicious software and computer crime

All operating systems contain bugs, and use of homogenous operating systems allows their wide-scale exploitation. As it is unlikely that operating system diversity can be achieved, other solutions should be pursued, such as running systems with administrative privileges turned off. Also, most systems allow any code executed on a system to receive all rights of the system user, called over-privileged code. To fix this security flaw, the operating system would need to restrict rights given to code, such as use of a virtual area or sandbox.

A key tool to combat viruses is to use antivirus software, which maintains lists of known viruses and prevents them from being installed or helps recover a computer once removed. Such software scans both incoming and outgoing data. Automated downloads and regularly scheduled scans are important controls to keep such systems up-to-date. Some antivirus programs use nature-based models that look for any unusual code and can detect new viruses. Basic policies can also help, such as allowing only downloads from reputable locations with security seals. Other tools to consider include blockers for spyware, spam, macros, and pop-ups.

Methods of self-protection

One method of self-protection is to follow a minimum set of agreed-upon controls, called baseline controls. One example is the VISA® Cardholder Information Security Program (CISP), which has made a set of security guidance rules available to credit card network users. This advice, called the "Digital Dozen," can be found in GTAG 1, "Information Technology Controls."

Other broad controls that can make a difference include taking sensitive information offline and performing background checks on new employees and users with security clearance. Newer browsers contain phishing filters, which send data to the browser manufacturer for validation.

Controls associated with proper user identification and authentication of identity are critical. Authentication mechanisms must be secured and assessed. Users must be aware of the dangers of sharing or not securing or creating weak passwords. The best means of securing access to data may be through the use of biometric controls. Biometric controls use unique physical or behavioral traits to authenticate identity. Biometric controls might focus on a user's fingerprints, the palm of the hand, patterns in the iris of the eye, facial, or vocal features.

Privacy

Privacy is essentially the right to be left alone and free from surveillance by individuals, organizations, or the government. From an IT standpoint, privacy is the right to have a say over how personal information is used and collected. Personal information is any information that can link back to a particular individual. Any transaction entered into a computer, from simple purchases to medical records, can be stored indefinitely and potentially used for marketing or crime fighting as well as for illegal activities such as blackmail.

IT can make invasions of privacy easy and inexpensive. Privacy is an issue for corporate data, employees, and customers. Corporate data must be safeguarded for a business to stay viable. Employees and their employers are in conflict on privacy, because organizations want to protect both their interests and guard against improper activity, while the employees want to feel that they have a measure of privacy at work. Programs can be used to log Web sites visited and track every keystroke a user makes.

Higher levels of monitoring can provide control but at the possible price of lower morale. Clear communication of the privacy policy will help with morale. The policy should inform employees what is and isn't monitored as well as what is expected of them, such as using the Internet only for specific activities. Logical controls over possible sites that can be visited can reduce the need to monitor employee activities.

Privacy laws and regulations

US, Canadian, European, and other countries' privacy laws are based in part on fair information practices (FIPs). FIPs acknowledge that the two parties in a transaction have obligations to each other. Individuals have rights to privacy but need to prove their identity; organizations have responsibilities over the collection and use of information. FIPs include:

- **Notice.** Prior to collecting data, Web sites must disclose who is collecting the data, its uses, other recipients, what is voluntary, and what will be done to protect the data.
- **Choice.** Consumers should be able to choose how the information is used outside of support for the current transaction.
- **Access.** Consumers should be able to access and modify their personal information without great expense or hardship.
- **Security.** Data collectors must ensure that they have adequate data controls.
- **Enforcement.** FIPs must be enforced via self-regulation, legislation giving recourse rights to consumers, and other laws.

A number of laws exist to protect privacy against government intrusion, such as the Canadian Privacy Act, which sets rules on the government's ability to collect and use information on its citizens. The private sector has far fewer regulations over it, and self-regulation is the general tendency. One example of a private-sector act is the US Health Insurance Portability and Accountability Act (HIPAA), which governs the disclosure of medical records. Because many nations have privacy laws that often differ considerably, the Organisation for Economic Cooperation and Development (OECD) and similar organizations are working to create consistency in privacy laws and laws on the transborder flow of information.

Many government constitutions also protect an individual's privacy. In the EU, the EU Data Directive obliges its member states to protect the fundamental rights and freedoms of persons, in particular their right to personal data privacy. This directive will be superseded by the EU Data Protection Regulation, which was released as a draft in 2012 and was in a review period at the time of this writing.

Auditors and privacy

The primary role auditors fill in privacy is to ensure that relevant privacy laws and other regulations are communicated to the responsible parties. Personnel must be told what is expected of them and what the individual and organizational penalties are for noncompliance. Auditors may need to work with legal counsel to identify other steps that should be performed to meet all requirements. Note that proof of compliance is required, not just compliance, so documentation must be addressed. Auditors must also determine if management is spending more on privacy controls than is warranted (e.g., expensive encryption for routine data).

Topic 3: Describe Application Authentication (Level A)

Application authentication is a form of security in which a software application is able to prevent unauthorized access to itself. One form of application authentication, possible in Microsoft Windows, for example, is the creation of accounts for authorized users with required identification. Web applications can also authenticate users, who may be assigned to roles, such as customer, user, manager, etc., and assigned a log-in code, which is sent to the Web server for verification.

Application authentication depends on implementing logical access controls.

Logical access controls

Logical access controls are the ways that computer program logic can identify authorized users—a challenging task in a large and complex enterprise in which many groups must have access to data. The various policies, procedures, activities, and technologies used to identify authorized users comprise a process called identity and access management (IAM). GTAG 9, "Identity and Access Management," poses three fundamental questions whose answers should inform access decisions and management:

- Who has access to what information?
- Is the access appropriate for the job being performed?
- Are the access and activity monitored, logged, and reported appropriately?

The IAM process is designed to allocate identities and provide appropriate access. An **identity** is defined as a unique descriptor (or combination of descriptors) of a person or machine—for example, a name, a password, an ID number, or a biometric identifier. Proper identity provides access to information systems and data. **Access** may be defined as the right to perform certain transactions (e.g., copying or transferring data). These access rights are termed the user's **entitlements.**

Three processes are involved in an IAM system:

- **Provisioning.** The most visible aspect of IAM is provisioning—the creation, changing, termination, validation, approval, propagation, and communication of an identity.
- **Identity management.** Identity management refers to the establishment, communication, and management of IAM strategies, policies, and processes. It entails monitoring, auditing and reconciling, and reporting system performance.
- **Enforcement.** Enforcement occurs automatically, through processes or mechanisms, as identities are authenticated and authorized and activity logged.

Exhibit VI-5 on the next page illustrates the way in which the IAM process manages identity and access.

The primary logical access control is password authentication. Authentication techniques include digitally enforcing use of alphanumeric passwords, enforced password changes, and password management such as deleting unused passwords and user accounts (provisioning) or detecting user accounts that have no password or use a default password. Unlike a physical signature, use of a valid password doesn't prove the authenticity of a user. Authentication can be reinforced by a physical device such as an access card or by software designed to recognize a user's keystrokes. Also, password protection can be bypassed if there are other access points, such as a logical/software backdoor created by a flaw in design or on purpose.

End-user security training can make a huge difference to application authentication security. Password and log-on methodology training teaches users to avoid common mistakes. Users will be trained to avoid storing their password near their computer or using easily deduced passwords such as their child's name or the word "password."

Exhibit VI-5: IAM Process

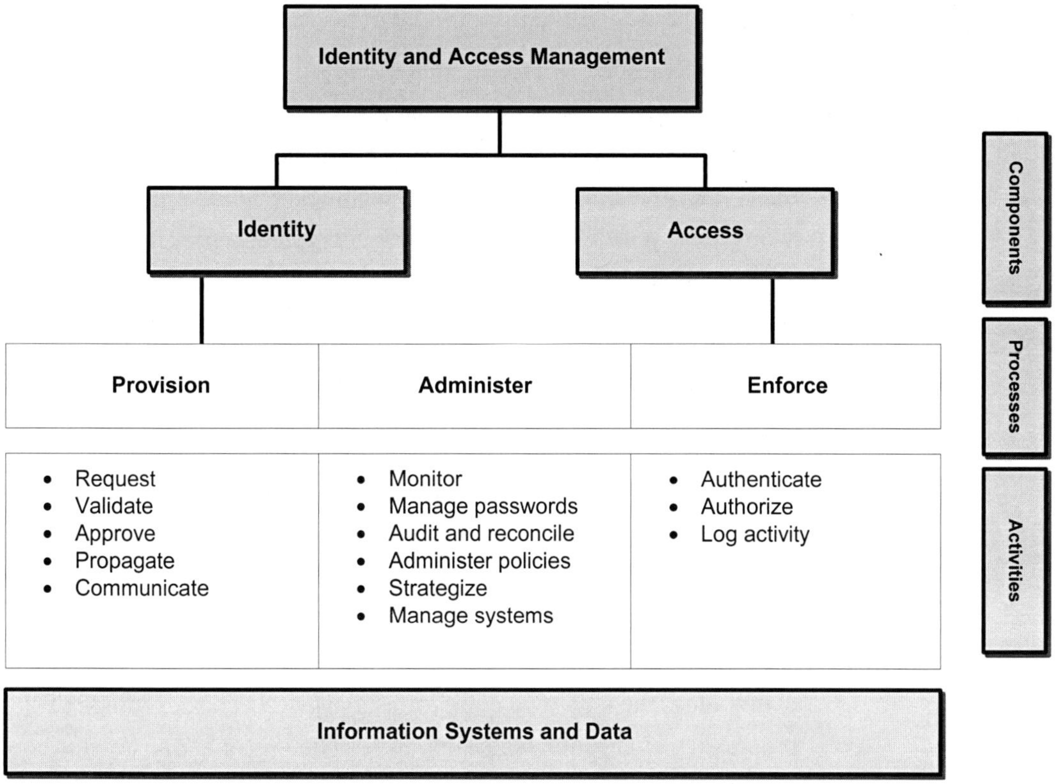

Source: GTAG 9, "Identity and Access Management."

Under least privilege, users and/or departments are assigned roles or profiles granting them access only to areas where there is a genuine business need. Access rights are based on a role name set in a hierarchy, which should be audited to see if roles are too broad and some users get unnecessary rights. Roles can be used to enforce laws and regulations, such as preventing a nurse role from creating prescriptions. Finally, roles can allow for some users to have read-only access (no modifications).

Other logical access controls include:

- Automatic log-off procedures.
- Monitoring and controlling access to computers with remote control privileges (e.g., help desk).
- Access logs (application and Internet logs).
- Single-use access codes or codes with defined start and end dates for contractors.

Topic 4: Demonstrate an Understanding of Encryption (Level A)

Encryption uses a mathematical algorithm to scramble data so that it cannot be unscrambled without a numeric key code. Encryption is used on stored and physically transmitted data (e.g., on a flash drive) and electronically transmitted data. Server access control is the use of internally encrypted passwords to keep technical persons from browsing password files. Wireless data can also be encrypted to prevent compromise if it is intercepted.

Two basic types of encryption exist: private key encryption and public key encryption.

- **Private (or symmetric) key encryption** is a method where a sender creates an encryption key and sends it to a trusted recipient, who can use it to decrypt all messages in that session. The method of sharing the key needs to be controlled, since the key could be intercepted in transit (though it might itself be encrypted). Poor controls at the receiver's end could allow the key to be compromised as well. The advantage of private key encryption is its simplicity: There is only one key for both encryption and decryption.

- **Public (or asymmetric) key encryption** is a more secure type of encryption. Public key encryption methods create two keys, a private key and a public key. The sender places the public key in a directory, or an application automatically applies it to lock sent data. To decrypt the data, the private key must be used. The private key needs controls to keep it secret, but since it never needs to be shared, it is more secure. The public key is known by many, but the private key is known by only one system. Public keys are generally used for brief messages since they are resource-intensive. Another consideration is the number of users of the public key. If the key needs to be changed, all of these users must be informed and the new key distributed.

To illustrate public and private key encryption, review Exhibit VI-6 on the next page, which presents both of these encryption processes.

Digital signatures verify the authenticity of a user of a public key. A digital signature uses public key encryption and a hashing algorithm, which is information about the transmitted data, to prevent the original message from being reconstructed. Conversely, a server certificate can establish the authenticity of a site.

Exhibit VI-6: Public and Private Key Encryption

Private Key Encryption Process (Symmetric)

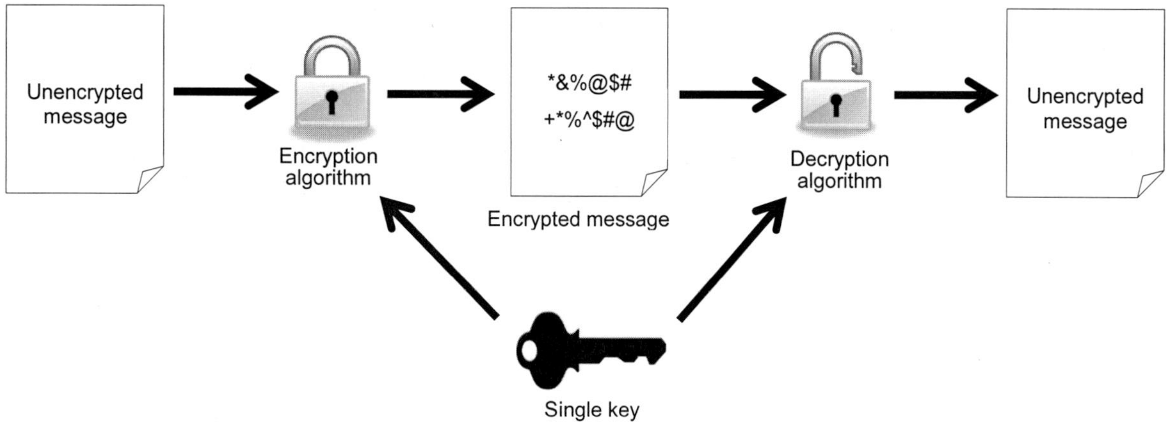

Public Key Encryption Process (Asymmetric)

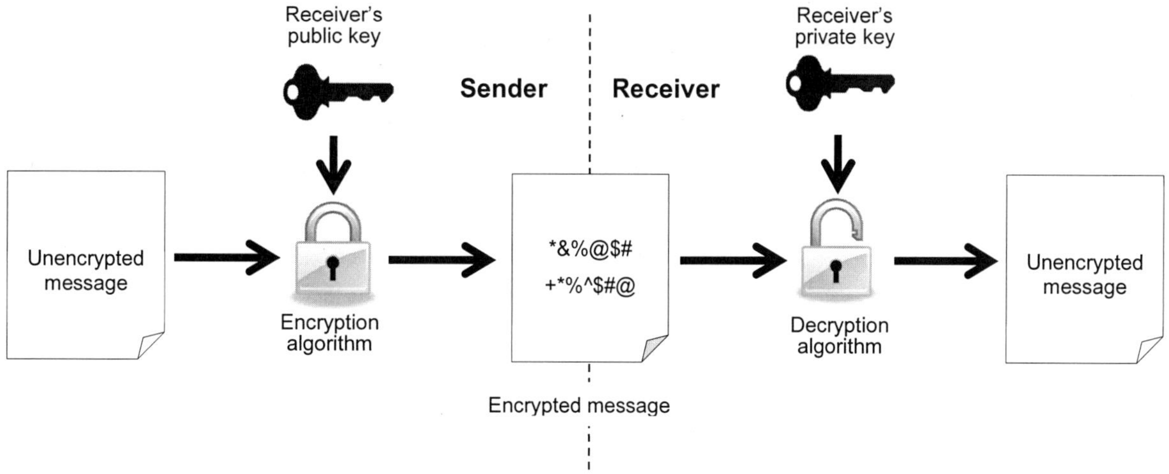

Auditing issues

Evaluating encryption includes evaluating physical controls over computers that have password keys, testing policies to see if they are being followed, and implementing and monitoring logic controls. Each security domain should be able to share its local identity and security data without compromising its internal directories.

The relative security of a key is determined by the bit length of the key. When passwords are used to create keys, effective password creation rules must be applied. External aids include cryptographic module testing (CMT) labs and validation programs for cryptographic modules and their algorithms.

Chapter B: Application Development

Chapter Introduction

Application development is the process of designing, customizing, or configuring software applications or information systems. It also involves evaluating and maintaining systems and IT application controls.

Audits of application development can take the form of participative consulting during a project, a post-implementation assurance review once a project is complete, or an assurance review of the general application development process. The objective can be to improve the efficiency of application development, to improve the internal controls in the process to reduce the necessary depth of future audits of the function, or to improve a specific application's effectiveness or controls

The topics in this chapter start with end-user computing and how it can be audited, followed by a discussion of change control. The third topic discusses the systems development methodology, which is a normative model of the process of developing applications. Internal auditors need to understand models of how the process is expected to work so that they can compare this against how the process is observed to work. The process of application development itself is then addressed, followed by a discussion of various levels of application controls. Finally, information systems development is discussed, which is the development of the overall framework for networking and computing at an organization.

Topic 1: Describe End-User Computing (Level A)

End-user computing is where end users are given the freedom to develop their own simple programs or analytical tools using commonly available software tools such as spreadsheets and database tools. Databases and spreadsheets can be run on smaller systems, giving individual users more control over their work.

Some of the possible risks of end-user computing include developing reliance on applications that can be maintained by only one person. If that person leaves the organization, the application may be difficult for another user to understand or maintain, especially if the user does not provide or update sufficient system documentation. The applications themselves may also become very complex over time, which is itself a risk since this type of development may not follow a formal development approach with proper planning and other controls to manage complexity. End-user computing applications often start out simple, but as more spreadsheets or database files are interlinked, they can grow more complex.

The first control over end-user computing is whether it is allowed to occur or not. Some organizations restrict this practice entirely; other organizations restrict it to specialists such as analysts. If it is allowed and end-user-developed applications exist, internal auditors can develop an understanding of the application by getting a developer to perform a walk-through. If no flowchart exists, the auditor can develop one with the assistance of the expert. The internal auditor should review system documentation for existence and completeness as well as how often it is updated and whether it matches the actual system. Internal auditors should also determine if the application has the proper application authentication controls and other controls specific to the application or that should be included because they are part of the organization's general IT controls.

Some safeguards are available to control the risks in end-user computing:

- Commercial backup software
- Encryption of stored data
- Security "cards" that ask for passwords and store information about time of use
- Use of master versions of software installed on all department (or related) PCs (This can eliminate subtle differences in software, for example, different rounding conventions.)
- Strong manual controls when PCs process transactions (manual review of reports, etc.)

Internal auditors can also determine how efficient the application is at performing the relevant task, how effectively it achieves the objectives it was designed to do, and how easily the system can be maintained. For example, if it is a financial forecasting tool, how long does it take the forecaster to enter the new period's information on assumptions and other data? What is the average time it takes between when a decision maker needs the information and it is ready? Is there an automated way to enter the data or for the decision maker to see the results? Do observations or other audit techniques reveal situations where there is an error in outputs and it takes a very long time for the end user to find the source of the error? Are errors easy to enter into the system (e.g., a spreadsheet with unprotected cells) but hard to locate? How are files checked out and checked back in for modification? Who is able to modify the files, and could more than one person be changing things from different locations? Answers to such questions will reveal the amount of risk that this application presents to normal business operations. Comparison to benchmark systems can reveal how efficient and effective it is in producing timely results.

A recommendation may include replacing such a system with a commercial system that has better controls and is less complex or time-consuming to maintain. Many organizations are finding that the custom solutions an area developed when the organization was small or midsize no longer work well when the organization grows larger such as by merging with other organizations. However, end users are likely to resist change and loss of direct control, so they must be shown the advantages of improvements and dealt with sensitively.

Topic 2: Demonstrate an Understanding of Change Control (Level A)

Changes in the IT environment may be frequent and significant. The auditor should look for adequate change controls, including security, audit trail, quality assurance, provision for emergency changes, source, and tracking.

According to GTAG 2, "Change and Patch Management Controls," change management includes application code revisions, system upgrades, and infrastructure changes such as changes to servers, routers, cabling, or firewalls. The process and results should be predictable, defined, and repeatable. Patch management is the installation of released bug fixes to applications that are already in production. Patch management should be handled as its own category. High-performing organizations perform far fewer patches than low-performing organizations. Organizations with poor change management controls have low success for IT changes due to project delays or scope creep. They suffer from unexpected outages and are always in crisis mode with many emergency or unauthorized changes. (For the latter, even one is too many.) Constant crisis creates stress and high turnover for IT staff, indicates a lack of control over problem escalation, and increases risks that a change will cause unintended consequences. If IT staff has no time for new projects, deteriorating service results.

If a change results in downtime or, even worse, a material error in financial reporting data, it carries a higher risk of loss than that of a system attack. When a possible patch or change comes up, IT staff and management should perform triage, or sorting out the true emergency situations from those that can be handled as routine. Criteria should be based on business need and the relative risk of waiting. Changes should be tested in a sandbox environment first. To make this cost-effective, multiple changes are bundled. Production changes should be performed in off hours.

Change management process steps

GTAG 2 lists the following change management process steps:

1. Identify the need for change.
2. Prepare. Document the step-by-step procedure for the change request, the change test plan, and a change rollback plan.
3. Justify change and request approval. Determine impact and cost-benefit; review associated risks and regulatory impact.
4. Authorization. Reject, approve, or request more information. Set priorities relative to overall schedule.
5. Schedule and implement change. Schedule a change implementer and change tester, test in preproduction, communicate to affected parties, get final approval, and implement change.
6. Review implemented change. Measure change success, use of process, variances, and regulatory compliance. Report lessons learned.
7. Back out change if unsuccessful.
8. Close change request and report to stakeholders.
9. Revisit change management process for improvement.

Reducing change risks

Complex production environments require more independent controls. Adherence to development methodologies such as the systems development life cycle (discussed in the next topic) is critical. Routine maintenance changes are easier to audit because their results can be objectively determined and management override risk is low. More scrutiny is needed for software controls that detect when controls are being overridden due to higher risk of management override and the need for auditors to subjectively judge their effectiveness. Software applications also have detective controls to verify production changes against authorizations.

The development department should report to a high enough level of management to keep department heads from scheduling low-priority projects. Top management needs to set the proper tone. Other supervisory controls include preventive controls such as enforcing change and patch management policy as well as having key stakeholders assess change risks. Detective supervisory controls involve measuring and correcting poor performance, such as by measuring mean time to repair.

Exhibit VI-7 summarizes risks, controls, and related metrics for change and patch management.

Exhibit VI-7: Metrics for Determining Change and Patch Management Success

Risk	Control	Metric
Unauthorized changes	• Policy for zero unplanned changes • Proactive management • Detective software	• Number of unplanned changes • Number of unplanned outages • Number of changes authorized • Number of changes implemented
Changes fail to be implemented or are late	• Change management process	• Greater than 70% change success rate • New work created by change
Unplanned work displaces planned work	• Triage • Planned changes bundled • Patches treated as a normal process to expect	• Less than 5% of work is unplanned • Percentage of time on unplanned work • Percentage of projects delivered late • Percentage of patches installed in a planned software release

Source: GTAG 2, "Change and Patch Management Controls."

Topic 3: Discuss Systems Development Methodology (Level A)

IT systems have a life cycle, from design through implementation to maintenance. Early system designs were left largely to IT specialists. A better approach is team design. The purpose of team design is to ensure that all stakeholders have their needs considered.

The steps in the process are:

- Request for system design.
- Feasibility study.
- High-level design.
- Detailed systems design.
- Program coding and testing.
- Conversion (of old data files).
- Implementation.
- Maintenance.

Internal audit has a strong role to play, especially when reviewing the feasibility and system study, such as being assured that the team is adequately staffed, control deficiencies are remedied, the system can accommodate growth, budgets are reasonable, users agree to the change, and so on.

The use of a formal or normative model for systems development helps developers in much the same way that the use of project management keeps a project progressing toward its goals while handling problems in an orderly fashion rather than as emergencies. Internal auditors can use a normative model to observe where actual practice differs from expected practice in the model. One such normative model is the systems development life cycle.

Systems development life cycle

Use of a development methodology is a vital tool because it forces management to be involved rather than relegate IT to specialists. Requiring a feasibility study, policies, objectives and standards, and testing forces IT to be treated as a resource that must be managed. Formal processes help managers understand how they can be involved. In fact, all stakeholders for a system should be involved in the formal process.

Indicators of effective IT controls for systems development include the ability to execute new system plans within budget and on time. Resource allocation should be predictable.

The traditional systems development life cycle (SDLC) is a sequential process moving between formal stages where one step is completed before beginning the next. In the traditional SDLC, end users are not involved in the process other than as interviewees and reviewers of completed work. Systems analysts and programmers design and build the system. Many organizations have altered the traditional SDLC because they found that engaging end users thoroughly from the start results in a better product that is "owned" by its users. The traditional process is still used by some organizations for complex, multidepartment projects such as an ERP system, but even these benefit from organized user involvement.

Exhibit VI-8 shows the traditional SDLC. Each step is described in detail following the exhibit.

Exhibit VI-8: Systems Development Life Cycle

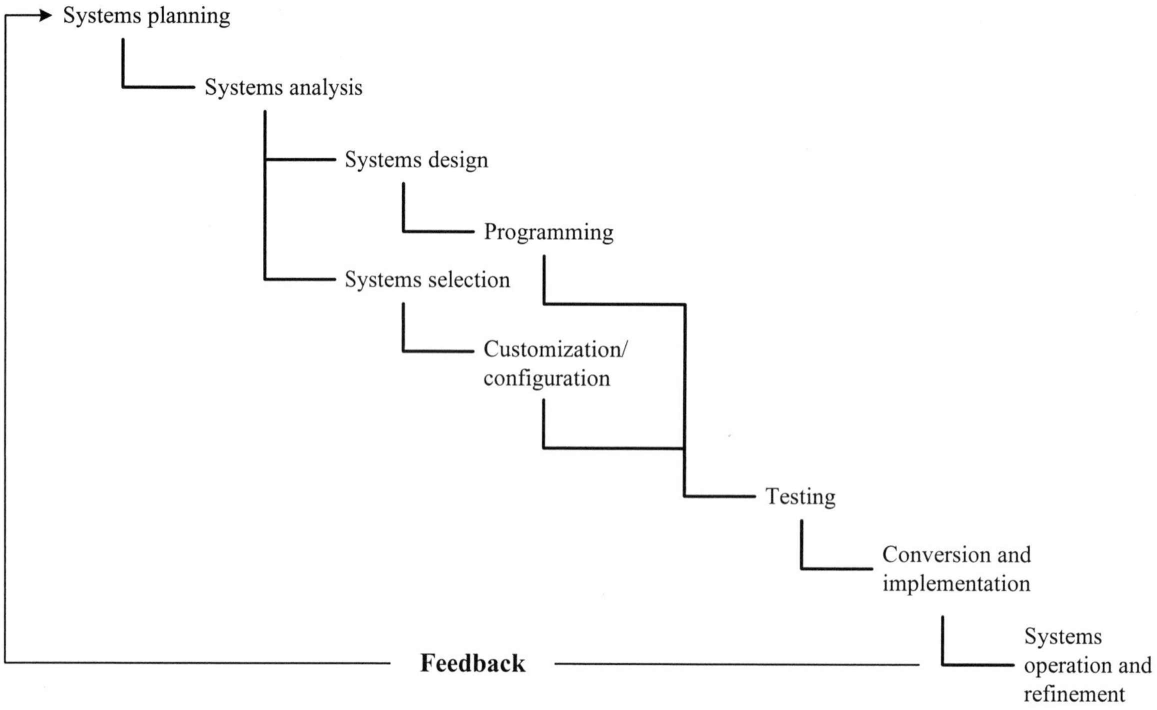

Systems planning

In the systems planning phase, executives and IT management establish a long-term technology strategy that measures success by its fulfillment of business strategy. Capital investments are allocated in accordance with business priorities. Systems planning is often conducted by an IT steering committee, made up of members from top management and IT. While management alone may not be able to assess if standards are adequate, the committee should be able to do so collectively. They set IT policy, approve both long- and short-term plans, provide monitoring and oversight, and assess the impact of new IT. A master plan schedules resources for all approved projects. Needs are defined and related business processes are streamlined. The basic question asked at this level is "What problems exist, and are they worth fixing by use of scarce resources?"

Systems analysis

While systems planning is used to identify problems or challenges that are worth addressing in the design and development of new systems, systems analysis is used to point out deficiencies and opportunities in existing IT systems. Systems analysis could indicate that existing system modification is more cost-effective than developing a new system, or vice versa. The result of systems analysis is a request for systems design or selection. This is a written request submitted either to the steering committee for large projects or to IT management for smaller projects. The committee catalogs the request, and, if approved, they allocate money for a feasibility study.

Feasibility studies indicate the benefits to be obtained if a proposed system is purchased, leased as a service, or developed, including its operational impact. Off-the-shelf software and out-sourced software development are evaluated against internal development costs and time to markct.

Feasibility studies:

- Identify the needs of all related parties—management, IT professionals, users—and develop metrics for future assessment (e.g., time frame, functionality, cost).

- Analyze the proposed system against:
  - Needs.
  - Defined resources (e.g., budget, personnel).
  - Additional costs and future impacts (e.g., impact on existing systems/hardware, additional training/staffing).
  - Technology trends.
  - Alignment with enterprise strategies and objectives.

- Perform cost-benefit analysis.

- Identify the best risk-based alternative (e.g., no change, development of new system, reengineering of existing system, purchase of off-the-shelf product, purchase and customization, lease of online software as a service).

Feasibility study conclusions should provide the basis for a go/no go decision. The feasibility study results require written approval of the committee or IT management. Internal auditors should be involved in the process at this point to ensure that control and auditability requirements are included in the scope of the project. Specific controls are defined in the next step.

Systems design/systems selection

Systems design occurs in two phases: high-level systems design and detailed systems design. In between these steps, sometimes prototyping is performed, which is a rapidly created, experimental bare-bones system. Prototyping makes a functioning model for users to interact with and suggest improvements. The prototype may have more than one revision.

High-level systems design has four steps:

1. Analyze inputs, processing, and outputs of existing or proposed system.
2. Break down user requirements into specifics such as support for a particular inventory valuation method or costing technique.
3. Define functional specifications to accomplish business goals, e.g., accounts receivable data updates customer credit.
4. Compare make or buy alternatives, including any needed configuration or customization.

Flowcharts showing the path of inputs/outputs can help clarify processing tasks and ensure that user needs are being met. Structural design can facilitate development by identifying and organizing sub-processes. At this time, data files and the database structure must also be considered as well as how existing files and databases can be converted to the new system.

If the decision is made to buy a system, systems selection begins. Assuming approval, a detailed systems design is created for both internally developed systems and for purchased software that needs modification. This is a blueprint including program specifications and layouts for files, reports, and display screens. Planners flowchart each process, including the method of implementation and testing. Specific areas of customization are authorized (controls need to minimize this) and configuration settings are determined.

Programming and customization/ configuration

If internal development is selected, programmers follow the detailed systems blueprint to write or reuse code, debug code, convert existing data and processes to the new system, reconfigure and acquire hardware as needed, and train staff. Online programming, performed on workstations, allows programmers to write and compile code using real data. It also speeds development time. However, it does introduce risks that must be controlled:

- Creation of multiple versions of programs
- Unauthorized access
- Overwriting of valid code

If the system is being adapted or purchased, customization and configuration are performed according to the blueprint. Programmers must get sign-off from superiors at appropriate milestones. Source code must be protected during the project by a librarian.

Testing

Testing involves creating a testing plan, collecting or creating testing scenarios, executing the test and managing test conditions, collecting and evaluating feedback, and reporting the results. Testing and quality assurance are done in two phases: unit testing and system testing. Unit or performance testing keeps the application in isolation to find internal bugs. It is useful to conduct unit testing as early as possible to prevent errors from affecting ongoing work in other units. System testing strings together all programs in the application to find intercommunication bugs. In addition, the new or acquired system's operation must be tested in an interface with all other systems with which data is transferred. Before implementation, the system faces final acceptance testing for quality assurance purposes and for user acceptance.

Testing terminology includes:

- Load testing—examining a system's performance when running under a heavy load (e.g., a large number of simultaneous users).
- Throughput testing—validating that a system can process transactions within the promised time.
- Alpha testing—conducted by developers.
- Beta testing—conducted by users.
- Pilot testing—a preliminary and focused test of system function.
- Regression testing—confirming that revisions have corrected problems and not introduced new ones.
- Sociability testing (SOCT)—testing the system in its intended environment, with actual hardware and limited resources, while running with competing and collaborating applications.
- Security testing—validating the ability to control vulnerabilities.

In some instances, testing may be conducted automatically, during off-peak use times, thus speeding testing and development.

Teams not involved in programming deliberately try to make the system fail. Security applications should be tested by deliberately trying to hack into the system. Auditors must guard that testing is not given a shortage of resources, time, or attention.

Conversion and implementation

Conversion is the process of closing down the old system and migrating any data to the new system. This area is of particular concern to audits because errors can be introduced at this point (after testing) and not detected until they cause material harm. Errors include incorrectly converting code, truncating fields, use of the wrong decimal place in calculations, or loss of records. Manual conversion is physical data entry of old records and should be avoided if possible. To reduce data entry errors, hash totals, record counts, and visual inspections should be used. Both automated and manual data migration should include a data cleansing step.

Adequate preparation and training of staff and end users must be planned and implemented as well.

Implementation is turning on the new system. Management must sign off on the conversion review. Different implementation approaches can be used. Big bang or cutover approaches have the entire system go "live" at the same time. Phased approaches are implemented by department or plant. Pilot approaches implement a test version and run it for a given period prior to full implementation. Parallel approaches run the old and new systems simultaneously for a period, requiring double entry of all transactions. This safeguards business continuity and provides independent system verification through comparison of process totals. Regardless of the method, internal auditors should ensure that a backout procedure exists.

User support, such as help desks and documentation, must be available at the time of implementation.

After implementation, the new/acquired system and project should be reviewed, using the metrics defined at the beginning of the project. Attention should focus on whether:

- The system has met user requirements (in terms of resource use and performance delivered).
- Specified controls have been created and are adequate.
- The development process was conducted in compliance with policy.

Systems operation and refinement (feedback)

Operations and maintenance is an ongoing activity that continues for the life of the software. Change controls can keep numerous noncritical changes from swamping productivity and budgets while allowing for problem escalation in emergencies. Changes must be approved by management, follow development standards, and be tested in a sandbox environment.

Documentation

The traditional SDLC produces large amounts of documentation and formal specifications. Documentation should cover the software and the related business process. Security features and backup processes are also noted. Documentation can be a boon to auditors if it is easy to use, so it should be clear and concise and follow a structured and well-communicated methodology. The problem with documentation and the traditional SDLC appears when a long-duration project needs to be changed due to shifting business requirements, new technologies, or releases of an application. In this case, the documentation becomes yet another hurdle, as all of it needs to be updated. Therefore the urge to fix design flaws discovered later in the process is sometimes suppressed by freezing the specifications, which could result in a less-than-useful tool.

Another risk is that programmers could shirk their documentation duties, preferring to move on to the next task. Early auditor involvement and having a designated person review the documentation as it is submitted can help lower this risk. Asking developers for personal notes can help fill in some blanks. Attempting to change a system without documentation can be made even more difficult if turnover occurs. Documentation is also a control for preventing fraud, but it is useful only if all valid changes are recorded.

Rapid application development (RAD) techniques

The SDLC can create inefficiencies through its rigidly enforced sequence of events. Simultaneous development efforts are one adaptation of the SDLC, in which portions of the development effort are begun as soon as possible instead of waiting for a prior step to finish. Tools such as CPM/PERT (see Section V, Chapter E) can help determine earliest start times and shortest project duration. Another method is to create the new system module by module, releasing each into production as soon as it is ready. Many programmers are also employing reusable software code to speed development efforts.

Rapid application development (RAD) is a set of methodologies and tools for fast software development. RAD reduces documentation, users participate in design, and source code can be automatically generated. RAD uses a process called joint application development (JAD), in which an executive champions meetings between IT and other stakeholders to work out the requirements for the system rather than each working independently. Such groups often use group support software to encourage participation. Agile development also uses frequent in-person meetings between users and developers to allow system blueprints to change during development. Agile development can reduce the risk that a long project will be outdated before it is finished.

Exhibit VI-9 highlights some variations of RAD.

Exhibit VI-9: Rapid Application Development Techniques

RAD Method

	Object-oriented programming	**Component-based development**	**Reengineering**	**Reverse engineering**	**End-user computing**
Process	Reusable objects 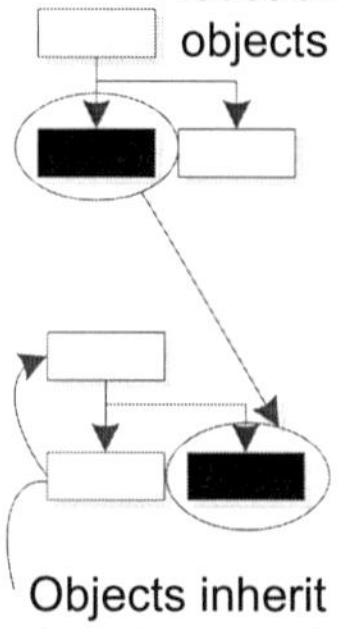 Objects inherit the classes of senior objects.	Components independently developed, then encapsulated. 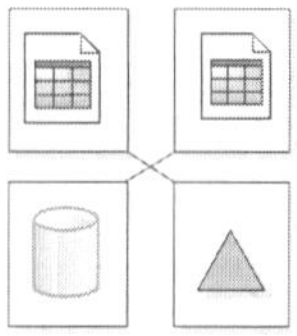 Encapsulation makes systems compatible.	Old system components are reused and rearranged. 	System to be emulated is studied, possibly decompiled, and then a similar system is built. 	End users develop applications themselves. 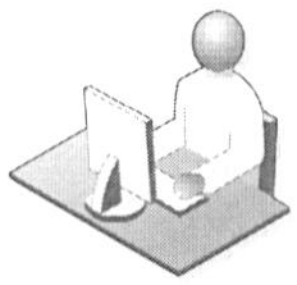
Pros	Objects collaborate with one another to get a job done. Iterative cycle	Can use development from different platforms or programming languages. Saves time. Easy to convert to new platforms.	Saves time and effort. Less risky than starting from scratch.	Saves time and effort.	Custom results. Faster results. User acceptance.
Cons	Making objects easily reusable may require more development effort.	Components may not all integrate as promised. Overall system may be poor vs. a SDLC system.	May miss opportunities to improve security or performance. Can perpetuate problems.	Risk of software license/copyright infringement. Decompiling can introduce errors.	Lack of process. Lack of standards. Difficult to audit. Difficult to update/ maintain.

Auditing RAD projects

Weaknesses to watch for on RAD projects include lower quality due to emphasis on speed. Poor documentation can weaken an audit trail. Information may have been missed, and the system may function but not provide the right functions for business needs. Gold plating can occur, which means the project's budget or scope has exploded because the project has too many requirements or many are added during the project. Naming conventions could be inconsistent in simultaneous development. The system could have poor scalability. To demonstrate success early on, projects may favor easier systems and push the difficult ones back. All of this makes audits of faster methods more difficult than audits of formal systems.

Topic 4: Demonstrate an Understanding of Application Development (Level A)

Application development, or systems development, is the process of making or modifying a software application. Application software includes general-purpose and application-specific software but not system software. General-purpose applications are broad use programs such as word processing or spreadsheet applications. Application-specific software is software that supports specific business functions, such as a customer relationship management system and database.

The assurance of application development is a critical area since failures to control risk here can directly damage business operations and can waste resources spent in creating and correcting faulty applications and remediating damage. While some enterprises develop their own applications, the majority of non-software business organizations do not develop their own applications other than simple queries or scripts. Most companies purchase applications off the shelf after a rigorous selection process, and some perform extensive customization. Whether applications are developed in-house or purchased and used as is or customized, the process must be controlled and audited.

According to GTAG 1, "Information Technology Controls," the following controls should be evident in all systems development and acquisition work:

- Documentation of user requirements for applications and measurement of achievement of those requirements
- Use of a formal process that ensures that user requirements and controls are reflected in both design and actual development
- Testing of elements and interfaces with actual users
- Planned application maintenance
- Controlled change management process

All of these activities should be steps in an organization's application development process, even out-sourced steps. Internal auditors must include out-sourcers in their IT audits, including an assessment of their efficiency relative to potential internal costs. Especially important is an assessment of the vendor's ongoing viability, since long-term support is essential for software systems.

Examples of advanced applications

There are a number of advanced analytical applications used as tools for management and for collaboration with other organizations or integration with internal/external systems:

- **Decision support systems (DSS).** DSS is a broad category of systems designed not to make decisions but to enhance information available to management in making decisions. DSS software must be attached to an organization's database, such as an ERP system. Management forms questions around a business scenario, and the DSS system analyzes the database to find alternatives. Raw DSS output can be voluminous, so most systems include role-based display of select data called dashboards.

- **Expert systems.** Expert systems capture the knowledge of a professional using a series of decision points. They are used to automate complex situations requiring judgment, such as the probability of loan default. They always behave in exactly the same way and are expensive and difficult to reprogram. Expert systems can assist auditors in checking voluminous records without sampling, such as continuously monitoring daily transaction processing for unusual numbers or transactions.

- **Cross-enterprise collaboration and optimization.** A number of software tools exist to facilitate easier collaboration between organizations, including collaborative planning, forecasting, and replenishment (CPFR), which includes group communication tools. Such tools and collaborations extend auditing across organizational boundaries. Partner organizations should have adequate controls.

- **Enterprise application integration (EAI) or middleware.** Enterprise application integration (EAI) is a portfolio of technologies that help disparate applications communicate. Middleware is EAI used for large systems with vast databases, such as integrating various ERP or legacy systems after a merger. EAI is generally expensive and time-consuming to develop, but newer forms called business process management (BPM) create a central information hub for all applications to use organized around common business processes, cutting out repetitive development. Auditors should check that BPM starts with business process mapping and streamlining of business processes. Auditors should see that managers measure the cost of EAI against increases in productivity. When EAI links organizations with their extended supply chain partners, auditors should see that managers ensure proper controls. Any EAI project should also include a data cleansing phase.

Topic 5: Describe Various Levels of Application Controls (Level A)

Internal audit review of SDLC activities

In assessing risks associated with the design stage in the SDLC, internal auditors should examine controls specifically related to:

- **User approval,** which aids user acceptance. However, evaluators must separate good advice from a desire to use familiar but inefficient processes.
- **Authorization procedures** for program changes and new code development. These are a vital control enabled through proper segregation of duties and management involvement such as review and sign-off by end users and managers at key points. Without authorization and access restrictions, errors or fraud can compromise application integrity. Good program change controls include security access such as use of a librarian to restrict source code and audit trails recording all changes.
- **Software testing and quality control.** Program change control can form the basis for quality assurance reviews.
- **Staff proficiency.** Internal auditors should check that the project staff is technically proficient. Auditors working with systems analysts and programmers should remember that these are specialists who may explain things with jargon. Auditors must remain independent, yet helpful and tactful.

For systems selection, auditors need to ensure that specific controls are part of the selection criteria and should check that the controls actually exist once a package has been selected. Relying on marketing information from the software vendor is inadequate; actual product walk-throughs are superior. If the auditor finds that standards are not being met or if IT managers are reluctant to fix an internal control gap, the auditor should report the findings to top management.

IT application controls

GTAG 8, "Auditing Application Controls," defines application controls as those that pertain to "individual business processes or application systems, including data edits, separation of business functions, balancing of processing totals, transaction logging, and error reporting." Application controls may be preventive or detective.

Ensuring that the system includes all of the necessary application controls during development is vital because such controls will not be robust if added later. The development stage is the most important one for auditor involvement.

With electronically stored data, application controls become vital for satisfying audit objectives related to specific transaction sets or audit cycles. Application controls ensure that processing will be performed as management intends with timeliness and accuracy.

Application controls regulate the input, processing, and output of an application. Inputs and outputs have risks such as loss of data during transmission, duplicate inputs, and manual input errors or incomplete data. Processing risks include incomplete processing, unrecorded transactions caused either by accident or as part of fraud, automated transactions (e.g., raw materials reordering) failing due to complications, or files lost during processing. Output risks include files being sent to the wrong place or too late to be of use. With high-volume transactions, many small errors could be found that are too numerous to address quickly. Also, the sheer mass of transactions can lead to mass authorizations, risking that some transactions could be improper.

Input controls

Input controls are intended to prevent computer errors by controlling data as it manually or electronically enters the system. Input errors are the most common source of errors, and internal auditors should emphasize tests of these controls. Garbage-in, garbage-out (GIGO) refers to the fact that regardless of one's processing and output quality, if inputs are poor, outputs will be too. Manual input controls include requiring authorizations both before the input and after a review, use of concise prenumbered forms, and training for data entry personnel.

Electronic aids for manual inputs include user-friendly screen formats that prompt users for required information and use of required fields. A field check is a check to see if information in an entry field is complete. Drop-down menus and similar features only allow specific preset inputs. To protect sensitive information, keystroke verification requires data to be entered twice, by different persons if possible, and highlights any differences. File labels and labeling conventions identify proper records or transactions.

Batch controls accumulate transactions and then apply tests on the batch such as a batch total. The batch total is reconciled at various transfer points. Real-time systems cannot use batch controls and must rely on visual verification. For example, after a supplier number is entered, the system may display the supplier's name and ask for verification.

Input error correction controls are problematic because an error already exists and the correction could cause more errors. Internal auditors must carefully review error reports before deciding on a course of action. Once settled, the files are updated with new inputs and balances are adjusted.

The following are other input controls:

- **Format checks.** These are checks to see that data is entered in an acceptable format, e.g., a date is entered as mm/dd/yyyy and not as mm/dd/yy (or in Europe as dd/mm/yyyy).

- **Edit checks.** Edit checks are automated tests on data fields. Some of these controls could also be considered processing controls. There are a number of types of edit checks:
  - Control totals. Hash totals are sums of nonfinancial numbers such as account numbers that have no meaning. A change in the hash total indicates a record change. Item counts count total numbers of items; financial totals sum monetary amounts.
  - Range tests. These allow entry between a range of numbers or characters.
  - Numerical checks. These prevent alphabetic entry in number fields.
  - Sequence checks. These are checks for an alphanumeric sequence in a field.
  - Limit checks. Entries above a particular number are prevented or result in a prompt for approval.
  - Check digits. An extra digit is added that has an algorithmic relationship to the remaining digits to show if the number was incorrectly entered by transposition. This is used for credit cards.
  - Record count. This tallies the number of records.
  - Historical comparison. This measures variance from past records.
  - Overflow checking. This places a memory or length limit on a field to prevent larger numbers than the maximum being entered.

- **Reconciliation and balancing.** Reconciliations analyze variances or test two balances to see if they are equal.

- **Inquiry logs.** These track all read-only access to records.

- **Automated inputs.** Automation reduces errors and increases input speeds. Some types of automated inputs include:
  - Optical character recognition (OCR). OCR is an example of an imaging system that stores, retrieves, and processes graphic data. For example, a company scans shipping receipts into a database, from which it can retrieve a given receipt to verify a signature.
  - Magnetic ink character recognition (MICR). MICR codes are commonly included on checks, and they indicate check number, account numbers,

routing numbers, and possibly the check amount. MICR characters can be run through a scanner at very high speed with an extremely low error rate.
- Scanners. A scanner is any device that digitizes graphic images.
- Bar codes. A bar code is a machine-readable representation of data, allowing for rapid reading and processing of associated data (such as price or inventory level). It uses vertical, parallel lines of varying width and spacing, and two-dimensional patterns are also used.
- Radio frequency identification (RFID). An RFID system uses identifier tags that can be included in packaging. The system can "read" these tags via radio frequency and identify where the product is. RFID systems are useful in tracking inventory through the supply chain.

Auditors should also manually review some records. For example, if the database shows that some account numbers are one character too short, it shows a weakness in internal controls. Interviews with programmers and examinations of edit reports, documented approvals, and other steps outside the computer help provide assurance for input controls.

Processing controls

Processing controls are automated error checks built into computer processing as well as segregation of duties such as controlling programmers' access to files and records. Data center operators' access to applications should be restricted to equipment and software installation and responding to errors. Auditors should examine restart procedures and verify that reconstructed files have accuracy checks. A console log or system control file should track operator interventions. Data center operators should not be allowed to override file names or device errors. Policy controls include rotating operators or requiring two operators to work on a system.

Access to configuration parameters within applications must be controlled, especially since more people will have the proficiency to alter configuration than reprogramming would require. Auditors should reconcile actual versus planned configuration.

Automated controls include the following examples:

- Date and file total checks are logs of item and monetary totals with date and time stamps. Exact duplicate entries are flagged as errors; applications designated for once-daily runs will log any additional run as an error.
- Completeness tests reject saving a record until all fields are complete.
- Control totals are totals recorded in a system control file when an application generates temporary files; an error occurs if each control total doesn't match.

Auditors test for processing controls by inserting known test data and comparing it against expected results. Auditors should be able to follow transaction trails back to the input point. IT audit specialists review program operation summaries and manually recalculate test sets.

Other processing controls include:

- **Reasonableness checks,** which find unreasonable entries in large volume, repetitive updating transactions by comparison to other existing records.
- **Suspense file,** which is a file used to retain transactions processed with errors. Auditors should measure delay in clearing suspense items.
- **Activity logging,** which records actions of users by date, time, and access terminal; it may record a before and after image of changes.
- **Processing logic tests (e.g., posting check, zero balance check, cross-footing check),** which are various checks that verify if accounts or transactions are at expected levels. An example would be checking that an account actually has a zero balance after payments are processed.
- **Run-to-run totals,** in which the data control group monitors batch run totals.
- **End-of-file procedures,** which prevent additional operations from taking place in a file when the end of the file is reached.
- **Primary and secondary key integrity check,** which verify encryption key security.
- **Access control list (ACL),** which is a list of all valid users. Auditors should verify that the list cannot be altered without proper authorization.

Output controls

Output controls are detective controls that find errors and verify the accuracy and reasonableness of output data after processing is complete. Requiring users to immediately review the output of their work is the most basic and vital of the output controls because users have the best knowledge about the process at that moment. Three totals can be reconciled: The auditor can manually produce control total samples and compare them to the system inputs and the system outputs. Similarly, automated comparison of inputs to outputs can reveal unreasonable relationships. Prenumbered output forms such as check blanks show control output gaps.

Record retention is an output control reinforced by law or regulation, especially for financial records. Other records can be stored electronically. Data backup procedures can ensure their safety.

The following are output controls:

- **Error listings.** Auditors ensure that errors are followed up without exceeding backlog limits, and corrected reports are resubmitted.
- **Reference documents.** When systems are interrupted, these logs show what was in memory at the time of the interruption.
- **Spooling controls.** A spool is a temporary memory allocation for a system output. These controls regulate data spooling methods.
- **Working documents.** Legal records such as checks, invoices, or stock certificates are safeguarded. These are audit evidence that can detect if inputs really match outputs. Dual custody, or needing two persons to access the records, is used for bonds, checks, or payroll.
- **Reports.** Report controls include ensuring that the reports are accurate, as simple as possible, timely, and aggregated to a meaningful level and that sensitive data is secured using distribution controls. Checklists ensure receipt of all scheduled reports, and report lists summarize batch-processed reports. Sensitive reports should be shredded.
- **Exception reporting.** By highlighting only out-of-the-ordinary data, exception reports relating to output should help managers determine the source of the error (human error, processing error, etc.).

Integrity controls

Integrity controls monitor data as it is processed and while it is stored to ensure that it remains accurate, consistent, and complete and that specific records are unique (not duplicated, perhaps under a slightly different name). Integrity controls are applied to the database and database management system (DBMS), so these controls will differ depending on the type of database management system being used. Databases and DBMSs are addressed later in Chapter C, Topic 2. The primary type of database discussed there is a relational database.

Integrity controls for relational databases include the following:

- **Unique primary keys.** The primary key, or identifier for a specific row of data, must be unique, for example, exactly one record for customer XZ.
- **Complete primary keys.** The primary key cannot have a null value.
- **Referential integrity.** If a database table (called a relation) contains a reference to a column (called a tuple) elsewhere in the table or in a different table, that column must be verified to exist.

Management or audit trails

Management or audit trails provide a history of all transaction processing, showing each stage from inception to conclusion. This allows an auditor to trace a transaction backward from an output to its source. This may be useful when trying to identify the source of errors or fraud.

Preventive maintenance and housekeeping

Preventive maintenance and housekeeping are two of the most important aspects of an IT operation. It is imperative that controls are in place that will reduce equipment breakdowns or inaccurate processing.

According to Sawyer, some examples of this are:

- Written procedures for operators in the event of unanticipated equipment failure.
- A written schedule of preventive maintenance procedures.
- Preventive maintenance programs providing for periodic maintenance according to the manufacturer's recommendations.
- Malfunctions described in console logs or an incident reporting system that notifies IT management of all errors occurring on each shift.

In addition, corrective actions must be determined, adhered to, and accurately documented.

Topic 6: Demonstrate an Understanding of Information Systems Development (Level A)

Development of an information system refers to the development of the entire organization's information network of people, processes, data, and technology. Therefore, the development of the computer hardware, software, and databases are really just one puzzle piece of information systems development. It also involves hiring, promoting, training, and developing human resources talent from the chief information officer, to expert specialists such as database administrators or programmers, to data entry clerks.

Like any development effort, it is best to begin with the end in mind. The end in this case is achievement of organizational strategy, so organizational strategy guides the creation of an information strategy. Exhibit VI-10 shows a high-level overview of the process involved in the development of an information system. Note that the next chapter addresses system infrastructure and its related databases, networks, hardware, software, and configuration.

Exhibit VI-10: Development of Information Systems

Chapter C: System Infrastructure

Chapter Introduction

System infrastructure is part of the design of an information system, as Exhibit VI-10 above indicates. The primary components of a system infrastructure are the database and its management system; networks such as a local area network or telecommunications networks; hardware including workstations, servers, and mainframes; software including operating systems and general software; and configuration, which refers to set-ups such as a client/server configuration of computers or the use of a cloud. While configuration is not addressed further in these materials, this chapter addresses the other components just listed. In addition, there is content on IT control frameworks and IT job roles.

Topic 1: Demonstrate an Understanding of Workstations (Level A)

Workstations are computers with their own processing power and memory, such as desktop or laptop computers. They have specialized functions in an organization's information system, for example, data-entry workstations, end-user workstations such as for accounting, computer-aided audit testing (CAAT) workstations, or computer-aided design (CAD) workstations. The term "workstation" historically refers to a more powerful version of a desktop or laptop computer that could handle more processing than the average computer but was still small enough to rest on a desk, but the lines of distinction have been blurred over time as computers of all types have become much more powerful. Workstations vary greatly in power and size, and some may be connected to several terminals as part of a mainframe system or may serve as the central computer for smaller organizations.

Another term historically associated with workstations is "microcomputer," which is just any computer with a microprocessor as its central processing unit (CPU). Personal computers (PCs) available from multiple manufacturers and Macintosh® computers (Macs) from Apple Computer® are varieties of microcomputers designed for general consumers. For simplicity, this text will use the term "workstation" when referring to any type of workstation or microcomputer.

Workstations are typically connected to other computers and peripherals such as printers through a network, but they can stand alone. With the constant increase in computer power and decrease in component size, workstations now outperform the mainframes of the past.

Hand-held computer devices may also be considered workstation equipment. Some hand-held devices may be specialized (e.g., for data input only), while others have a full range of functionality.

Workstations are part of the hardware of the IT system infrastructure and therefore may be included in audits of hardware controls.

Auditing hardware

Among the ways the auditor can evaluate hardware controls are by:

- Interviewing operators and users to obtain reliable information about equipment.
- Determining what actions operators or software takes in the event of hardware malfunction.
- Confirming oral statements by cross-checking against maintenance reports and error logs.
- Checking temperature and humidity control devices to see that they are installed, functional, and adequate.
- Reviewing failure logs to determine loss of time due to malfunction.
- Reviewing daily and periodic computer logs and reports to determine whether or not maintenance schedules conform to manufacturers' specifications.
- Determining whether or not the timing of maintenance is appropriate.
- Comparing actual downtime with normal expectations.
- Checking fire detection and suppression systems.

It is critical that internal auditors understand that they must cross-check what is actually done by the organization against what they should be doing.

Topic 2: Demonstrate an Understanding of Databases (Level A)

A database is any repository of data in a computer system. A database management system (DBMS) is an application that links users and programs to the database and allows the database to be manipulated by multiple applications. A DBMS serves as a buffer between the various applications or modules and the database. Database and DBMS combinations are often just called a database. Skilled database administrators are required to keep a DBMS working. Audit uses of databases include:

- Audit programs.
- Risk and control inventories.
- Personnel data related to staff members.
- Departmental or organizational fixed assets.
- Record retention control.
- Histories of audit findings.
- Data on organizational units or audit sites.

Advances in software and hardware technology make ever-larger databases possible, allowing storage of graphics, audio, and video as well as documents.

Databases that are shared among multiple applications, such as an ERP system's database, have more robust controls than a series of databases for each application because the database can be centrally located and fewer avenues of access need to be protected. Data can be used in strategic analysis, redundant files are eliminated, modifications are easier, and standards and a framework for control can be applied consistently. Because data is independent of the applications, applications gain some consistency and ease of programming.

Another option is to use a distributed database system such as a cloud, which creates a virtual centralized database. This creates the advantages of a single source of data storage and adds the advantage of geographic diversification to reduce some risks, but it creates its own set of control risks, especially if the distributed database is out-sourced and the organization therefore cannot maintain complete control over the data. Management and oversight must typically be increased in such scenarios and consideration must be given to the countries in which the data is stored. Some countries have fewer intellectual property protections or less enforcement, for example.

In either method, controls must be put in place to limit access to sensitive data by user role, such as allowing only payroll personnel access to payroll files. Other drawbacks include greater complexity and expense, and failure of the database or the transmission method to and from the database can halt all computer work. Use of backup procedures is vital. Auditors need to understand how DBMSs are structured, including the underlying rules used to ensure proper controls.

Database terminology

Databases are at the top of a hierarchy: bit, character, field, record, file, database. Each item listed is a larger and larger grouping of data. A **bit** is a binary digit, a **character** is any alphanumeric key, a **field** is a business object such as a name or an asset, a **record** is a logical grouping of fields, a **file** is a collection of related records, and a **database** is a collection of files. When a record relates to a person, place, or thing (i.e., a noun), it is called an **entity.**

The fields relating to entities are called **attributes.** An employee entity would have a first name attribute. A **key field** is the field used to identify an entity, such as employee number. **Data items** are the specific data in fields, while a **primary key** is a unique key field number (i.e., a proper noun) used to identify a specific entity such as employee ID #12345.

Other database terminology includes the following:

- The **data definition language** describes the data and the relationships between data in a database, including logical access paths and records.
- Schema and subschema contain the specifics. **Schema,** from "schematic," are the overall rules for the database; **subschema** are files describing a portion of a database, including authorized read-only/full access users.
- The **data dictionary** is a master record concerning the data in the database (metadata), e.g., pseudonyms, lists of users responsible for maintenance, ranges of values, and other controls. Auditors can use the data dictionary to check facts if it is up-to-date.
- The **data manipulation language** has commands for viewing or changing the database.
- The **data query language** is a user-friendly method of querying the database for information. Ad hoc queries are possible. A popular language is structured query language (SQL), which allows users to select data from a particular location and qualify search parameters.

Relational databases

Older database types were rigid and resulted in data redundancy. For example, a spreadsheet is an example of a flat database, which is fine for simple single-user work but would become untenable for vast amounts of data. Most databases are now relational databases, so this is the only type that will be discussed here. Exhibit VI-11 on the next page shows a relational database.

A relational database is a DBMS that is arranged into two-dimensional files called tables, with links between tables that share a common attribute. A **table**, or **relation**, is a file with rows and columns similar to a spreadsheet. Each table contains a business entity such as those in Exhibit VI-11—CUSTOMER, SALES_TRANSACTIONS, or ACCOUNTS_RECEIVABLE. Any row in the table is an **entity** (also called a **tuple)**, while columns contain **attributes** for entities.

The key to a relational database is that any particular data field is entered in only one place in the database and then its relationships are mapped to all relevant tables. Links are the relationships between tables or within the same table that share at least one common attribute. The exhibit shows CUSTOMER_NUMBER and SALES_NUMBER attributes linking tables. As many links are created as necessary, as shown with the PART_NO attribute linking to the PART table.

Exhibit VI-11: Relational Database

Attribute (column)

CUSTOMER TABLE

CUSTOMER _NUMBER	CUSTOMER_NAME	ADDRESS	CUSTOMER _CITY	CUSTOMER _STATE	CUSTOMER _ZIP
8259	K. Bear	3510 Rocky LN	Wounded Knee	SD	57794
8261	B. Poquelin	1667 Rehearsal RD	Paris	TX	75460
8263	K. Jackson	5 Tito BLVD	Gary	IN	46405
8444	B. Bumble	601 32nd ST	Chicago	IL	60616

Entity (row)

Link

SALES_TRANSACTIONS TABLE

Link to PART Table

SALES _NUMBER	CUSTOMER _NUMBER	SALE_ DATE	PART_ NO	DESC	SALES _DEPT	LIST_ PRICE	DISC_ PRICE	QTY	DISCOUNT _TOTAL
111	8259	11/20/Y6	32234	Plastic Sticks	001	$0.35	$0.33	4,000	$1,320.00
112	8261	11/20/Y6	43423	Versailles Replica	012	$1.29	$1.20	10,000	$12,000.00
113	8263	11/20/Y6	45264	ABC Wood Blocks	003	$0.45	$0.40	20,000	$8,000.00
115	***8444***	11/20/Y6	78974	Cheddar Hat	012	$2.29	$2.00	80,000	$160,000.00

Link

ACCOUNTS_RECEIVABLE TABLE

SALES _NUMBER	SALE_ DATE	CUSTOMER _NUMBER	DISCOUNT _AMT_DUE	DISCOUNT _ENDS	DUE_AFTER_ DISCOUNT_END	CASH_ RECEIVED	CASH_DUE
111	11/20/Y6	8259	$1,320.00	11/30/Y6	$1,400.00	$0.00	$1,320.00
112	11/20/Y6	8261	$12,000.00	11/30/Y6	$12,900.00	$2,000.00	$10,000.00
113	11/20/Y6	8263	$8,000.00	11/30/Y6	$9,000.000	$4,000.00	$4,000.00
115	11/20/Y6	***8444***	$160,000.00	11/30/Y6	$183,200.00	$10,000.00	$150,000.00

Key Field

Relational databases require more processing power than older types, but they provide more useful ways of manipulating data. Using a data query language such as SQL, a manager could create a query that eliminated irrelevant rows (entities) from the report, called selecting. Or they could pare down the number of columns to make the data more relevant, called projecting. Finally, a query could combine data from two or more tables, called joining. Relational databases are intuitive and allow new links or relationships to be formed easily without reprogramming the model.

Batch versus real-time processing

Batch processing is the processing of records at specific intervals; real-time processing is the processing of a record as soon as it is submitted. Batch processing can be less expensive and is therefore still used for many types of data. Batch controls can be more robust. Real-time processing is used for data that could have a real effect on company efficiency if received immediately, such as inventory levels.

Halfway between the two is memo posting, which is used by banks for financial transactions and others to create real-time entries that are posted to a temporary memo file. The memo file allows the updated information to be viewed; at a designated time the memo file is batch-processed to update the master file. In this way data is available immediately for viewing but batch-processing controls are applied before the changes become permanent.

Database controls

Database controls focus on maintaining the integrity, efficiency, and security of the database. This may involve:

- Enforcing attribute standards and ensuring that data elements and database relationships are accurate, complete, and consistent.
- Managing concurrent access to the same data by different users to maintain data integrity and availability.
- Integrity controls to ensure that all primary key fields are unique and none are left blank and that all relational links lead to where they should.
- Protecting against loss of data during processing through the use of data checkpoints and restart routines.
- Protecting against loss of stored data through specified backup routines.
- Optimizing database size and efficiency by periodic reorganization (confirming that all data relationships remain accurate and functional).
- Managing access to ensure proper authorization for access to data and rights to update the database and to restrict access by those outside.
- Monitoring and reporting on database performance and conditions.

Access management

Organizational databases support role-based access, so each user should be assigned a role and a unique ID and password to enforce accountability. Various areas of the database should be segregated by checkpoints, such as the payroll area. Fine-grained access control is when the data itself is restricted. In a relational database, attributes (columns) can be programmed with the controls described in Chapter B, Topic 5, such as numerical checks, range tests, or drop-down menu choices. The attribute's domain is the description of all of its controls. Schema, subschema, tables, rows, and views can also have similar protections. A view is like a stored query, or a presentation of data from several tables. Changing data in a view changes the data in the underlying tables.

Performance monitoring

Regular audits are an integral part of database controls. Audits should review any data needing extra access controls and verify that the controls are functioning properly. Audit policies should be designed to include an "alarm bell" that is not triggered unless access or other controls have already failed.

Database maintenance and utility programs

Database maintenance is the use of transaction processing systems to add, delete, or change data. Utility programs such as data cleansing tools (see below) can monitor a database for inconsistencies.

Data cleansing

Data cleansing is the removal of redundancies and errors in a database. It is vital when two or more databases are integrated, such as for integrating with an external partner. Data cleansing may be out-sourced or kept in house. It is not a one-time affair but a regularly scheduled process.

The following are data cleansing terms:

- **Concatenation** is linking fields and columns.
- **Standardization** is expanding abbreviations and the use of common terms, prices, and units of measure.
- **Taxonomy** is the use of standard names, while **normalization** is application of taxonomy standards such as the United Nations Standard Products and Services Code (UNSPC).
- **Deduping** removes duplicate data such as one supplier with two records.
- **Categorization** puts items in classes and groups for proper aggregation.
- **Enhancement** is combining additional internal and external data sources to improve data quality.

Data warehouses

Data warehouses are databases designed to collect the information from one or more transactional databases for purposes of multiyear storage of records, planning and analysis, and reporting. Queries to databases can generate pertinent information for planning and decision making but can also slow down the transactional database due to the processing power required. Data warehouses are critical for organizations that have grown through merger and acquisition and cannot always integrate all of their transactional databases in a cost-effective manner. Therefore, entire organization queries can be done on a data warehouse. A data mart is a subset of a data warehouse or database that contains focused information for a particular function, such as customer relationship management. Virtual databases are data partitions in a database, i.e., a virtual data mart.

OLAP and data mining

Online analytical processing (OLAP) is software that allows multiple perspectives for a set of data to be analyzed. Analysis of complex data is fast, and users can aggregate the data into useful information. OLAP draws a set of data to the user's computer and allows the user to manipulate that data in multiple ways or dimensions without having to perform a new query. This is useful because querying a data warehouse can often involve some delay. With OLAP, data can be compared in three or more dimensions, such as sales by item, sales by region, and actual versus planned sales. OLAP allows these multidimensional databases to be rotated to show different relationships and sliced and diced or drilled down or up in aggregation level.

Data mining software is designed to look for unforeseen similarities and correlations among large amounts of seemingly unrelated data. Internal auditors could use data mining tools to look through every record for potential fraud.

Topic 3: Describe Common IT Control Frameworks (Level A)

IT controls

The *Internal Control—Integrated Framework* of the Committee of Sponsoring Organizations of the Treadway Commission (COSO) defines an internal control as:

> A process, effected by an organization's board of directors, management, and other personnel, designed to provide reasonable assurance regarding the achievement of objectives in the following categories:
> - Effectiveness and efficiency of operations.
> - Reliability of financial reporting.
> - Compliance with applicable laws and regulations.

A key control concept is that IT controls must provide continuous assurance for internal controls. A related key control concept is that auditors must provide independent assurance of this coverage.

Effective IT controls provide continuous assurance supported by a reliable and continuous trail of evidence. In addition, this assurance is itself assured through the internal auditor's independent and objective assessment of the control. According to GTAG 1, "Information Technology Controls," the goals of the IT controls and the control framework are to provide and document:

- Compliance with applicable regulations and legislation.
- Consistency with the enterprise's business objectives.
- Continuity with management's governance policies and risk appetite.

Control objectives

Control objectives describe how an organization should function, assuming that auditors have provided reasonable assurance over internal controls. More specific objectives of internal IT controls include:

- Protect assets/owners' equity.
- Ensure that information is available, reliable, and appropriately restricted.
- Hold users accountable for functions performed.
- Protect customer privacy and identity.
- Protect employees' jobs. (Employees can prove that they did the right things.)
- Maintain data and system authenticity and integrity.
- Assure management that automated processes are controlled.
- Provide an audit trail for all automated and user-initiated transactions.

Exhibit VI-12 lists some indicators of effective IT controls.

Exhibit VI-12: Indicators of Effective IT Controls

• Ability to execute and plan new work (e.g., IT infrastructure upgrades to support new products/services) • Projects that come in on time and within budget, saving the organization time and resources and improving its competitive position • Ability to allocate resources predictably • Consistent availability of reliable information and IT services across the organization and with customers, partners, and other external interfaces	• Clear communication to management of key indicators of effective IT control • Ability to protect against new threats and vulnerabilities and to recover from disruptions quickly and efficiently • Efficient use of a customer support center or help desk • Heightened security awareness throughout the organization

Source: GTAG 1, "Information Technology Controls."

Control classification

GTAG 1, "Information Technology Controls," describes a hierarchy of controls that affect an organization from the top down, including controls aimed at assuring good governance, management, and technical control. This hierarchy is depicted in Exhibit VI-13.

Exhibit VI-13: Hierarchy of IT Controls

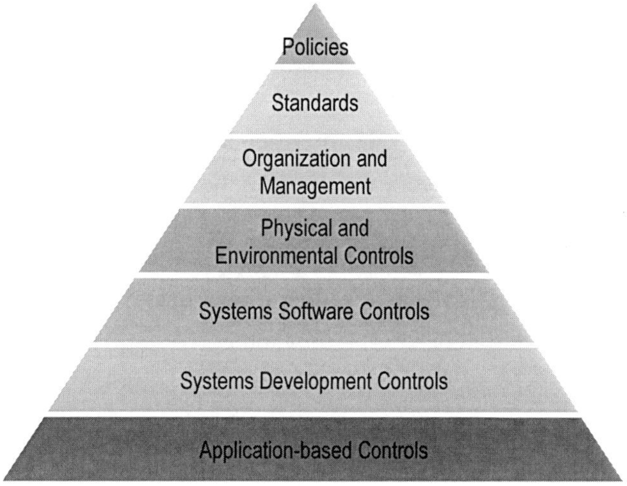

Source: GTAG 1, "Information Technology Controls."

- **Governance** controls include policies about the use of IT throughout the organization, including security, privacy, ownership, level of autonomy to create and use applications, and measures to assure business continuity.

These policies must be approved by management and communicated throughout the organization to set the "tone at the top" and expectations.

- **Management** controls focus on identifying, prioritizing, and mitigating risks to the organization, its processes, and its assets. They include:
  - **Standards** for systems development processes (both those developed internally and those acquired from vendors), systems software configuration, and applications controls, data structures, and documentation.
  - **Organization and management** of lines of responsibility and reporting, incorporating separation of duties as appropriate, financial controls for IT investment, IT change management, and personnel controls.
  - **Physical and environmental controls** to mitigate risk from hazards such as fire or unauthorized access.
- **Technical** controls are the foundation of almost all other organizational IT controls. Automated technical controls implement and demonstrate compliance with policies. Technical controls include:
  - **Systems software controls** such as those controlling access rights, enforcing division of duties, detecting and preventing intrusion, implementing encryption, and managing change.
  - **Systems development controls** such as documentation of user requirements and confirmation that they have been met, a formal development process that incorporates testing, and proper maintenance.
  - **Application-based controls** that ensure that all input data is accurate, complete, authorized, and correct and is processed as intended; all stored and output data is accurate and complete; and all data processes are tracked from input, through storage, to eventual output.

Controls may be classified in different ways, according to the way they are viewed throughout the organization.

Exhibit VI-14 shows how GTAG 1 classifies controls by different perspectives, meaning that any given control can be classified in more than one way.

Exhibit VI-14: Control Classifications

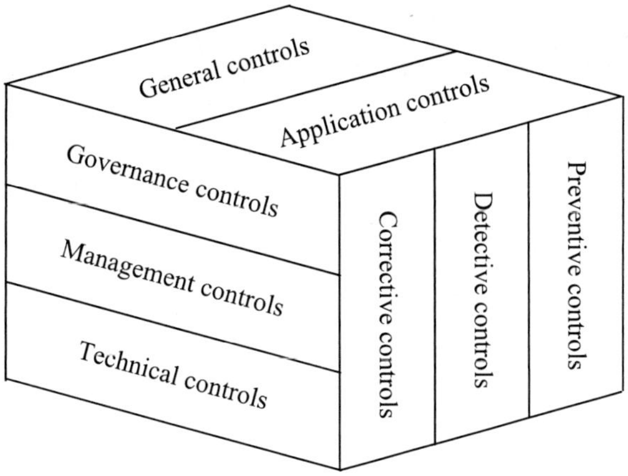

Source: GTAG 1, "Information Technology Controls."

General controls and application controls

A **general control** is a control that applies generally to the IT environment or overall mix of systems, networks, data, people, and processes (also known as the IT infrastructure). The use of an IT control framework requires implementing a general control framework such as the COSO *Internal Control—Integrated Framework.*

An **application control** is a control related to the specific functioning of an application system that supports a specific business process. Balancing of process totals is an example.

These type of controls are also covered in Topic 5 of Chapter B in this section.

Governance, management, and technical controls

This classification rests on who will be the responsible party.

Governance controls are oversight rather than performance controls that rest with the board of directors and their committees, such as the audit committee, in consultation with executives. Examples include setting IT security policy and evaluating metrics.

Management controls determine and mitigate risks to critical assets, sensitive data, or operations, including standards, organizational structure, and physical and environmental controls. Such controls have a broad reach over many organizational areas, requiring collaboration between executives and the board.

Technical controls are the specific controls that must be in place for management and governance controls to be effective.

Preventive, detective, and corrective controls

Preventive controls are designed to stop errors or fraud before they occur, such as using firewalls, a drop-down menu, or assigning access privileges by job role.

Detective controls are controls that should be triggered after an error occurs, e.g., automated flagging of inactive users or review of exception reports for completed transactions to detect credit limit overrides.

Corrective controls are used once errors, fraud, or other control issues have been detected. They need their own preventive and detective controls to ensure that the process isn't corrupted. Corrective controls range from error corrections to continuity plans.

Control frameworks

According to GTAG 1, a control framework is an outline that identifies the need for controls but does not depict how they are applied. IT control frameworks are internal control systems that help managers set IT control objectives, link IT to business processes and overall control frameworks, identify key IT areas to leverage, and create a process model that logically groups IT processes. Control frameworks help determine the appropriate level of IT controls within the overall organizational controls and ensure the effectiveness of those controls.

Why are control frameworks needed? Managers need assurance that their IT processes are contributing to business objectives and competitive advantage. The organization needs assurance that it is resilient because it can mitigate risks of fraud or cyber attacks. Stakeholders need to know that the organization can be trusted. The only way to gain such assurances is for management to increase their understanding of IT operations without getting bogged down in the increasingly complex execution details. Breaking systems down into understandable processes helps managers combine business with IT strategy, align organizational structures, and set performance goals and metrics.

Control frameworks provide a methodology for seamlessly linking objectives to requirements and requirements to actual performance. A process model breaks IT down into easy-to-understand activities organized around the control objectives to be achieved and identifies resources to be leveraged. Control frameworks also help prove to outside authorities and auditors that all regulatory requirements are being satisfied, such as for the US Sarbanes-Oxley Act or industry-specific regulations (e.g., in regard to health care).

Use of standardized, well accepted frameworks means that there is a body of literature available for guidance and that users can benchmark against the standards or against competitors using similar methods. IT controls need to be everyone's responsibility, and the framework should clearly communicate specific roles. IT controls should provide a "defense in depth," meaning that multiple layers of controls reduce the likelihood of a control failure.

Selecting an IT control framework

Selecting an IT framework involves deciding which model will benefit the entire organization, since the model will be used by a large number of employees with control responsibilities. Frameworks are generalized for broad appeal, but no framework encompasses all business types or all IT. GTAG 1 states that each organization should "examine existing control frameworks to determine which of them—or which parts— most closely fit its needs."

Control frameworks can be formal, as discussed in this section, or informal, meaning that they are not written down but are communicated verbally and through action. Such systems are not appropriate once an organization has moved past the earliest stages of organizational development. Satisfying regulatory requirements requires use of formal approaches.

The chief audit executive should work with management to select a framework or portions of several frameworks. Any model, once selected, must be customized. Properly understanding risks is a prerequisite for selecting a control framework. The CAE should determine the organization's risk appetite, defined by COSO as "the degree of risk, on a broad based level, that a company or other organization is willing to accept in pursuit of its goals." Risk appetite is paired with risk tolerance, also defined by COSO: "the acceptable level of variation relative to the achievement of objectives. In setting specific risk tolerances, management considers the relative importance of the related objectives and aligns risk tolerances with its risk appetite."

The COSO model is a high-level control framework, developed in 1992 and accepted for the purpose of assuring compliance with financial reporting provisions, such as Sarbanes-Oxley. Its main features are illustrated in Exhibit VI-15. From a technology perspective, it incorporates:

- Monitoring (e.g., metrics, cost and control performance analysis, internal audit).
- Information and communication (e.g., IT performance surveys, help desks, IT and security training, internal corporate communication).

- Control activities (e.g., review board for change management, analysis of return on IT investment, enforcement of IT standards, assessment of compliance with business continuity risk assessment).
- Risk assessment (e.g., assessment of IT risks and inclusion in corporate risk assessment, IT internal audit assessment, IT insurance assessment).
- Control environment (e.g., management support of IT control environment, overall policies, corporate technology governance committee, technology and architecture standards committee).

Exhibit VI-15: COSO Model for Internal Control Frameworks

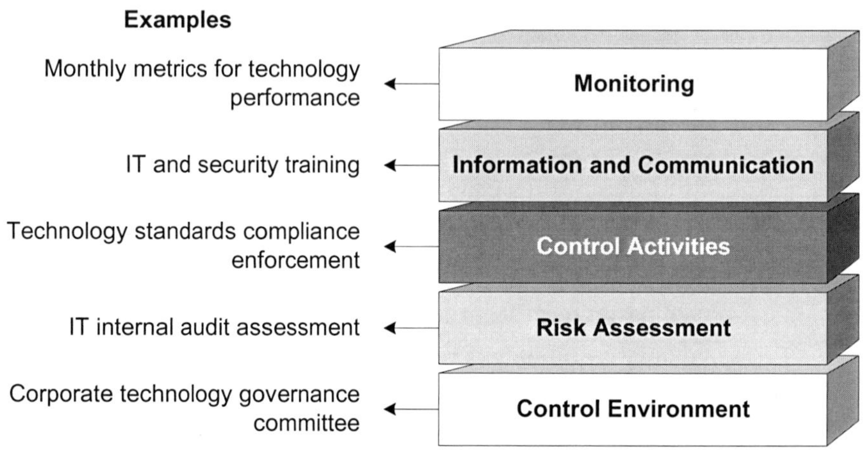

Source: GTAG 1, "Information Technology Controls."

COBIT 5®

"COBIT 5: A Business Framework for the Governance and Management of Enterprise IT" (hereafter called the COBIT 5 framework) is a family of products developed by ISACA and available at their Web site, www.isaca.org. It is internationally popular because it is kept up-to-date (version 5 was released in 2012), it helps management understand the role of IT and its place in organizational strategy, it helps users be more satisfied with IT security and outcomes, and it sets clear lines of responsibility. It also helps managers create more value from IT resources, meet regulatory compliance, and control IT risks by providing better risk awareness so that informed risk decisions can be made.

In addition to the framework document, the COBIT 5 family of products includes published guidance related to enabling processes (these are defined later) and other types of professional guidance such as an implementation guide. There is also an online collaborative environment.

The COBIT 5 framework is built on a generic set of five key principles and seven enabling principles that can be adapted for use by any size or type of organization to set and achieve separate governance objectives and management objectives for its information systems. Since the enabling principles are referred to in each of the key principles, the seven enabling principles are listed here first and then described later:

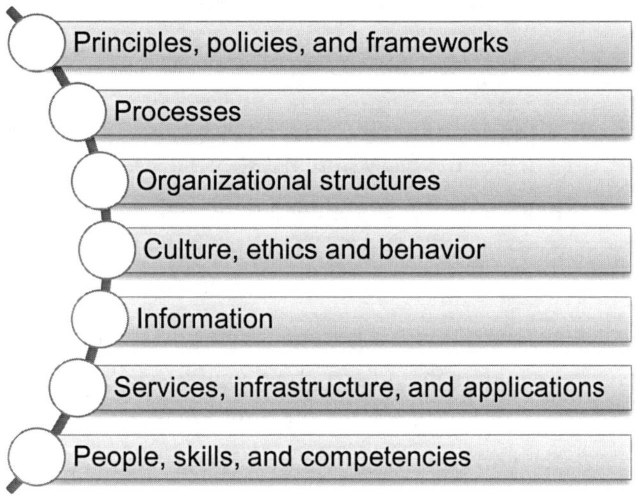

Exhibit VI-16 illustrates the five key principles that form the COBIT 5 framework. Each key principle is explained next.

Exhibit VI-16: COBIT 5 Principles

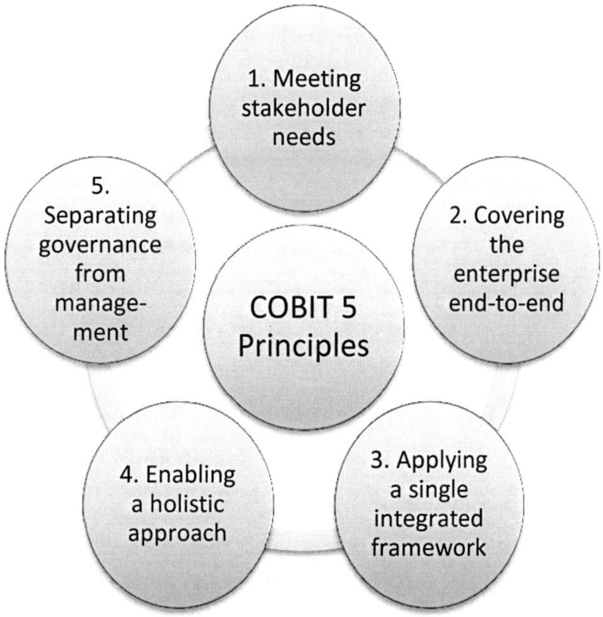

Source: "COBIT 5: A Business Framework for the Governance and Management of Enterprise IT," © 2012 ISACA. All rights reserved. Used with permission.

- **Principle 1: Meeting stakeholder needs.** Stakeholder needs drive value creation in an organization. Since the objective of governance is the creation of value in an organization, governance must define value creation as the realization of the benefits expected by stakeholders while optimizing use of resources and management of risks.

  The needs of stakeholders often conflict, such as shareholders' need for profit versus regulators' or society's need for environmental sustainability. Therefore, the COBIT 5 framework promotes governance as a process of negotiating among stakeholders' value interests and then deciding how best to create optimum value for stakeholders overall.

  Also, since this is a generic framework, what constitutes value for stakeholders may differ considerably, such as between for-profit and not-for-profit organizations. To help organizations define value, the COBIT 5 framework includes a values cascade, which is basically a set of tables that start with a set of 17 generic goals, for example, "financial transparency." Organizations select from among these generic goals, which cascade down to 17 IT-related goals, for example, "transparency of IT costs, benefits and risk," which in turn cascade down to a set of enabler goals. Enabler goals are the goals for COBIT 5's enabling processes, such as people, skills, and competencies. The point is to translate stakeholder needs and the derived governance goals into priority-weighted IT goals and from there to easily implementable processes, policies, and procedures.

- **Principle 2: Covering the enterprise end-to-end.** The second principle is that IT governance must be wholly and completely part of the organization's overall governance and internal control framework. The COBIT 5 framework integrates the most current governance models and concepts. It also applies to processes that have been out-sourced or are part of an extended enterprise of partners in a supply chain. Because the seven enabling principles listed earlier are organization-wide in scope, focusing on each of these enablers allows governance to be end-to-end. The last part of this principle involves defining governance roles as well as their relationships and activities. Owners or shareholders delegate to a governing body such as the board, who sets the direction for management, who provide instruction to operations so that it remains aligned to stakeholder goals. Each relationship also includes a feedback process of reporting, monitoring, and accountability.

- **Principle 3: Applying a single integrated framework.** The COBIT 5 framework is designed to integrate seamlessly into other governance frameworks to provide a single source of organizational guidance. It avoids getting into technical details and integrates all guidance from prior ISACA publications and is designed to integrate with other governance frameworks, such as ISO/IEC 38500, which is described briefly later in this topic.

- **Principle 4: Enabling a holistic approach.** The seven enablers listed previously are used to implement each goal determined using the goals cascade. The first enabler, "principles, policies, and frameworks," is central, because these provide practical guidance on how to shape desired behavior by doing specific management activities. The processes; organizational structures; and culture, ethics, and behavior principles are governance-directed management organizing activities that help ensure successful adoption of the principles, policies, and frameworks. Governance direction over culture, ethics, and behavior are critical success factors to achieving goals, although their influence is often underestimated. The remaining principles of information; services, infrastructure, and applications; and people, skills, and competencies are resource management enablers of the basic principles and framework. These enablers are interconnected and rely on one another to succeed. For example, processes need proper information, skills, and behavior to make them effective and efficient.

  For each enabler, the COBIT 5 framework has a set of enabler dimensions, that ensure that each of the following is considered for each enabler:
  - Does measurement of leading indicators (predictive metrics) show that the proper inputs, practices, and outputs are being followed?
  - Does measurement of leading indicators show that the proper system development life cycle is being used (e.g., feedback is incorporated)?
  - Does measurement of lagging indicators (historical metrics) show that internal and external stakeholder requirements were met?
  - Does measurement of lagging indicators show achievement of enabler goals (e.g., quality, efficiency, effectiveness, security, accessibility)?

- **Principle 5: Separating governance from management.** The governance body of an organization, typically its board of directors, needs to see itself as a separate discipline from the management of an organization. The COBIT 5 framework outlines five governance processes and 32 management processes that are developed in detail in a supporting document, "COBIT 5: Enabling Processes." For each governance process, the key roles are to evaluate, direct, and monitor. Governance processes include ensuring that the governance framework is in place and maintained, stakeholder benefits are delivered, risk responses are optimized, resource use is optimized, and transparency exists. The management processes are divided into the following categories that reflect a cyclical set of management roles:

- **Align, plan, and organize.** Processes include managing strategy, systems infrastructure, risk, security, human resources, and relationships.
- **Build, acquire, and implement.** Processes include project and change management, defining requirements, identifying and building solutions, and managing configuration, changes, knowledge, and assets.
- **Deliver, service, and support.** Processes include managing operations, incidents and problems, continuity, security, and process controls.
- **Monitor, evaluate, and assess.** Processes include monitoring, evaluating, and assessing performance and conformance, the control infrastructure, and compliance with external requirements.

The COBIT 5 framework and family of products, taken as a whole, can help organizations get the best value for their investments in IT by finding the optimum balance between achieving stakeholder benefits, effectively managing risks, and efficiently managing resource usage.

Electronic Systems Assurance and Control (eSAC)

The IIA's Electronic Systems Assurance and Control (eSAC) model was designed and published in 2001 to allow an auditor to express an opinion on the reliability of information created by IT. This framework is a risk-assessment-based, process-oriented methodology. eSAC facilitates communications between auditors, the board, and other audit clients.

eSAC starts with strategic inputs and ends with measurable results, enhanced reputation of the firm, and opportunities for improvement. The center of the model is COSO's broad control objectives (e.g., safeguarding of assets), followed by IT business assurance objectives:

- **Availability.** Transactions can be performed at all times.
- **Capability.** Transactions are reliably completed in a timely manner.
- **Functionality.** Systems are user-friendly and responsive and fulfill all business requirements.

- **Protectability.** Unauthorized access is denied through logical and physical security controls.
- **Accountability.** Data is nonrefutable, accurate, and complete.

Each specific process is related to one or more of these objectives and to the following building blocks: people, technology, processes, investment, and communication. The model also covers internal and external forces or the risks and control environment as well as their maturity, or how quickly such relationships change and evolve. Finally, monitoring and oversight is key.

ISO/IEC 38500

ISO/IEC 38500:2008, "Corporate Governance of Information Technology," is an international standard framework document that provides top management and boards of directors and other owners with a set of guiding principles to ensure that IT at their organization is acceptable, effective, and efficient. It specifically relates to management processes and management decisions in regard to information systems regardless of whether the actual processes are carried out as internal activities or are out-sourced.

ISO/IEC 38500 also provides guidance for senior managers; controllers and other resource managers; legal, accounting, and other business specialists; hardware, software, and communications suppliers; consultants and other internal or external service providers; and IT auditors. This guidance is designed to help these business professionals to provide better advice and insight.

Global Technology Audit Guides

The IIA's *Global Technology Audit Guides* are not control frameworks, but they can help in selecting the proper framework for an organization. GTAG 1, "Information Technology Controls," covers IT controls as an executive needs to understand them, including organizational roles and structure and how the IT controls fit within the overall control framework. The other GTAG documents cover specifics such as change and patch management controls. These guides contain specific advice for set-up, management, and measurement of application level controls.

The GTAG documents can be used to create a unique framework or to supplement an existing framework. One example of a tool that can be used to plan for sufficient audit coverage is the CAE checklist shown in Exhibit VI-17 on the next page. Studying the questions chief audit executives should raise for each of the actions listed shows how a general risk-based framework would be customized for each organization.

For further study, the GTAG documents can be found at www.theiia.org.

Exhibit VI-17: IT Control Framework Checklist

Action	Questions
1. Identify the IT control environment of the organization, including: a. Values. b. Philosophy. c. Management style. d. IT awareness. e. Organization. f. Policies. g. Standards.	1. Do corporate policies and standards that describe the need for IT controls exist?
2. Identify relevant legislation and regulation impacting IT control such as: a. Governance. b. Reporting. c. Data protection. d. Compliance.	2. What legislation exists that impacts on the need for IT controls? 3. Has management taken steps to ensure compliance with this legislation?
3. Identify the roles and responsibilities for IT control in relation to: a. Board of directors. i. Audit committee. ii. Risk committee. iii. Governance committee. iv. Finance committee. b. Management. i. CEO. ii. CFO and controller. iii. CIO. iv. CSO. v. CISO. vi. CLC. vii. CRO. c. Audit. i. Internal audit. ii. External audit.	4. Have all the relevant responsibilities for IT controls been allocated to individual roles? 5. Is the allocation of responsibilities compatible with the need to apply division of duties? 6. Are IT responsibilities documented? 7. Are IT control responsibilities communicated to the whole organization? 8. Do individual role holders clearly understand their responsibilities in relation to IT controls? 9. What evidence is there of individual role holders exercising their responsibilities? 10. Does internal auditing employ sufficient IT audit specialists to address the IT control issues?
4. Identify the risk assessment process. Does it cover: a. Risk appetite? b. Risk tolerances? c. Risk analysis? d. Matching risks to IT controls?	11. How is the risk appetite and tolerance of the organization determined? 12. Is the risk appetite and tolerance of the organization authorized at board level? 13. Is the risk appetite and tolerance clearly understood by all those with a responsibility for IT control? 14. Is a formal risk analysis process used by the organization? 15. Is the process understood by all those with responsibility for IT control? 16. Is the process used consistently throughout the organization?
5. Identify all monitoring processes, including: a. Regulatory. b. Normal in-house. c. Other than internal auditing.	17. What processes exist to monitor compliance with all relevant legislation plus internal policies and standards? 18. Are there monitoring processes carried out by management outside of internal audit?
6. Identify information and communication mechanisms: a. Control information. b. Control failures.	19. What metrics are provided to the board of directors, its committees, and management in relation to IT security? 20. What additional reports are provided to the board of directors and to management on a regular basis? 21. Is management always provided with reports when there are IT control failures? 22. Do the board of directors and its committees receive similar reports of IT control failures?

Source: GTAG 1, "Information Technology Controls."

Topic 4: Describe the Functional Areas of IT Operations (Level A)

Internal auditors must understand the IT environment to identify—and fully appreciate the roles and responsibilities of—the departments and individuals involved in IT activities.

As explained in GTAG 4, "Management of IT Auditing," IT has four layers:

- **IT management** comprises the people, policies, procedures, and processes that manage the IT function. This includes system monitoring (to identify failures), programming, planning to align IT resources and activities with the organization's strategic goals and objectives, managing out-sourced vendors, and assuring IT governance.

- **Technical infrastructure** refers to the systems involved in business processes: operating systems, databases, and networks.

- **Applications** are programs that perform specific tasks related to business processes. They may be **transactional** or **support** applications. Transactional applications perform **buy side** activities (e.g., procurement), **sell side** activities (e.g., order processing), **back office** activities (e.g., invoicing for payables, recording receivables), and **enterprise resource planning**, which integrates some of the other functions. Support applications include such software as e-mail, imaging, and design tools.

- **External connections** include external networks, such as the Internet, EDI systems, and data warehousing providers.

IT management and organization

The top level of managerial responsibility lies with the chief information officer (CIO), who reports directly to the chief executive officer (CEO). The CIO is responsible for IT in relation to business strategy and compliance. The CIO designs and maintains IT internal controls, IT resources, and IT metrics and determines which new IT to pursue. He or she manages an IT domain that includes a variety of functions, depending on the enterprise.

Exhibit VI-18 shows a generic organizational chart for an organization's IT. Note that not all of the following positions are found in all organizations. Positions can be combined, and, if so, internal auditors need to verify that segregation of duties is appropriate.

Exhibit VI-18: IT Organizational Chart

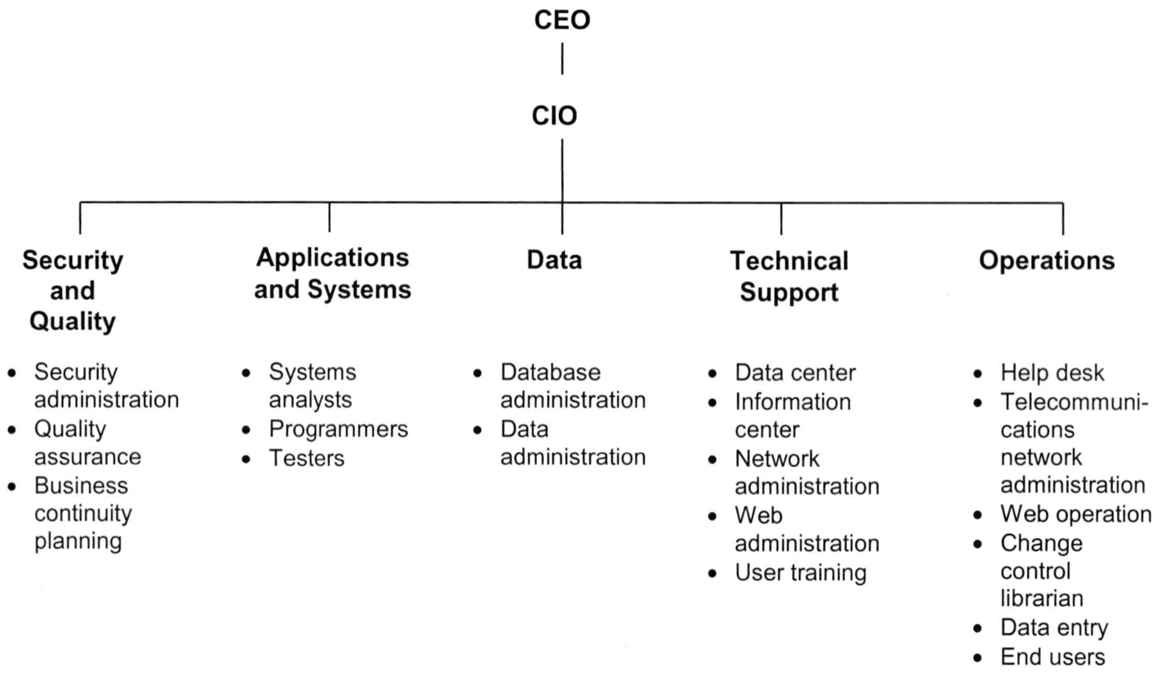

Operations

Operations supports all business units, with a focus on efficiency. The operations manager is responsible for capacity planning, or the efficient allocation of IT resources and the elimination of waste. The following functions are included in operations:

- The **help desk** reduces persistent system interaction errors by users.
- The **telecommunications network administrator** programs telephones.
- **Web operations** administers Web sites, extranets, and intranets.
- The **change controller** makes judgment calls whether to escalate an issue or to schedule it. A **librarian** holds the master versions of applications.
- **Data entry personnel** format data for computer use. Systems should minimize manual entry by capturing data at the point of the transaction.
- Each department will have **end users** with specialized job roles. Training is a key control to prevent input errors.

Technical support

Technical support keeps back-end systems functioning and trains end users:

- The **data center** is a secure location where servers or mainframes are kept, including controls over electricity, HVAC, and physical access.
- The **information center** is a centralized location for support staff, traditionally relating to end-user training and ongoing technical support.
- The **network/LAN administrator** monitors and maintains network usage.

- The **Web administrator** develops the company Web site, monitors it for inappropriate usage by employees or others, and maintains appropriate bandwidth and availability.
- **User training** may take place in computer classrooms with a "sandbox" environment, or an area in which applications can be used in a testing mode.

Data

Database administrators (DBAs) are trained to design, implement, and maintain databases; set database policy; and train users. The DBAs help auditors review raw data (e.g., find payees named "CASH").

Data administrators monitor data use and set policies on how data can be stored, secured, retained for archives, and released. They plan for future data needs and oversee database design and data dictionary development.

Systems and application development

Systems development functions include systems analysts, programmers, and testers.

Systems analysts determine the necessary system outputs and how to achieve these goals, either by hardware/software acquisition, upgrade planning, or internal development.

Programmers translate the systems analysts' plans by creating or adapting applications. Categories include:

- Application developers (end-user applications).
- Systems developers (back-end systems and networking).
- Web developers (Web functionality, Web-based applications).

Testers test at the unit and system level. (See Topic 3 of Chapter B.) Programmers should not be used to test code that they wrote themselves.

IT security and quality

IT security sometimes oversees other areas and external threats. Security staff enforce password and other security policies. They may also deal with business continuity. (See Chapter D.) The **quality assurance (QA) officer** determines whether IT systems satisfy the needs of executives and end users. He or she may head a data quality audit, which tests all or a subset of the data for accuracy, integrity, and completeness.

Out-sourced or co-sourced IT

Out-sourcing or co-sourcing (partly out-sourced) IT is common, especially for application development. If the software vendor is reputable, no further audit activity may be needed unless mandated by policy or law, but their support services can aid understanding. Managed security service providers (MSSPs) out-source security by monitoring network activity for intrusions and using simulated attacks. Internal auditors will need to work with the provider to assess security risks.

IT role of senior and non-IT management

IT governance begins at the top with the board of directors and key executives. Oversight, approval, and understanding of the basic infrastructure are the responsibilities of these parties. GTAG 1 notes that an organization's management layer has significant responsibility for and effect on IT policy, resources, and activities.

- The **board of directors** approves enterprise strategies, in which IT plays an important role. The board must be aware of IT issues and projects and how they affect corporate strategies. Board committees play additional IT roles:
  - To fulfill its governance responsibilities, the **audit committee** must ensure that appropriate financial reporting and ethical monitoring controls are in place and assessed and tested adequately.
  - The **compensation committee** can reflect the importance of IT performance goals in the compensation packages it approves.
  - The **governance committee** must include oversight of IT activity and ensure board attention to IT oversight and compliance with external regulations.
  - The **risk management committee** must ensure that IT-related risks have been identified, assessed in terms of the enterprise's risk appetite, and appropriately addressed.
  - The **finance committee** relies on IT for data used in preparing financial reports and making financial decisions, such as the replacement or repair of the IT system.

- **Management** implements enterprise strategies and includes the:
  - **Chief executive officer (CEO)**, who defines objectives and metrics for IT, approves resources, directs issues to the board, and holds ultimate responsibility for the adequacy of IT controls.
  - **Chief financial officer (CFO)**, who must understand the role of IT in the enterprise's financial management and who holds ultimate responsibility for IT controls related to financial systems and data.
  - **Chief security officer (CSO)**, who is responsible for all security, including IT continuity planning. The CSO documents and enforces security policy, is responsible for all external network connections

and logical and physical security controls, and is involved in compliance, legal, and audit.

- The **chief information security officer (CISO)**, who works under the CSO and with the CIO (chief information officer) to develop IT security policy, control IT resources, and oversee IT security. The CISO aligns security with business objectives and risk and educates key executives on security.
- **Chief legal counsel (CLC)**, who helps set policy on information disclosures, advises on legal risks for IT, and checks financials.
- **Chief risk officer (CRO)**, who manages risks, including IT risk exposures, and measures how they relate to overall business risk.
- **Chief ethics officer,** who looks at privacy issues and proper use of data.
- **Chief compliance officer**, who measures adoption of strategy.
- **Chief technology officer**, who explores new IT against needs.
- **Director of contingency planning/continuity planning**, who oversees contingency planning. See Chapter D.

- The **chief audit executive (CAE) and audit staff** ensure that IT is included in the audit universe and annual plan, advise on the development of controls, provide objective auditing of all types of controls, and monitor the IT risk management plan. **External auditors** perform annual audits of the IT system and related controls.

Topic 5: Demonstrate an Understanding of Enterprise-Wide Resource Planning (ERP) Software (Level A)

Enterprise resource planning systems are modular suites of business applications that share data between modules seamlessly and store all data in a single repository. A shared database reduces redundancy of data and creates synergies such as advanced analysis and automated forwarding of transactions to the appropriate departments. ERP systems are available as complete packages from vendors or may be assembled from multiple systems, often called best-of-breed because each application focuses on a particular business niche. ERP systems increase efficiency such as by keeping inventory levels low, reducing cycle times, improving the timeliness of data for decision making, and enforcing procurement agreements.

Older ERP systems and certain areas of new systems that don't need constant updates use batch processing, which accumulates data changes until a set time and then releases them to the database. Newer ERP uses online transaction processing (OLTP) or real-time updates of key data. For example, inventory levels will reflect items just purchased or sold. Also, while older ERP systems required using custom interfaces with external business partners and external sources of market information, now most ERP systems have much simpler interfaces and can transmit and receive data from Web-based sources. Users may also be able to log on and transact business in the ERP system from remote locations using secure Web-based interfaces.

ERP core modules and functionality

Core modules of ERP systems include finance, manufacturing, sales and distribution, and human resources. However, just about any business function has modules devoted to it. ERP are primarily transaction processing systems (TPS), which process vast amounts of data through multiple interconnected transactions. ERP also includes management tools and information systems. Management information systems (MIS) are analytical tools and productivity aids such as standard reports or dashboards. Other advanced features include customer relationship management (CRM) and supplier relationship management (SRM), which are efforts to integrate customer and supplier inputs to ERP systems, an extended supply chain.

Customized versus configured

ERP vendors try to cover the top 80% of functionality requested by their users. Therefore, even the best system is unlikely to cover all needs. A rule of thumb is that if the ERP system provides 80% or more of the items in a needs analysis, it is a good fit. The remaining differences can be achieved through customization or configuration.

Customization is changing the code of a system to provide unavailable processes. It should be avoided for the most part because it exponentially increases development costs and makes upgrades difficult. Configuration is changing preset parameters in the package, and it should be encouraged because it is cheap and doesn't impede upgrades.

Studies of organizations implementing ERP have found two common methodologies: those that used business process reengineering to study and streamline their business processes to fit the system, and those that felt their processes needed no improvement and tried to customize the system to match their existing processes. The former spent two to three times the price of the software overall; the latter spent seven or eight times the price of the software overall. Internal auditors can help management see the costs of organizational resistance to change while concurrently ensuring that process reengineering does not remove vital controls. Separating business processes from controls can help make this distinction.

Internal auditing for ERP

ERP systems provide a wealth of data for auditing, and a single data repository should simplify gathering audit evidence. Auditing an ERP implementation has its problems, but they generally beat auditing the alternative: a set of disparate applications that speak different languages, require multiple workarounds, and have redundancies. ERP systems are making such multiple legacy system set-ups less common. Internal auditors need to be sure that management has evaluated the efficiency of their ERP system relative to competitor systems.

Due to the high cost of ERP systems, auditors need to be fully involved in the systems development life cycle (see Chapter B, Topic 3), including evaluating the credentials of members of the implementation team and determining how the system will be audited. Due to the comprehensive nature of ERP in an organization, internal auditors must carefully monitor conversion or implementation. The same goes for the personnel training plan. Once the system is in place, management may be tempted to take a break, but with any large system, continuous improvement is possible and auditors are the ones who can point out those improvements.

A main issue with ERP systems is that the point of the system is to have only a single entry of any type of information. There will be no paper audit trail to follow between departments, and approvals tend to be automatic (e.g., must select from a vendor list, spending caps) instead of requiring individual intervention, exacerbating segregation-of-duty issues. In such cases, audits must focus on the quality of passwords and other logic controls as well as transactions that can be used to override controls.

Auditing when ERP implementations use business process reengineering

As noted above, when an organization implements ERP applications, it sometimes involves a major reengineering or reorganization of their business. The resulting internal controls may change drastically from traditional methods of auditing. Some of the concerns that may arise from ERP implementations involving business process reengineering are:

- Complexity of hardware and engineering that increases the difficulty of understanding operational efficiency.
- End-user acceptance of the new technology.
- Training effort and costs (in time and money).

In terms of internal auditing, there must be changes in the methodologies used. New approaches may be necessary, or existing approaches may need to be modified. Any new methodologies must fit within the overall control framework.

Once the methodologies have been designed, an internal auditor must, among other things:

- Evaluate the technology environment, including its complexity and efficiency.
- Decide if a legacy system is still being used for any part of the process.
- Have a detailed understanding of the ERP approach, including the specific modules that have been implemented.

In addition, the internal auditor should be involved from the very beginning of the implementation and reengineering process. This will ensure that any changes to methods or controls are clearly defined and understood.

Continuous auditing for ERP systems

ERP systems are too complex to reliably audit only once a year. The automated controls in ERP must be designed and implemented with audit involvement, including the availability of alarm triggers that will indicate either that errors were detected or the controls themselves are not working. Exception reports are alarm triggers that highlight unusual data or areas of operational concern. High risk areas may be monitored for extended periods to see if internal controls are being circumvented over time.

Topic 6: Describe Data, Voice, and Network Communications/ Connections (Level A)

A computer network is the sum of all infrastructure and applications required to connect two or more network nodes, which are computers and devices. More broadly, networks can include telecommunications networks. Also addressed in this topic are some controls over networks, such as firewalls.

Processing methods

Networks process data in one of three basic ways: centralized, decentralized, and distributed.

Centralized processing handles all data processing needs at a central data center, usually over a mainframe computer. Because IT resources such as maintenance staff, equipment, and physical security can also be concentrated, centralized processing has the highest level of control. However, a threat to this location could affect business continuity.

Decentralized processing is a strategy that keeps the processing and communications needs of various divisions or geographical regions separate. Decentralized processing is harder to control because each location has its own IT facility and each could have a different level of processing capability and needs. It might be used by divisions that do not want or need to communicate with other divisions, such as a chain of independent pharmacies.

Distributed processing is a strategy where remote locations each have their own processing power but all are networked together. The client/server architecture is typically used in distributed processing, though other options exist such as cloud-based networks. Excess processing capacity can be shared where needed, but physical resources must be distributed as well. A catastrophic event that destroys one facility will not interrupt the service overall, and data can be backed up through the network. Distributed processing often uses distributed databases with a centralized database and/or data warehouse (see Topic 2), which allows multiple databases to accumulate data and the data is replicated in all distributed databases. A master database gives some benefits and controls like those associated with centralized processing.

Network types

Networks have different control needs depending on their reach. All types of networks have some common issues. For example, determining where information originated can become complicated as networks grow ever larger. This, coupled with the vast increase in number of transactions, makes networks difficult to manage, let alone account for all of the potential access points.

Local area networks and wide area networks

Local area networks (LANs) connect computers (including laptops) and related devices (printers, for example) in a limited area, such as one building. The LAN allows users to share data and also expensive hardware devices, such as fast color laser or wide-format printers. LAN users can connect through various wired or wireless means. They can also connect to the Internet through data modems that accept a phone line or a cable connection. A modem is a device that modulates a data signal from analog to digital and vice versa (e.g., a telephone or cable modem).

Though LANs are limited in distance, they can connect to one another, thus becoming a wide area network. Wide area networks (WANs) are networks of LANs over a large area (e.g., nation or world) using multiple transmission media. WANs can connect through wireless transmission, thus becoming available to mobile computers.

Other types of networks

The following are other types of networks, listed from narrow to wide access levels:

- A **peer-to-peer network** is a direct connection between two computers.
- **Personal area networks (PANs)** support wireless connections within a room or small area.

- **Metropolitan area networks (MANs)** are networks of LANs for a city, campus, or other medium-sized area.
- **Consortium networks** are groups of organizations that form networks to assist in their intercommunications, such as the Society for Worldwide Interbank Financial Telecommunication (S.W.I.F.T.), a consortium that transmits international payment instructions (not funds).
- **Public data networks (PDNs)** are networks that allow public access, such as the World Wide Web. WANs can operate over PDNs by using special communication methods.

Network transmission options

Networks are not all hard-wired but include wireless methods. Wireless methods are inexpensive, but data transmissions can be intercepted more easily, making encryption and other safeguards more important. Transmission options include:

- Wired—telephone (twisted pair), coaxial cable, fiber optics.
- Wireless—radio waves (cellular), infrared, microwave, satellite.
- Virtual private networks (VPNs; discussed later in this topic).

Open Systems Interconnection (OSI) reference model

The Open Systems Interconnection (OSI) reference model is a method of defining how messages should be sent through a network so that unrelated products can work together. The OSI model is an international standard adopted by the International Organization for Standardization (ISO). The OSI model is divided into seven layers for communications and computer network protocol design, such as message addressing, flow control, error control, message encapsulation, and reliable message transfer. The first two layers are the only two that contain hardware; the rest are software only. The first three layers are common layers to the network, while the last four are specific to a particular computer, with the last layer closest to the user.

The following is some of the terminology for how information is grouped in a network:

- **Packet.** A general term describing a logical grouping of data passing through network layers. Packet headers have control information.
- **Circuit switching/packet switching.** Phone systems use circuit switching, or a continuous physical circuit. Packet switching sends fixed or variable length packets without a continuous circuit.
- **Frame.** Logical grouping of data transmitted as a data link layer unit (layer 2). A frame can refer to a message's header and trailer, which are used for error control and message synchronization.
- **Datagram.** The primary Internet data units that group data sent as a network layer unit (layer 3) without establishing a virtual circuit.

- **Segment.** A TCP (defined later) term describing a single transport layer (layer 4) unit of information.
- **Cell.** A fixed size unit of data for asynchronous transfer mode (ATM) switching and multiplexing (defined later).
- **Message.** Application layer (layer 7) logical grouping of data, often made up of a number of lower layer logical groupings.

Network protocols Descriptions of each layer are shown in Exhibit VI-19.

Exhibit VI-19: Open Systems Interconnection (OSI) Reference Model

OSI Layer	Description	Related Controls
Layer 1: Physical layer	This electrical/mechanical layer transmits digital signals; e.g., T3 carrier line.	Wiring and other physical protections.
Layer 2: Data link layer	This layer synchronizes layer 1 data movements and compresses data where possible; e.g., Ethernet or token ring.	Encryption (see Chapter A, Topic 4).
Layer 3: Network layer	This layer routes and forwards data to the right places; e.g., Internet protocol (IP) gives Internet addresses a unique number specifying the network and host.	• IP addresses can be tracked with help from Internet service providers (ISPs) after legal due process. • Firewalls (see later in this topic).
Layer 4: Transport layer	This layer ensures that data transfers are complete by managing end-to-end control and error checking; e.g., Transmission Control Protocol (TCP) is used by all Internet-based systems along with IP: TCP/IP. LANs and WANs using TCP/IP are called IP networks.	• This layer is a logical control layer. • Firewalls (see later in this topic).
Layer 5: Session layer	This layer initiates and terminates conversations between applications.	
Layer 6: Presentation layer	This layer is usually the operating system (O/S), which applies syntax and formatting.	O/S controls (see Topic 10).
Layer 7: Application layer	This layer isn't necessarily the application itself but the constraints on data, such as user and communication partner authentication and privacy.	• Configurable data constraints and authentication. • Intrusion detection/ prevention systems.

Network topology

Network topology refers to the physical connection points between devices on a LAN or similar network. The predominant network topology is a bus network, which has a main line (bus) and all devices are connected to the line. A ring network is arranged in a circle, so two paths for data are available. A star network wires each device to a central device that routes data to or from other devices, eliminating the need to wire between devices.

Networking hardware

Controls over network hardware include protecting wiring from damage and maintaining an inventory of vital replacement parts. Networking hardware terms include the following:

- **Ports** are physical connection points to a device.
- **Hubs** serve as the center of the network and switch or direct communications. Active hubs check data and regenerate the data signal before sending it on.
- **Repeaters** extend the range of a network by amplifying or regenerating signals that may have weakened or become corrupted during transmission.
- **Switches** are devices that connect telecommunications circuits and may allow network management capabilities at layers 3 and 4 of the OSI model.
- **Routers** are intelligent processors that link network segments, allowing them to communicate but also remain separate and independent. Routers are generally not as efficient as switches.
- **Bridges** are an early software-based device that function similarly to switches and routers but are not as efficient as switches. They connect two or more LANs with similar network architectures, allowing them to act as a single logical (but not physical) network.
- **Gateways** convert protocols between networks with dissimilar network architectures.
- **Multiplexers** for data combine multiple channels into a single channel, such as multiple phone lines sharing a single physical phone line. This single channel is the aggregate or composite link. At the other end, another multiplexer reverses the process.

Firewalls

Constantly available broadband connections need constant monitoring. A firewall is a hardware/software combination that routes all communications to or from the outside world through itself, blocking unauthorized traffic. Firewalls compare access rules against the IP addresses, names, files, and applications attempting to enter the system. Network administrators control these access rules. Firewalls can:

- Improve security by blocking access from certain servers or applications.
- Reduce vulnerability to external attacks (e.g., through viruses) and ensure IT system efficiency by limiting user access to certain sites.
- Provide a means of monitoring communication and detecting external intrusions (through intrusion detection systems, which are described below) and internal sabotage.
- Provide encryption internally (within an enterprise).

Corporate firewalls are often two-tiered: a firewall is placed before the Web server and any other public access servers, and a second firewall is placed between the public access servers and the private network areas. Additional firewalls can be used to protect sensitive data such as payroll. An organization's firewalls should be installed on dedicated hardware that has no unnecessary software.

Several types of firewalls exist. They can be located at the network or transport layers (layers 3 and 4). The following are layer 3 and 4 firewall types.

- **Packet filtering.** This type of firewall works by comparing source and destination addresses to an allowed list, specifically examining headers and other fields in packets of data. Because it examines packets in isolation, it can miss many types of attacks. Packet filtering can be enhanced in the following ways:
  - **Stateful inspection.** This firewall enhances packet filtering by monitoring packet flows in general. State tables are used to track the data flowing through multiple packets, and the firewall analyzes whole conversations for appropriateness and legitimacy.
  - **Network address translation (NAT).** Firewalls with packet filtering and stateful inspection can use NAT to hide their internal host computer IP addresses from sniffer utilities.

- **Gateways.** A gateway firewall stops traffic flowing to a specific application such as file transfer protocol (FTP), e.g., rules may block outgoing FTPs but permit incoming FTPs. One common type of gateway is the **application gateway/proxy server.** Proxy servers are an intermediary for communications between the external world and private internal servers. They intercept external packets and, after inspection, relay a version of the information, called a proxy, to private servers, and vice versa. Proxy servers are specific to an application.

Auditors need to determine if firewalls can be bypassed or controls overridden by alternative transactions. User prompts for allow/deny communications can be the most risky. Auditors should work with the network administrator to determine the efficacy of a firewall, how specific its rules are, and whether the lists of acceptable users, IP addresses, and applications are kept up-to-date such as by promptly removing terminated employees. Because a firewall is a chokepoint, it can be used to audit controls or trace the source of an incoming attack. Firewall logs could be used as legal audit evidence if the data was collected, processed, and retained properly.

A firewall has limitations. For example, data can still be stolen via telephone, CD, DVD, or USB flash drive. Employees or visitors could either have a conflict of interest (industrial espionage), or they could simply be gullible and "help" someone by providing access. Firewalls can be configured incorrectly; they can also be circumvented by using a personal modem on a voice line. Auditors should assume that firewalls are always being probed for weaknesses and that they cannot prevent all attacks.

DMZs (from military jargon for demilitarized zones) are portions of a network that are not part of either the Internet or the internal network, such as between the Internet access router and host. If the access router has an access control list, it creates a DMZ that allows only recognized traffic to even contact the host.

Intrusion detection/prevention systems

Systems are now vulnerable through the multiple browsers at the application layer (layer 7) of a network. Normal firewalls cannot process the vast amount of data at this layer. Intrusion detection systems (IDS) reside at layer 7 to monitor systems for intrusions. An IDS combined with an application layer firewall is called an intrusion prevention system (IPS). Host IPS (HIPS) software functions at the operating system kernel level to detect and block abnormal application behavior before it executes. HIPS assumes that abnormal behavior is an unknown form of attack. Network IPS (NIPS) are hardware and software systems on a network that analyze incoming packet content, dropping malicious packets.

These types of intrusion detection/prevention systems usually are more conservative than other types of firewalls and provide more detailed reports.

Wireless networks

Wireless networks often use wireless application protocol (WAP) because it supports most wireless networks independent of operating system. Bluetooth technology is standard for short-range wireless communication under 100 meters. Wireless fidelity (Wi-Fi or 802.11x) is a wireless standard for Ethernet networks; Wi-Fi has better speed and range than Bluetooth.

Mobile devices are becoming standardized under WAP, because these specifications can adapt to the small amount of bandwidth and display size on such devices.

E-mail security

E-mail is the source of many types of attacks and nuisances, such as these:

- Spoofing. Fraudulent Web site links (phishing/pharming); see Chapter A, Topic 2.
- Spam. Unsolicited bulk e-mail. Legitimate businesses that send spam usually allow receivers to opt out; however, many spammers ignore such

requests. Viruses can be sent through spam; important e-mail messages can be lost due to spam blockers or having too much e-mail.
- Eavesdropping. Passive spying on the content of e-mail. This vulnerability is compounded if the message has not been encrypted.
- Message modification. Active modification and retransmission of intercepted messages, e.g., to misdirect business strategy.
- Denial-of-service attacks. Valid users are blocked from using the e-mail system.

E-mail management

E-mail is only as secure as the systems on which it operates, and at larger organizations, e-mail security could differ between sites with different e-mail administrators. The first test for e-mail security controls is therefore ensuring that a consistent policy for administrators is set and followed. Policies should include those for IT staff such as automatic deletion of confidential e-mail messages once the user has downloaded the e-mail from the server and other maintenance tasks. E-mail security settings should be set to "high," and all messages should be set to read as plain text. Digital signatures can ensure accurate identification of all senders outside the trusted network.

Three types of e-mail encryption exist: boundary, staging server, and end-to-end:
- Boundary encryption does not encrypt internal e-mails, but e-mails that pass through the gateway or boundary are encrypted at that point and are decrypted when they arrive at the other organization's boundary server. This method is less complex and works well when working with trusted partners but has low protection for unknown partners.
- Staging server encryption allows users to transmit a secure e-mail to a secure e-mail server; the system sends the receiver a standard e-mail telling them to retrieve the secure e-mail using a secure Web portal, adding another task.
- End-to-end encryption creates the encryption when the e-mail is sent and doesn't decrypt until it is opened, providing the best security, especially with unknown intermediaries.

For employees, policies should include privacy policies restricting the use of spam or other intrusive e-mails or allowing only designated employees to use spam. The policy should spell out the rights to privacy that the user has in regard to the content of their messages, which is often that the e-mails are subject to organizational review and are not considered private. Legitimate users can use e-mail to transmit organizational secrets, conduct personal business, or commit illegal acts. E-mail policies should clearly communicate organizational policy on such matters. The policy should ensure that users comply with any legislation affecting the use of e-mail or spam in the business, such as the US government's Controlling the Assault of Non-Solicited Pornography and Marketing (CAN-SPAM) Act.

Voice networks

Voice telecommunications networks includes telephones, voice mail, and Internet-based telecommunications that may include video. Auditors use phones for callback procedures, verbally corroborating audit evidence by directly contacting vendors, payees, banks, and others.

Risks

Many industries, such as airlines, are dependent on continuous, uninterrupted access to communications or telecommunications. Communication technologies (analog, digital, wireless) also impact the risk of unauthorized disclosure unless appropriate controls are in place.

Telecommunications (voice and data) involve some exposures:

- Changed, dropped, or duplicated data
- Downtime
- Eavesdropping
- Slow response time
- Insertion of fraudulent messages into the network by wiretapping

Some of these exposures can be controlled through:

- Message sequencing to spot gaps and duplicates.
- Encryption (encoding) of data by a scrambler.
- Self-checking algorithms that can detect changes in messages.
- Network monitoring software that allows central operators to locate problem points in the transmission lines and equipment.
- Automatic dial-back systems that foil hackers attempting to gain access to computer networks by automatically hanging up and dialing a number that will set up a secured connection with callers who can demonstrate authorization.
- Dedicated lines leased by carriers to organizations that have sole access.
- Restart/recovery procedures to guard against loss or ambiguity of data when telecommunication fails.

Standard service and voice mail

Telephone systems are generally multi-line systems with automated voice mail. Such systems require proper configuration and a trained administrator. Telephone systems are usually a vital part of an organization's operations, and any lost calls or periods of inoperability can carry a high opportunity cost. Even a system slowdown or slow response time for customers on hold has a cost. Restart/recovery procedures must be part of a contingency plan. Wires and hardware should be labeled for fast repair. Backup lines should be available.

Wiretapping to gain confidential information is one potential problem that can be mitigated by line monitoring devices if significant risk is perceived. Another risk associated with phone systems is that the person on the other end could be fraudulently representing himself or herself as a trusted party. Call-back procedures to official phone numbers may be needed for important transactions.

VoIP

Voice over Internet protocol (VoIP), or Internet telephony, uses packet switching over the Internet rather than circuit switching over telephone lines. Connecting through an ISP allows this set-up to avoid long-distance charges and reduces the amount of cabling required. However, if the network isn't configured optimally, the technology could slow the network down.

Data over computer networks is not automatically secure, so VoIP messages should in theory be encrypted. However, VoIP encryption is a current issue because the American government wants IP providers to allow the government a backdoor into any VoIP call for wiretapping purposes. The issue is in the courts. Allowing point-and-click wiretapping is a threat because organized crime could exploit it. Once hackers gain access to a VoIP system, they can use it to exploit the network itself. Proponents of end-to-end encryption say that this is the only way to secure communications. Only the sender and the recipient could be determined, not the content of the messages.

Virtual private networks (VPNs)

Controls to protect communications over Internet-based connections include using a third-party virtual private network (VPN)—a secure method of connecting two points on the Internet, often run by an Internet service provider (ISP). A VPN uses tunneling, or encapsulating data into Internet protocol (IP) packets before sending them. The data is encrypted at the firewall and sent to the ISP; then it is sent through a tunnel to another ISP.

Topic 7: Demonstrate an Understanding of Servers (Level A)

The server is a powerful computer system that provides service to other computer systems called clients. A client/server architecture uses servers for specialized functions. Clients—the recipients of these functions—are workstations that send requests to the servers. A server dedicates high bandwidth to a specific task such as a Web server hosting a Web site, a file server providing access to files, or an enterprise server managing the common application needs of an organization. Data requests are routed through a data request server, which formats and forwards the data to the proper database server.

In comparison to a mainframe computer, generally a server is more compact physically and the information it contains is delivered to a smaller network of workstations.

A server may consist of both hardware and associated operational software. A key requirement for servers is scalability; scaling up means adding more powerful processors, while scaling out increases the processing capacity through additional, less-powerful processors. The software must also be scalable.

Topic 8: Describe the Process of Software Licensing (Level A)

The software programs an organization uses to create documents, store data, draft blueprints, and the like must be purchased to be legitimate. The not uncommon practice of borrowing a software program from a friend or colleague and loading it on your computer, especially for the purpose of making money with it, is illegal, a violation of the creator's intellectual property rights—and an enormous global problem.

Organizations that use dozens or hundreds or thousands of copies of the same program can buy licenses for all the users who may be using the program on the organization's network. It's an auditor's responsibility to evaluate controls that management is using to implement software licensing requirements and monitor usage for any violations.

Software copyright

A software license agreement is a contract between an organization and the software vendor specifying terms of use such as permitting usage by one of the following methods:

- Per server
- Per computer (per processor, per individual)
- Site
- Number of users (concurrent or total)

- Load (total frequency of use)
- Floating (flexible contract)

Most licenses specifically prohibit decompiling or reverse-engineering software to determine the source code unless the organization buys a source code license. For many types of software, it is important to include in the license a right to copy the software to make a legitimate backup for disaster recovery. If organizations need to transfer a license to an out-source provider, it should be negotiated into the original contract. The license or a separate contract also covers the rights of the organization, covered later in this topic.

Software piracy is making illegal duplicate copies of software or installation of software beyond what is allowed in the license agreement. Violation of a software license agreement is easy to do because many types of software do not prevent installations beyond the number allowed in the agreement. This can make it tempting for individuals in an organization to take a few shortcuts, especially when bureaucracy slows the normal software requisition process or a requisition is denied. Some software requires each copy to be registered or activated with the vendor, so copyright is easier to determine in these cases. In addition to being an ethical issue, penalties for copyright infringement can be severe. A number of software vendors have won lawsuits regarding copyright violation. Copyright is more difficult to enforce in some countries where piracy violations are not prosecuted.

Auditors need to review all software contracts or licenses and become familiar with agreement restrictions. They must also ensure that software copyright and piracy policies exist and are communicated to all applicable parties. The policies should disallow making illegal copies/installations and state the personal consequences for breaking the policy (e.g., termination, criminal liability) as well as the potential cost to the organization.

Lists of approved and licensed applications should be compiled so that auditors can compare end-user computers with this list and identify potentially pirated or illegally copied software. Since illegal copies may be difficult to detect, the auditor's list of applications should include the acceptable number of copies. The auditor can then make a count of actual copies. In addition, policy and logical controls should prevent end users from downloading an illegal copy (usually with copy protections cracked) from a peer-to-peer network or Web site.

Other possible controls include:

- Securing site or concurrent user licenses, rather than specific user licenses, from vendors. Site licenses allow access to all network users; concurrent licenses allow access to a certain number of users at one time.
- Reconfiguring workstations to prevent employees from installing and running programs from the workstation rather than from the network.
- Centralizing software purchasing and installation.

Software purchasing

Software purchasing should follow a defined acquisition methodology, including a cost-benefit analysis. Purchased software has some advantages over internal development for audit purposes: The application usually is better documented, testing is generally more thorough, it often costs less than internally developing the equivalent, and most applications benefit from regular update releases that add features or remove bugs. Also, the vendor may be able to provide support by contract or in an emergency such as if internal staff quit.

On the other hand, internally developed software can be flexible, but users could inadvertently alter the configuration and cause errors. The flexibility may also require better hardware processing capability. Organizations may also be tempted to customize a system, which can be expensive and cause upgrade problems. Change controls include keeping a "patch deck" that contains all customizations for an application for install after an upgrade. All involved parties may under-anticipate the need for training. Also, seemingly vital program patches can be a problem (see Chapter B, Topic 2).

Software purchasing steps

When searching for software, organizations can purchase or lease off-the-shelf software or they can hire a firm to make custom software for them (or customize existing software). Software leasing is addressed below. Simple and straightforward off-the-shelf applications can be purchased after an internal evaluation of the possible choices, including a presentation of the pros and cons of each choice to the relevant stakeholders. More complex off-the-shelf systems and arranging work for hire involve a methodology such as the systems development life cycle, the results of which are used to submit requests for proposals (RFPs) to all vendors identified in the feasibility study. Controls for this step include requiring all vendors to sign nondisclosure agreements prior to receiving sensitive information (often contained in an RFP). The vendors prepare detailed responses stating how their package will fulfill each of the criteria.

A short list of vendors will be asked to make a sales presentation. Criteria for good vendors include their stability and the longevity of their application, the size and satisfaction of their user base (verified by interviews), and their quality control and maintenance standards, such as support for and regularity of upgrades. Auditors need to ensure that the organization does not rely on marketing information to make their decision: They should see a functioning model that proves vendor claims, preferably as a walk-through on the organization's own systems and data. Price should not be the primary factor; the application should satisfy at least 80% of requirements without customization and definitely the top ten requirements.

Software contract

In addition to (or appended to) the software license, both parties need to sign a contract that indicates other responsibilities. The contract should specify detailed costs, ongoing maintenance subcontracts, and delivery dates and milestones and should include recourse if either party defaults on its obligations. Contracts need to be specific on entitlement to upgrades, releases, ongoing maintenance and customer service, or the right to use internal or third-party software maintenance or development. The license will also specify legal liability limits for the vendor if the software fails to perform or if it causes a user's system to be compromised. Legal counsel should examine the clauses to ensure that the organization's rights are not being overly restricted.

The organization should withhold final payment until the system is up and running and they have verified that each of the functions works as promised for the organization's actual volume of transactions. The vendor may require that this payment be kept in an escrow account to prove the funds are available. The organization could also require that the vendor keep a copy of their source code in an escrow account in case the vendor quits business.

Software leasing

Some types of software, called software as a service (SaaS), allow users to subscribe to it on a leased basis. The software is accessible via a Web browser and is maintained entirely by the third-party vendor (unless it is an internally developed SaaS application for distributed organizational use). These applications allow users to perform regular transaction processing, analysis, or forecasting. Many applications allow users to set up automated interfaces with the organization's ERP system. Advantages of leasing software include that there is only one version of the system because updates to the system are seamless and entirely in the hands of the vendor. The systems have low up-front costs and no or very low risk of software implementation or development project failure. They are almost immediately available once the decision to subscribe is made. However, the ongoing costs may be higher in the long run as there is an ongoing fee. There is an added risk in that loss of Internet connectivity prevents access to the system. There may also be a need for more monitoring and control since sensitive data is being processed and stored by a third party. Finally, the third party could go out of business and the service might no longer be available.

Topic 9: Demonstrate an Understanding of Mainframes (Level A)

A mainframe computer is a large computer capable of supporting massive inputs and outputs and many concurrent users. The mainframe is the grandfather of business computers. Mainframes are powerful and generally connected to a large number of terminals and peripheral devices, such as high-volume printers. Mainframes are primarily used for processing and storing large amounts of data.

A data terminal, or dumb terminal, is an input/output node for a mainframe system consisting of either just a display and entry devices or a workstation running terminal emulation software (it acts as if it had no processing capacity).

Mainframes were once the mainstay of business computing. Now, however, servers and clients have taken over the role of the mainframe and terminals for a large number of applications. The mainframe has evolved into a niche application, such as for handling actual transfers of funds for banks. Modern mainframes specialize in highly stable and reliable operations that can continue uninterrupted processing for long periods, which is achieved in part by containing redundant hardware and having strict backward compatibility with older operating system versions. For example, system maintenance, such as adding more hardware capacity, can occur while the mainframe continues normal processing. Mainframes are also capable of vast data throughput because they have extensive input and output hardware. Mainframes have high security, and the specialized nature of the operating systems and other features makes them difficult to hack into; instances of this occurring are very low. Mainframes also allow running multiple operating systems on the same unit, so one mainframe can act as a set of virtual servers that can perform very different tasks.

Controls associated with mainframes include locating them in a secure data center, including proper heating, venting, and air conditioning, electrostatic control, and properly trained system engineers. Other controls include automated log-off of inactive users and placing data terminals where they will not be unattended.

Topic 10: Demonstrate an Understanding of Operating Systems (Level A)

The operating system (O/S) is the software that, in essence, runs the computer. Microsoft Windows, Unix, Linux, and the Mac OS are examples of operating systems. The operating system mediates between the computer hardware and the applications accessed by a user. Windows allows the user to create a slide show in PowerPoint or a spreadsheet in Excel. Different operating systems, or different versions of an operating system, may be appropriate for different types of computers. Operating systems exist for computers, devices, servers, and mainframes. Computers have a built-in operating system (BIOS), a hardware-based O/S that initiates the software O/S.

The auditor should pay special attention to operating systems, since a crashed operating system can leave a great many employees without access to their work (if it's on a mainframe or a network).

Functions of operating systems

The O/S performs a variety of critical functions that coordinate hardware (e.g., keyboard and mouse, display, scanner, Webcam, and microphone); memory storage and access (both internal and external storage); processing tasks; and network communication. These tasks include:

- Creation of a user interface for user interaction with the computer—e.g., a graphical user interface (GUI).
- Operation of computer hardware (e.g., keyboard).
- Communication with application programs.
- Allowing network capabilities (sharing of network peripherals and data).
- Managing memory to ensure rapid retrieval of data and processing.
- Scheduling of resources.
- File management and tracking. The O/S tracks where files are stored and who is allowed to view/change them.
- Control of access—even by multiple simultaneous users. Access controls restrict access by ID/password and keep a log of users, the duration of their use, and any attempted security breaches.
- System recovery after failure.

Process management includes allocating resources to processes and users for multiprogramming/multitasking (simultaneous tasks). Memory management determines how much random access memory (RAM) and virtual memory to allocate to an application and locates data by its physical address (location in memory) given a logical address (online label). Applications interact with the O/S via an application program interface (API), which can be programmed without needing to understand hidden O/S features.

Audit issues

Auditors of operating systems should be IT audit specialists. Internal auditors reviewing the controls over operating systems security face the challenge that such systems are continually evolving, requiring continuous training. General areas of review include monitoring change procedures, checking that O/Ss are up-to-date, determining if system programmers have enough training, checking update status of O/S tables (e.g., employee information), and ensuring that an adequate system of error tracking exists.

O/S controls include error notification for failed hardware and detection of abnormalities in the system using ZAP programs, or programs that change or fix data or programs but can bypass security safeguards and may not leave an audit trail. Two examples are data handling utilities (DHUs) and data file utilities (DFUs) (e.g., registry fix applications). These utilities are designed to automatically correct some errors caused by ABENDS (abnormal endings), crashes, and data corruption. They can make changes to files without use of processing programs. Sometimes, no record of the changes or transactions is kept, creating a potential source of error or method of abuse. Restricting access to system programmers who must get approval and provide documentation for each use is one method of controlling usage. Security software may or may not detect when these utilities are used.

Another area to control is changes to operating systems, usually by update or replacement. System programmers should not be allowed to perform applications programming because they could commit and conceal fraud. Because an O/S affects an entire data center, it is high risk and should be performed in a sandbox area first or done at night with a backout plan available to reverse the changes. A log of all changes is key. Sometimes O/Ss are customized with software called "hooks," and these will need to be reinstalled at each upgrade.

Topic 11: Demonstrate an Understanding of Web Infrastructure (Level A)

There may be two ways to look at the phenomenon that most people interchangeably call the World Wide Web and the Internet—as shared information or as interconnected machines. Either way, "Web" or "Net" have very similar connotations of complicated linkages. The physical infrastructure is the myriad computers that allow users to send e-mail and visit Web sites.

Connection to the outside world is a source of risk for organizations. They are vulnerable to viruses and intruders who enter their internal network of computers through transferred files or e-mail attachments. Internet access increases the risk of inappropriate or illegal use of company assets for personal activity.

Terminology

The **Internet** is a network of networks that have devoted a portion of their processing power and data to public use, the ultimate distributed network. The **World Wide Web** or **Web** is the largest subset of the Internet. Internet use is now automatic for most users; the difficulty lies in sorting out good information from a vast selection of data.

An **intranet** is an internal network for employees built using tools, standards, and protocols of the World Wide Web and the Internet. Intranets empower employees by giving them remote access to company information and possibly even by giving business units responsibility over their own content. Obviously both of these benefits will require improved controls to prevent their misuse. An **extranet** is like an intranet service designed for customers, external partners, or suppliers. Extranets require even greater controls over user authentication and privacy.

The following is other Web infrastructure terminology.

- **HTTP/HTTPS (Hypertext Transfer Protocol/Secure HTTP).** Regular and encrypted versions of the communications standard for Internet message formatting and transmission.

- **Internet protocol (IP) address.** Numeric address for a specific computer located on the Internet, e.g., 128.6.13.42.

- **Domain name.** Plain language label referring to a numeric IP address.

- **Domain name system (DNS).** Hierarchical server network that maintains the domain names for conversion to IP addresses. The National Institute of Standards and Technology (NIST) has developed DNS security extensions (DNSSEC) to authenticate the origin of DNS data and either assure data integrity or provide authenticated denial of existence.

- **Uniform Resource Locator (URL).** The combination of transfer protocol, domain name, directory path, and document name, as follows.

http://www.theiia.org/itaudit/index.cfm?catid=29&iid=509

Protocol Domain name Directory path Document name

- **File Transfer Protocol (FTP).** Allows transfer of large files between computers on a network or the Internet.

- **E-mail.** Electronic messages that could contain viruses or spam.

- **Instant messaging.** Text message services that can be co-opted by hackers as an avenue for remotely controlling user computers.

- **Telnet.** One way of gaining remote control over a computer.

Internet structure

The Internet backbone is a series of high-capacity trunk lines owned and operated by network service providers (e.g., long-distance telephone companies or governments). The remainder of the backbone is owned by regional telephone and cable organizations, who lease access to organizations and Internet service providers (see below). The points of connection between the backbone and the regional areas are called network access points (NAPs) or metropolitan access points (MAPs). Other than this physical infrastructure, the Internet is neither owned nor managed. Internet organizations exist such as the World Wide Web Consortium (W3C), which sets programming standards and protocols. Organizations such as these do not control the Internet; they just work to improve its efficiency or security. Due to this, some nations heavily regulate or outright ban use of the Internet.

An Internet service provider (ISP) is an organization that provides connection to the Internet via a TCP/IP (Transmission Control Protocol/Internet Protocol) connection or provides network services (IP network). Control issues for ISPs include choosing a reliable service from a reputable organization to minimize risk of business interruptions. Use of an IP network is inexpensive, but because the data flows over the Internet, the company's data is only as secure as its encryption. Broadband involves high-speed transmission methods over a single high-capacity medium or multiple lower-capacity media. Broadband access has many methods, but satellite, cable modem, and digital subscriber lines (DSL) are common. Narrowband refers to standard telephone/modem service. Controls to protect intranets or extranets include using a virtual private network (VPN). (See Topic 6.)

Browser security

Browsers, like other applications, have bugs and associated patches. Browser security flaws are a potential source of attack, but the upgrade process must be managed. Even when browsers are up-to-date, a number of security risks still exist. In general, administrators should disable all unnecessary features of browsers. Pages using active content languages such as ActiveX or Java allow more interactivity but could conceal malicious code in their scripts, which operate independently of the browser. Java, for example, operates in a sandbox environment that limits interaction with the rest of the system, but this protection can be compromised by attackers. Active content that runs inside the browser, or plug-ins, should also be treated as suspect. Therefore many organizational sites block such interactivity and allow viewing only in plain text. Web sites create cookies on a user's computer, which are files intended to be accessible only by the creator that are used to store data about the user's preferences. Administrators should disallow cookies in general and allow their use only for trusted sites.

Other browser security measures include blocking pop-up windows using a utility program because they could contain malicious programs. Administrators should set browser security for external sites to "high." With this setting, administrators need to define "trusted" sites, or sites allowed normal access. This will often include only secure sockets layer (SSL) or HTTPS sites that can verify their authenticity plus a few sites such as the operating system software provider's update site. Other sites that are trustworthy should still not be set as trusted in case they are compromised. An example of such a compromise is cross-site scripting, where a vulnerable site is used to gain access to its trusted site list. Intranet sites can have lower security, but this content is not immune from attacks. Finally, although it isn't a complete control, a set of unsafe sites can be designated as restricted.

Web services and service-oriented architecture (SOA)

Web services use open Internet protocols and standards to create stand-alone, modular software called services that are capable of describing themselves and integrating with other similar services. Web services work independent of platform, operating system, or computer language, and the offerings of other providers can be leveraged without any middleware.

Web services can work with traditional applications by creating a universal wrapper around the message content. They speed software development efforts because common services such as a credit check tool can be found on a registry server. Web services are especially good for making automated or one-time connections such as with trading partners.

A service-oriented architecture (SOA) is a software system design that allows for sharing of Web services as needed: A service consumer sends out requests for services to service providers, which either provide the service or forward on the request. SOA has an architecture goal of loose coupling, which means that the data is separated from the application and each service says what it needs another service to do, not how to do it. Advantages include the ability for remote users to access ERP systems using mobile devices and for various applications to work together to synthesize data into information faster. In addition, developers have easier and faster upgrades.

SOA packages include Microsoft .NET as well as offerings from IBM® and each of the ERP vendors.

What does this all mean for internal auditors? Despite the many advantages of this set-up, control issues abound. Internal governance models that were created for traditional software models will not suffice and will need to be reengineered. This is especially true if the organization must comply with Sarbanes-Oxley Section 404 rules or an international equivalent on internal controls. The openness of SOA creates new risks to internal controls.

For example, in a traditional IT system, segregation of duties would safeguard electronic sales documents by creating barriers between the sales, credit, and billing modules. The barrier would rely on logical access controls and role-based access to lock out unauthorized users. Customers entering through a Web portal would be assigned a customer role and temporary unique ID. Furthermore, their access would be restricted to the Web portal and moving further would require knowledge of the proprietary interface that resides between the portal and the rest of the ERP system. Customers could create a purchase but not modify it or change their credit.

In SOA architecture, all modules such as sales, credit, billing, and the general ledger are each Web services connected to the Web. The system would still have a firewall and other protections, but the SOA would be like a trunk line to which each set of modules and databases is connected. The entire ERP system would become a Web service. Now the customer's ERP system gets approval for and establishes a direct link to the organization's ERP system. The two parties can automate their trading. Therefore, some of the segregation of duties created by user interaction will be missing. A compensating control is to designate the machine or system making the interface as a user in its own right with its own role-based access. The ID of the user commanding that "user" also needs to be mapped to prove compliance with controls (e.g., nonrepudiation, authentication, segregation of duties). Auditors may need to seek external assurance that the SOA system can either authenticate the external system, the system user, and the user's role or deny all service.

In the worst-case scenario, an organization with this set-up could conceivably allow the SOA modules, such as the general ledger, to communicate over port 80, which is an open channel that bypasses the firewall for direct Internet access. Any service anywhere could then modify the general ledger. Horrifying as this seems, it is how some systems have been set up. Greater emphasis must be placed on application level controls than with a traditional set-up. General audit recommendations include implementing SOA in stages, starting with nonfinancial business functions. The organization can then assess risks and upgrade controls using less-sensitive data.

Chapter D: Business Continuity

Chapter Introduction

An important risk management process is for an organization to have a plan in place to deal with crises and disasters as they arise. Having a plan in advance helps to mitigate losses as effectively as possible. Crisis management plans incorporate plans to deal with the immediate crisis and stakeholder communication as well as longer-term plans to ensure the continuity of the organization. Some organizations may call these disaster recovery plans, business interruption plans, or business continuity plans.

Topic 1: Define and Describe Business Continuity Planning (Level A)

Business interruptions can result from natural occurrences and accidental or deliberate acts. A crisis could include events such as the unexpected death of a CEO or product tampering. Such interruptions can have significant financial and operational ramifications. Crises distract attention from the status quo of operating the business and have the potential for productivity and profitability losses and reduced stakeholder confidence. Auditors should evaluate the organization's readiness to deal with such business interruptions.

GTAG 10, "Business Continuity Management," defines business continuity management (BCM) as a "process by which an organization prepares for future incidents that could jeopardize the organization's core mission and its long-term viability." Business continuity is made up of enterprise-level and end-to-end solutions, from design and planning to implementation and management, with the focus on being proactive. A business continuity plan is a set of processes developed for the entire enterprise, outlining the actions to be taken by the IT organization, executive staff, and various business units in order to quickly resume operations in the event of a business disruption or service outage.

To ensure that an organization can remain functional during and after disasters, it must have a plan for continued operation in the event of disaster. A comprehensive plan would provide for emergency response procedures, stakeholder communications protocols, alternative communication systems and site facilities, information systems backup, disaster recovery, interim financing, insurance claims, business impact assessments and resumption plans, procedures for restoring utility services, and maintenance procedures for ensuring the readiness of the organization in the event of an emergency or a disaster.

Internal auditors can play two distinct roles: reducing risks before disaster strikes and restoring functions and controls in the aftermath of a risk event.

Internal audit's role before a disaster

The internal auditor's role during normal operations is to determine whether or not the organization could survive disruption of business or IT and how well they are equipped to mitigate the effects of the disaster. One of the questions for which the auditor will be seeking answers is "How well can the organization function when access to information systems has been disrupted?" The answer varies considerably with the type of organization. Stock brokerage, for instance, is difficult without computer, phone, and network access. Retail outlets may be less dependent upon continuous access to information systems. IT disruptions are addressed further in the next topic.

Other questions the auditor will be concerned with are:

- Is there a disaster plan in place?
- What is the organization's current disaster capacity?
- Have the critical applications been defined?
- Does the disaster plan provide for all contingencies, for instance, fire, earthquake, floods, or water damage from leaks or activated sprinklers?
- Has it been tested?
- Are the backup facilities adequately equipped and readily available?

The answers to these questions will determine whether the organization is prepared as well as it can be and, if it isn't, what it can do to improve the situation.

The internal auditor should observe the off-site testing process and realistically consider any subtle differences that may result in technical issues and potentially delay start-up.

Keeping plans up-to-date

The internal auditing activity should assess the organization's business continuity management process on a regular basis to ensure that senior management is aware of the state of disaster preparedness. To support an organization's readiness to deal with business interruptions, the internal audit activity can:

- Assist with the risk analysis.
- Evaluate the design and comprehensiveness of the plan after it has been drawn up.
- Perform periodic assurance engagements to verify that the plan is kept up-to-date.
- Observe and provide feedback on tests of the plan.

Because business continuity and disaster recovery plans can become outdated quickly (due to turnover of managers and executives and changes in system configurations, interfaces, software, and the like), such audits should provide assurance that the plan is not outdated. The audit objective is to verify that the plan is adequate to ensure the timely resumption of operations and processes after adverse circumstances and that it reflects the current business operating environment.

Internal audit's role after a disaster

An organization is extremely vulnerable after a disaster occurs and it is trying to recover. Internal auditors have an important role during the recovery period.

Internal auditors should monitor the effectiveness of the recovery and control of operations. The internal audit activity should identify areas where internal controls and mitigating actions should be improved and recommend improvements to the entity's business continuity plan.

The internal audit activity should participate in the organizational learning process following a disaster. After the disaster, usually within several months, internal auditors can assist in identifying the lessons learned from the disaster and the recovery operations. Those observations and recommendations may enhance activities to recover resources and update the next version of the business continuity plan.

Senior management determines the degree of the internal auditors' involvement in the business continuity and disaster recovery management processes, "considering their knowledge, skills, independence, and objectivity."

Topic 2: Describe the Process and Best Practices of IT Contingency Planning (Level A)

In addition to general business interruption risks, since organizations are becoming increasingly dependent upon access to information systems, business continuity planning must include IT contingency planning as part of the overall information systems security package. The goal of IT contingency planning is to mitigate business risks due to a mission-critical functional failure caused directly or indirectly by noncompliant hardware or software, a vendor, a package, embedded devices, a supplier, or an external interface or environment.

Internal auditors addressing IT contingency planning should consult Standard 2120, "Risk Management": "The internal audit activity must evaluate the effectiveness and contribute to the improvement of risk management processes."

Business interruptions can be accidental or by deliberate act. In either case, not having an IT contingency plan risks the loss of business continuity and possibly the demise of the organization. From an IT perspective, an IT contingency plan within a BCM framework would entail a system of internal controls for managing the availability of computer and other resources and data after a processing disruption. It would include:

- Regaining access to data (e.g., records, applications) and equipment.
- Reestablishing communications (e.g., e-mail, phone).
- Locating new workspace.

IT contingency planning consists of forming and testing a plan, incident handling, and disaster recovery. Incident handling includes procedures for dealing with a problem as it is occurring; disaster recovery includes procedures for restoring business processes in the order of their priority. Exhibit VI-20 on the next page illustrates the model for the BCM process from GTAG-10, "Business Continuity Management." Note that IT contingency planning is integral to several steps in this process. The BCM process encompasses the following steps:

- IT management gains commitment from senior management to ensure material and organizational support for the plan's results.
- Probable, high-impact events (e.g., natural disasters, employee errors, fraud, computer virus or denial-of-service attack) are identified by the organization, and mitigation strategies are developed.
- A business impact analysis (BIA) is conducted to:
  - Identify and define critical business processes.
  - Define recovery time objective (RTO) and recovery point objectives (RPOs) for processes, resources, and so on.
  - Identify resources and partners that can assist in recovery.
- A recovery and continuity plan is developed that defines alternative sources for staff, functions, and resources and identifies alternative locations for operations (e.g., alternative information networks, backup data centers).
- The BCM program is communicated throughout the organization, and all employees are trained in crisis procedures and communications strategies. BCM plans and staff performance are tested.

Developing an IT contingency plan

IT contingency planning begins by creating a contingency planning team. Contingency plans cannot be the responsibility of just one individual, but the team must have a project leader whose responsibilities include orchestrating the plan document and explaining the plan to management. A contingency plan must delegate specific responsibilities and roles to those who are closest to the associated risks. The team should have adequate authority and also visibility, meaning plan development is communicated clearly.

The process of developing a contingency plan document can be out-sourced, or it can be developed in-house, but on-site employees must be used for actual incident handling and therefore need training.

Exhibit VI-20: BCM Process

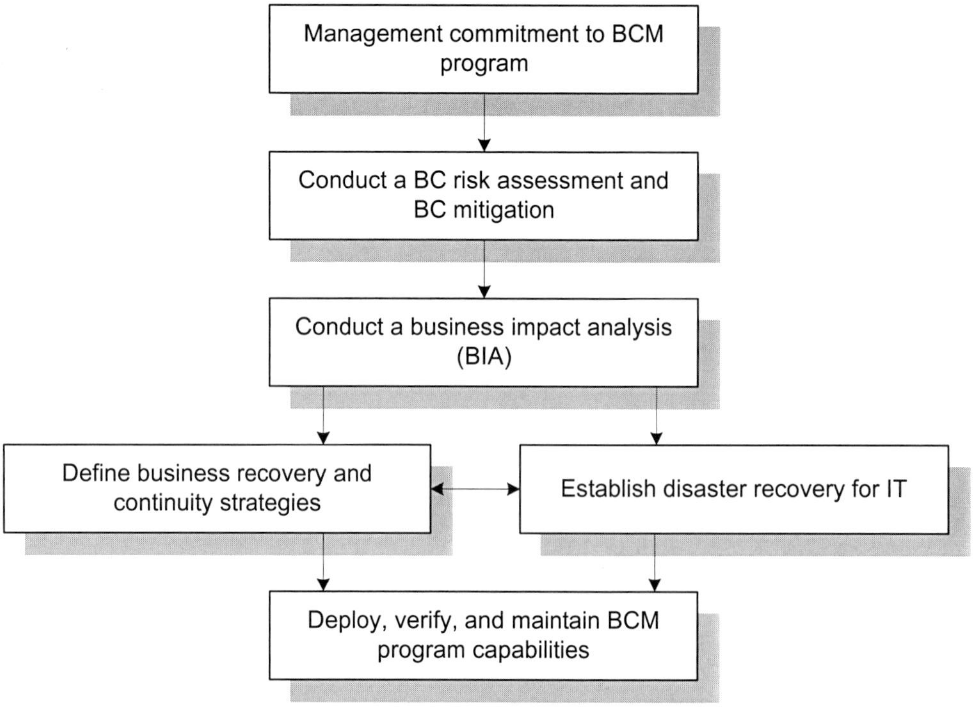

Source: GTAG 10, "Business Continuity Management."

Setting objectives and determining risks

IT contingency planning must be integrated with IT systems planning methodologies and overall BCM and risk management frameworks. Management must be educated on effective disaster recovery procedures. Contingency plans start with a risk assessment, called a business impact analysis or assessment (BIA), often as part of the risk management framework. For each risk, a probability is assessed as well as the impact it would have on each separate facility.

Determining systems relevance and setting risk-based priorities

After determining risks, the order of restoration of services and the level of protections for each service are worked out. Each category would have an acceptable downtime and a cost associated with that downtime. This becomes the organization's benchmark data. Each organization will have different priorities or categories, such as:

- **Critical systems.** Telecommunications and core processes such as order processing, invoicing, and shipping.
- **Vital systems.** Finance (A/R, A/P, general ledger), customer service.
- **Sensitive systems.** Payroll, end-user data restoration.
- **Noncritical systems.** Human resources, budgeting, purchasing.

When making a plan, organizations combine the risks ranked by severity and likelihood with their restoration priorities. Each type of disruption has an appropriate response. Events that endanger employees require employee evacuation plans with row or area leaders to ensure that everyone gets out. Part of the plan is to provide adequate business interruption insurance to cover operational losses (opportunity costs of lost work and sales) and adequate equipment and property insurance to cover physical losses. Evidence of data backup and recovery controls and business continuity plans will likely reduce insurance costs.

Recovery methods include redundant systems at multiple sites, identifying and training backup staff in other parts of the organization who can perform critical functions, and out-sourcing critical IT processes (including staffing as well as processes). In terms of IT components that may need to be replaced, GTAG 10 lists the following.

- IT systems:
  - Data center
  - Applications and data needed by the enterprise
  - Servers and other hardware
  - Communications devices
  - Networks, including third-party networks
  - IT infrastructure (e.g., log-on services, software distribution)
  - Remote access services
  - Process control systems used in manufacturing, such as supervisory control and data acquisition (SCADA) or distributed control system (DCS)
- Information management systems:
  - File rooms
  - Document management systems (both electronic and manual)

Recovery strategies must meet the business's needs; they must be complete and elements must work together, leaving no significant gaps and allowing access to all users. The goal is to find the best and most cost-effective solution for each affected system—even if the solution is unconventional.

Off-site storage and libraries are used for all data, operating systems, documentation, etc. Such sites may not be available for resuming operations, so organizations usually arrange a space for operations to resume.

The following are types of off-site facilities:

- A **hot site** is a dedicated location that is kept fully stocked with the hardware needed for operations configured to client specifications. Hot sites will not have the organization's data, so the first step is to load the most current backup from off-site storage. Hot sites can be fully functional within 24 hours after a business interruption. Fixed hot sites require the firm to relocate; portable sites deliver a trailer where needed.
- A **cold site** is an empty space that has no computers but is set up and ready for a data center, including raised flooring and computer cooling. The organization is responsible for providing computers. Cold sites can take days to go online.
- A **warm site** is a site partway between a hot site and a cold site.
- A **reciprocal agreement** can be made with one or more organizations to share resources if one party suffers a failure. Auditors must ensure that all parties stay technically synchronized.

Such services have a cost, so recovery priorities may require noncritical systems to use temporary manual workarounds. Or a hot site can be used while a cold site is being prepared. Often, management decides not to mitigate a particular type of risk at all because the cost of mitigation exceeds the likely loss or the likelihood is extremely low.

Documenting the plan

An IT contingency plan has several components:

- A clear and simple introduction
- A list of team responsibilities and emergency contact information
- Backup schedules and locations of off-site backups
- An escalation procedure for problems
- Action plans including recovery time frames, recovery strategy, and subplans for hardware, software, networking, and telecommunications
- Insurance documentation

An out-of-date action plan with the wrong phone numbers or hot sites that haven't been informed of a necessary hardware upgrade can be a disaster, so the documents must have an owner who is responsible for keeping them current. Plan documents contain confidential information and so must have access controls.

Testing the plan

According to GTAG 10, a testing plan should include the following elements:

- Tests should be held at periodical intervals, set by the BCM steering committee and based on business goals and objectives. Intervals will vary according to the nature of the enterprise. Most enterprises test plans one or two times a year, but testing might be more frequent based on:

- Changes in business processes.
- Changes in technology.
- Changes in BCM team membership.
- Anticipated events that could result in business interruption (e.g., an anticipated pandemic).

- Tests should address a variety of threats/scenarios and different elements within the BCM plan (i.e., broad-based exercises or targeted site or component exercises).

- A method should be established for identifying performances gaps and tracking their successful resolution.

Exhibit VI-21 on the next page describes some types of BCM tests and their characteristics.

Internal auditors should regularly assess the IT contingency plans. The best evidence that contingency planning is working is to test the plan. The test should indicate the organization's current disaster recovery capacity, or the time it takes to load all systems and data and get running again. Variance is determined by comparison to the organization's benchmarks. The test should duplicate typical transaction volumes, and auditors should record processing times. This will lead auditors to ask questions such as "Was the replacement telecommunications system adequate?" Mainframes rarely restore correctly, even on identical hardware, so in such situations the auditor should measure progress toward the goal rather than the immediate result. Other tests are physical, such as a fire drill. The test results could be used to set realistic benchmarks or as a call for more resources to get to the desired benchmark.

Incident handling/ disaster recovery

Determining the severity of a disaster is the first task of employees in charge of incident handling. Employees follow their plan, starting by contacting all persons on the list and communicating the issue and what they need to do. Planned alternate workspaces or equipment is accessed if part of the plan. Organizations with a public presence should have a designated spokesperson who has guidelines on what to say and what not to say to the press. In the aftermath of a disaster, internal auditors play a vital role in assessing what parts of the plan worked and what parts need to be revisited.

Exhibit VI-21: Types of BCM Tests

Test	Characteristics
Desk check or plan audit	Written plan is reviewed in detail and updated. • Involves only the plan owner and an objective assessor. • Ensures relevancy and currency of plan.
Orientation or plan walk-through	All BCM team members meet to review their roles in the plan; does not constitute a "test."
Tabletop exercise (boardroom-style exercise)	BCM team participates in brief (two- to four-hour) simulation of a scenario; includes group self-assessment of ability to meet exercise objectives, performance gaps, and planned remediation.
Communication testing	Actual contact is established with all key stakeholders (as opposed to simply compiling a list of stakeholders to be contacted in case of a disaster). Helps: • Validates stakeholders' contact information. • Train participants in how to use mass communication tools. • Configure communication tools. • Identify communication gaps/bottlenecks.
IT environment (systems and applications) walk-through	Participants walk through an announced or unannounced simulation and execute system recovery procedures. • A less costly and disruptive alternative to a full test. • Verifies that critical systems and data can be recovered. • Identifies impact of the loss of multiple systems/applications. • Coordinates resources across multiple locations and lines of business. • Ensures adequacy of resources.
Alternate site testing	Participants test the ability to transfer staff to an alternate site, restore processes, and recover data, as designed. • Demonstrates actual capacity of alternate site. • Identifies whether privacy, security, and financial can be maintained at the alternate site. • Trains staff in processes and equipment at site. • Confirms sufficiency and effectiveness of IT assets at alternate site.
End-to-end testing	All stakeholders participate, including IT, business partners, suppliers, and customers; demonstrates ability to perform key processes at an agreed level.

Source: GTAG 10, "Business Continuity Management."

Next Steps

You have completed Part 3, Section VI, of The IIA's CIA Learning System®. Next, check your understanding by completing the online section-specific test(s) to help you identify any content that needs additional study.

Once you have completed the section-specific test(s) and feel confident that you have mastered the information, you can advance to studying Section VII.